The Northwestern Pacific Railroad

Redwood Empire Route

Fred A. Stindt

FIRST PRINTING — DECEMBER 1964
SECOND PRINTING — OCTOBER 1966
THIRD PRINTING — APRIL 1978
FOURTH PRINTING — AUGUST 1982

THE NORTHWESTERN PACIFIC RAILROAD

Printed and bound in the United States of America

Library of Congress Catalog Card No. 64-24033.

Published by Fred A. Stindt
3363 Riviera West Drive
Kelseyville, California 95451

ACKNOWLEDGEMENTS

Coming into being in 1907 as the ultimate consolidation of some forty railroad companies, the Northwestern Pacific was the creation of two of the giants of western railroading - the Southern Pacific and the Santa Fe. With its many passenger trains and steam locomotives; with its narrow gauge line from Sausalito via Point Reyes and Duncan Mills to Cazadero, its standard gauge (more commonly known in Marin and Sonoma counties as the "broad" gauge) line from Sausalito and Tiburon eventually all the way up to Eureka and beyond to Trinidad, it titled itself the "Redwood Empire Route." But today scores of miles of road have been abandoned; the steam locomotive has fallen into oblivion, the bustling little passenger trains have been all but forgotten, and the present Northwestern Pacific is little more than another operating division of the parent Southern Pacific.

But like all publications similar to this one, the finished product - notwithstanding the work and dedication of the author - could not have been realized without the assistance, in varying forms, of many people. So while the bulk of the material came from the personal files and libraries of the author, much additional - photographs, maps, facts and information - was graciously contributed by others. It is, therefore, with sincere thanks that 1 acknowledge the help of:

Roy Graves, well-known authority on early western railroads, and one-time (1904-1907) fireman and machinist on the North Shore and Northwestern Pacific narrow gauge.

Willis A. Silverthorn, fireman and engineer on the Northwestern Pacific from 1911 until his retirement in 1955.

Robert Hancocks (deceased) and David F. Myrick of the Southern Pacific Company, who furnished much valuable information as did Cliff Hanssen, Master Mechanic, and his secretary, Lois Sanders; and the late George Morrison, Vice President and General Manager of the Northwestern Pacific, who gave me so much data on locomotives and passenger cars along with Company photographs.

Al Rose, for his masterful photo reproductions and his interest in seeing the book in print, and Stanley Borden and Richard Houghton for their map work.

The author would appreciate being informed of significant errors in the book, and also is much interested in obtaining additional quality pictures having to do with the Northwestern Pacific.

Fred A. Stindt, Redwood City, California

November 1, 1964

ACKNOWLEDGEMENTS

Mike Barnes
Gerald M. Best
William Billings
Stanley Borden
Darrell Brewer
O. B. Cavanaugh
James Cloney
John Farley
Carl Fennema
Frank Gori
Francis Guido
Al Graves
Peter Hahn
Robert Hanft
George Harlan
Donald Howe
Richard Jackson
Guy King
Arthur Lloyd
Marvin Maynard
R. P. Middlebrook
Warren Miller
E. R. Mohr
Joe Moir
Edward Nervo
Robert Parmelee
Douglas Richter
Clemente Roberts
Al Rose
Vernon Sappers
Charles Savage
Louis Stein
Walt Sievers
Thomas Taber
Brian Thompson
Wally Thompson
William Tuggle
Bert Ward
Wilbur Whittaker
Redwood Empire Association
San Francisco Maritime Museum
San Rafael Independent
Santa Rosa Press Democrat
Southern Pacific
Turrill & Miller
Western Railroader

And to the heirs of the collections of:

Art Alter
R. Bave
Carl Beggs
D. L. Joslyn
Andy Kirkpatrick
Gilbert Kneiss
Stuart Liebman
R. H. McFarland

TABLE OF CONTENTS

LIST OF MAPS

CORPORATE STRUCTURE

RAILROADS FORMING THE NORTHWESTERN PACIFIC

The Northwestern Pacific Railroad was incorporated January 8, 1907, as a consolidation of -

Northwestern Pacific Railway　　　　Fort Bragg & Southeastern Railroad　　　California Northwestern Railway
Eureka & Klamath River Railroad　　North Shore Railroad　　　　　　　　　　San Francisco & Northwestern Railway
　　　　　　　　　　　　　　　　　　San Francisco & North Pacific Railway

The following list names in alphabetical order all of the railroad companies involved in the background of the Northwestern Pacific. Most were consolidated into one of the seven shown above, while a few were taken over by the N.W.P. after January 8, 1907.

				SEE PAGE
1.	Albion Lumber Co.	5-26-91	FB&SERR	54
2.	Albion River Railroad	9-24-85	FB&SERR	44
3.	Albion & Southeastern Railway	5- 8-02	FB&SERR	44
4.	California Midland Railroad	4-26-02	SF&NWRY	40
5.	California Northwestern Railway	3-17-98	NWP	10
6.	California & Northern Railway	3- 5-00	SF&NWRY	38
7.	Cloverdale & Ukiah Rail Road	8-17-86	SF&NPRY	15
8.	Contra Costa Steam Navigation Co.	8-31-52	SF&NPRY	10
9.	Eel River & Eureka Rail Road	11-14-82	SF&NWRY	40
10.	Eureka & Klamath River Railroad	1- 6-96	NWP	38
11.	Fort Bragg & Klamath River Railroad	3-25-03	NWP	30
12.	Fulton & Guerneville Railroad	5-23-77	SF&NPRY	13
13.	Humboldt Railroad	3-13-01	NWP	41
14.	Humboldt Bay & Trinidad Logging & Lumber Co.	12-29-91	E&KRRR	38
15.	Marin & Napa Rail Road	8-17-86	SF&NPRY	15
16.	North Pacific Coast Railroad	12-19-71	NSRR	13
17.	North Pacific Coast Railroad Extension Co.	12- 6-82	NSRR	26
18.	North Shore Railroad	1-11-02	NWP	20
19.	Northwestern Pacific Railway	11-24-06	NWP	48
20.	North Western Railroad Co. of California.	8-19-85	NSRR	26
21.	Oregon & Eureka Railroad	8-14-03	NWP	38
22.	Pacific Lumber Co.	2-27-69	SF&NWRY	40
23.	The Pacific Lumber Co.	1883-?	SF&NWRY	40
24.	Petaluma & Haystack	1862	SF&NPRY	10
25.	Petaluma & Santa Rosa	6-20-03	Note 1.	54
26.	San Francisco & Eureka Railway	3-15-03	NWP	48
27.	San Francisco & Humboldt Bay Rail Road	3- 2-68	SF&NPRY	11
28.	San Francisco & North Pacific Rail Road	11-16-69	SF&NPRY	12
29.	San Francisco & North Pacific Railroad	7-12-77	SF&NPRY	12
30.	San Francisco & North Pacific Railway	12-19-88	NWP	12
31.	San Francisco & Northwestern Railway	5-12-03	NWP	41
32.	San Francisco & San Rafael Rail Road	10-21-82	SF&NPRY	14
33.	San Francisco, Tamalpais & Bolinas Railway	9- 6-89	NSRR	28
34.	San Rafael & San Quentin Rail Road	2-25-69	NSRR	13
35.	Santa Rosa, Sebastopol & Green Valley Railroad	1889	SF&NPRY	15
36.	Sonoma & Marin Railroad	11-13-74	SF&NPRY	13
37.	Sonoma & Santa Rosa Rail Road	3- 2-81	SF&NPRY	15
38.	Sonoma County Railroad	1-10-68	SF&NPRY	52
39.	Sonoma Valley Prismoidal Railway	2-18-75	SF&NPRY	18
40.	Sonoma Valley Railroad	7-24-78	SF&NPRY	15
41.	Sonoma Valley Railroad	8- 7-85	SF&NPRY	15
42.	Vance's Mad River Railroad	1875-?	E&KRRR	38

Note 1: The Petaluma & Santa Rosa Railroad is still an existing corporation. It is owned by the Southern Pacific Company, and has been operated by the Northwestern Pacific since 1932.

Documentary sources of information:

Valuation Reports, Interstate Commerce Commission.
Railroad and state Commission engineering records and reports.
Poor's and Moody's manuals of railroads.

Official Railway Guides.
Employee and public timetables of the N.W.P. and predecessor companies.
Official locomotive and car records of the Northwestern Pacific.

STATISTICS

Line	Subject	Broad Gauge	Narrow Gauge	Total
1	Miles	474	96	570
2	Locomotives	83	15	98
3	Psgr. Train Cars (Total)	295	65	360
	Steam (Wooden)	139	65	204
	Steam (Steel)	54	....	54
	Interurban (Wooden)	78	....	78
	Interurban (Steel)	19	....	19
	Gas-Electric	5	....	5
4	Boats	5	10	15
5	Roundhouses	16	7	23
6	Turntables	26	6	32
7	Bridges	56	6	62
8	Trestles	44	13	57
9	Tunnels	40	7	47
10	Agency stations	60	20	80

The figures shown in this table indicate what the road has had in its entire past, not for any one year or period.

Line 1 includes certain portions of track that at one time were dual gauge, viz: Sausalito-Manor; San Anselmo-San Rafael; Mill Valley Junction-Mill Valley; Monte Rio-Duncan Mills. Also includes 20 miles of interurban trackage.

Line 2 includes only locomotives on the N.W.P. regular roster, not the three steam dummies that were used in building the Baltimore Park-Greenbrae cut-off in 1908, nor engines of predecessor companies that were not renumbered into the regular roster.

Line 3 includes mail, baggage, express and combination cars, private or business cars as well as regular passenger cars.

Line 4 includes ferry boats, freight car boats and tugs.

Line 5 includes roundhouses, enginehouses and engine sheds.

Line 6 includes both power and manual turntables.

Line 7 includes bridges only in excess of 300 feet.

Line 8 includes trestles only in excess of 300 feet.

Line 9 includes all tunnels, some of which have now been "daylighted."

Line 10 is an approximation.

The NWP emblem depicts Richardson's Bay with the Mill Valley hills and Mt. Tamalpais in the background. The redwood tree indicates the trees in Muir woods and along the California Coast to the Oregon-California State Line.

The idea of the emblem originated with Warren S. Palmer in 1909 who then was the General Manager, with probably some help from Joe Geary who was General Freight and Passenger Agent. The suggested design was developed under the direction of James K. Brassill, Master Mechanic at Tiburon shops with a Clarance E. Harris, Foreman Painter, assisting in the details of the final design. It became the official emblem at the beginning of the year 1910 and was then placed on all time tables, letterheads, etc. and then on some locomotives and cars in the twenties.

Today it is all but forgotten, except on letterheads and envelopes, as the NWP owns no revenue cars.

SOUTHERN SECTION OF THE
NORTHWESTERN PACIFIC

As shown on the map on the page to the right, specially drawn for use in this book, the heavier concentration of rail lines of the Northwestern Pacific - in certain areas a complex of broad gauge, narrow gauge and electric operation - was from the Sausalito and Tiburon terminals northward for a distance of approximately sixty miles. While they did not all exist at the same time, this map - a composite - shows all the lines that were constructed. Other and more detailed maps are published elsewhere in this book (see Table of Contents), and more specific and complete information will be found in the stories of the San Francisco & North Pacific Railway and the North Pacific Coast Railroad, but the following will give a quick over-all summary:

Primarily there was a narrow gauge and a broad (standard) gauge. The main line of the former started from Sausalito (Saucelito in the old days), veered to the right at Alameda Point, then continued in a northwesterly direction to Corte Madera, San Anselmo, White's Hill, Point Reyes (Station), Tomales, and Monte Rio; west to Duncan Mills, and north to Cazadero. There were branches from San Anselmo to San Rafael and San Quentin; from Pedrini to Shafters; from near Duncan Mills to Azalea, and from Duncan Mills to Markham and Willow Creek. Improvements to the system included a new and shorter line between Alameda Point and Corte Madera via Mill Valley Junction; between Roys and Maillard via Woodacre, and a branch from Mill Valley Junction to Mill Valley. The rest of the southern lines were broad (standard) gauge, except the section between Ignacio and Glen Ellen, built as narrow gauge but converted to broad gauge in 1890.

From about 1902 to 1920 three-rail operation was in effect to accomodate both broad and narrow gauge trains between Sausalito and Manor, San Anselmo and San Rafael, and Monte Rio and Duncan Mills, all of which sections were changed to broad-gauge-only in later years. Also, certain lines that were narrow-gauge-only were changed to broad gauge, viz: Ignacio-Glen Ellen; Almonte-Mill Valley; San Rafael-San Quentin; Manor-Point Reyes; Duncan Mills-Cazadero; Duncan Mills-Markham. The lines between Markham and Willow Creek, and between Point Reyes and Monte Rio remained narrow gauge until they were abandoned. All other sections were constructed and operated as broad gauge. Because the Southern Pacific played an important part in interchanging with the Northwestern Pacific, their line in Sonoma Valley is shown entering at Schellville from the east and ending at Santa Rosa.

Suburban electric service was provided between Sausalito and Mill Valley; Sausalito and Manor via Almonte (Mill Valley Junction); Baltimore Park, Ross, San Anselmo and Fairfax; and between Sausalito and San Rafael via Baltimore Park and Detour, as well as via San Anselmo and West End. So for the eighteen year period between 1902 and 1920, Sausalito was a particularly busy terminal, and three types of operation could be observed between that point and Baltimore Park: main line standard gauge steam trains; narrow gauge steam trains; and standard gauge electric trains.

N. W. P. MAP

The compilation below indicates when sections were abandoned;

Section	Gauge	Miles	Year
Alameda Point - Corte Madera	N	6.10	1884
Sears Point - Sonoma Landing	N	3.50	1888
Duncan Mills - Azalea	N	1.25	1902
Roys - Maillard	N	4.74	1904
Camp Vacation - Bohemia - Smith Creek	B	1.99	1907
Guernewood Park - Mission Gulch	B	3.50	1908
San Rafael - San Quentin	*N	3.26	1909
San Rafael - San Anselmo	*N	2.54	1911
Mill Valley Junction - Mill Valley	*N	1.74	1911
Pedrini - Shafters	N	2.33	1913
Bridge - Willow Creek	N	5.14	1917
Duncan Mills - Markham	*N	2.80	1917
Sausalito - Point Reyes	*N	29.91	1920
Markham - Laton	B	1.10	1924
Duncan Mills - Markham	B	2.80	1925
Monte Rio - Cazadero	N	10.57	1926
Point Reyes - Monte Rio	N	37.35	1930
Santa Rosa 4th St. (P&SR)	B	1.07	1932
Duncan Mills - Cazadero	B	7.04	1933
Manor - Point Reyes	B	17.51	1933
Madrone - Glen Ellen	B	2.54	1934
Santa Rosa - Sebastopol (P&SR-NWP)	B	6.33	1934
Junction (Petaluma) - Donahue	B	5.67	1934
Fulton - Duncan Mills	B	22.99	1935
Glen Ellen - Los Guilicos	B	6.32	1941
Larkspur - San Anselmo; Fairfax - Manor	B	3.83	1942
Sonoma - Glen Ellen	B	6.59	1942
San Rafael - Fairfax	B	4.43	1942
San Quentin Branch	B	1.22	1946
Liberty - Two Rock (P&SR)	B	5.43	1952
Almonte - Mill Valley	B	1.73	1955
Baltimore Park - Larkspur	B	.51	1959
Ross - Forestville (P&SR)	B	1.08	1961

Southern Pacific section between Schellville and Madrone, and between Los Guilicos and Santa Rosa was abandoned in 1936.

* - Complete narrow gauge abandonment in favor of broad gauge operation.

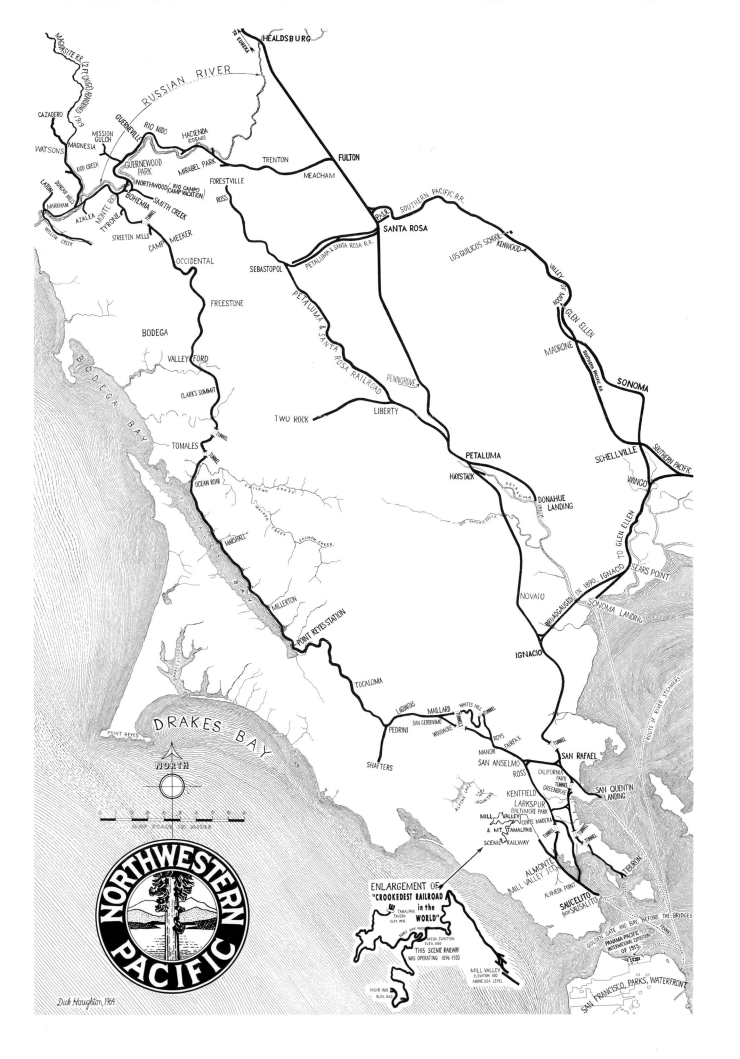

FOREWORD

"Go West, young man!" had been on the lips of many, but from San Francisco, "West" was the broad Pacific. With the cry of "Gold!" no longer heard, many a man started looking for new lands to conquer and develop. North of the "City by the Golden Gate" was the vast Redwood Empire. Prospectors were settling down which meant homes and factories and the lumber to build them. Lumber interests were felling the redwood giants around the Russian River and the area to the north, but the ponderous ox teams were too slow and cumbersome in moving the logs and timber to market. A new form of transportation was sorely needed.

In early 1862 Charles Minturn, the "Ferry Boat King," (so known for his many ferry boat enterprises around the Bay Area) started the wheels in motion to capture the freight and passenger traffic from the wagon and stage lines. Minturn applied for the right to build a horse-drawn railroad between Petaluma and Italian Garden - where the N.W.P. drawbridge is now located over Petaluma Creek. The plan was immediately attacked by the citizens of Petaluma as a poor solution to the high cost already assessed for transport to San Francisco. It seemed that a vessel came up from San Francisco, transferred its goods to a smaller boat which went a total distance of one mile and then the freight was again transferred for surface conveyance to Petaluma. The citizens maintained that the little boat operation, which cost over a thousand dollars a month, should be eliminated and the railroad built directly from Petaluma to Haystack Landing where the larger steamer took off. The Legislature, however, approved the original plan on April 18, 1862.

There are no records available to indicate when official sanction was given, but when the road finally opened in July 1864, it was completed to Haystack Landing and the power was that of a steam engine. The ferry boats assigned to the run from San Francisco were the "Clinton" and the "Contra Costa."

Shortly after 8:00 a.m. on August 27, 1866, after some sixty passengers had climbed aboard from the trip to Haystack Landing, the engine blew up at the Petaluma Station, killing four persons and injuring many more. Fortunately, the engine blew sideways and there were very few injuries to passengers in the coaches. The coroner's jury reported it had found evidence that "there was not sufficient water in the boiler, and the explosion occurred from an over-pressure of steam."

The following month the railroad was busy adjusting the cars and fitting the track for application of horse-power until another steam engine could be purchased. The "iron horse" never arrived; consequently, the cars were hauled by mules until the beginning of the Donahue Railroad in 1869.

Upon the death of Charles Minturn, the property passed into the hands of Benjamin M. Hartshorne, administrator of his estate, who conveyed the property on February 28, 1874, to the Contra Costa Steam Navigation Company (a San Francisco Bay ferry operator organized in 1852) of which Minturn had been the head for many years.

The little rail line known as the Petaluma & Haystack Railroad was the first of the forty-one roads in the Redwood Empire whose properties eventually became part of the Northwestern Pacific Railroad. By 1906 these forty-one roads had been consolidated into six, variously under the control of the Southern Pacific and the Santa Fe. These two companies formed the Northwestern Pacific Railway on November 24th of that year. On January 8, 1907, the name was changed to the Northwestern Pacific Railroad, bringing into being the organization about which this book is primarily written.

While this volume is basically a photographic and historical record of motive power and passenger equipment and property as it has existed since January 8, 1907, we will touch, though relatively lightly, on things prior to that date. Return with us now to the inspiring days when the steam locomotive and passenger train were the backbone of transportation in the Redwood Empire.

SAN FRANCISCO & NORTH PACIFIC RAILWAY
(CALIFORNIA NORTHWESTERN RAILWAY)

The first railroad to get under way (after the Petaluma & Haystack) was The Sonoma County Railroad Company. This road was incorporated on January 10, 1868, and it was intended to build a line from Petaluma to Healdsburg via Santa Rosa with a branch to Bloomfield. Construction failed to even start and, by Deed of Sale dated July 28, 1868, the corporation transferred its right to The San Francisco & Humboldt Bay Railroad Company. This company fared a little better and some grading was accomplished between Petaluma and Santa Rosa, but no rail was put down.

Meanwhile, the California Pacific Rail Road offered to build a railroad from the Napa County Line (Napa Junction) to Petaluma, Santa Rosa, Healds-

burg and on to Cloverdale with a branch to Bloomfield if the county would vote a $5,000 per mile subsidy to the road. A county election on June 14, 1869, voted in favor of this subsidy with a three year deadline.

However, Colonel Peter Donahue, having sold his San Francisco & San Jose Railroad to the Southern Pacific Railroad in 1868, had become interested in the Redwood Empire and on August 2, 1869, bought a portion of the rights of The San Francisco & Humboldt Bay Railroad which had been held by the county. The price was $40,000. Rights-of-way were donated by a number of property owners and grading and the laying of rail was started. By October 10, 1869, ten miles had been completed from Petaluma

"Dedicated to Mechanics by James Donahue in memory of his father Peter Donahue," is the inscription on this statue that stands at Bush, Sansome and Market Streets in San Francisco, honoring the builder of the San Francisco & North Pacific Railway. This photo was taken one month after the San Francisco earthquake and fire in 1906.

north. Donahue was going to establish Petaluma as the southern terminus, but due to arguments with the city fathers over depot rights, he conceived the idea of making the southern terminal of the railroad almost eight miles south thereof, or at a point which became known as "Donahue Landing." By November 8, 1869, five miles were completed toward the Landing. Then came the birth of The San Francisco & North Pacific Rail Road, for on November 17, 1869, (the date of organization) the remainder of the rights of The San Francisco & Humboldt Bay Railroad were conveyed to the new company. December 8th of the same year saw another five miles constructed to the north of Petaluma and three miles to the Landing to complete that leg. By January 1, 1870, the line was completed to Santa Rosa, but it was almost a year later (October 31, 1870) before the first regular passenger train reached that point.

The California Pacific Railroad, with the "paper" subsidy it had obtained by vote the year before, suddenly started to grade a line alongside the Donahue route. This brought Colonel Donahue down to the offices of the "Cal. P." to see what could be done to stifle this rival operation. Out of this came a startling announcement, for on April 13, 1871, Donahue sold his interest in the SF&NP to the "Cal. P." Sonoma County was flabbergasted and did not view the deal with satisfaction because of the immediate increase in freight and passenger rates. On August 1, 1871, the "Cal. P." came under the control of the Central Pacific and this group lost no time in extending the rails to Cloverdale in order to qualify for the subsidy which was due to end in June, 1872. There was talk of making Saucelito or Tiburon the western terminal for transcontinental trains but, like so much conversation of the times, nothing came of it. Then came the next surprising development: in January, 1873, Donahue bought the SF&NP back again.

All in all Donahue, with his moves and countermoves, was quite happy. The railroad in the Redwood Empire had been realized, was operating, had received at total of $300,000 from the county in a building subsidy, and had obtained a great deal of the right-of-way through gifts from property owners.

When Donahue came over from the San Francisco & San Jose Railroad, he brought with him one locomotive, No. 2, the "San Jose," which was given the number "1" on the SF&NP, but kept the same name. This engine, which became affectionately known as "Little Josie," was used extensively in building the road and when it was scrapped in 1920 by the Northwestern Pacific, it was reported to have been the oldest active steam engine in the country at that time.

Time Table No. 1 shows the official start of the SF&NP to Healdsburg as Sunday, July 9, 1871, with

North end of the Ferry building in 1880 where SF&NP passengers boarded the boats for Tiburon.

a daily (except Sunday) passenger train along with a freight and accommodation train. Trains to Cloverdale started on April 15, 1872, with a total of 52.76 miles in operation. Civic officials of Petaluma, however, looked on Donahue with disfavor. They therefore gathered some of the capital in the locality and proceeded to try to spite the gentleman by building a line from Petaluma to San Rafael to connect with the San Rafael & San Quentin Railroad which had a connection to San Francisco by ferry. The proposed right-of-way, which at the time was in the hands of the Contra Costa Navigation Company, was conveyed on September 30, 1874, to Milton S. Latham, one-time Governor of the State, a U.S. Senator, and one of the incorporators of the North Pacific Coast narrow gauge. He held the land as trustee only, deeding it to the Sonoma & Marin Railroad on March 23, 1875. This company would then build a narrow gauge road from Petaluma to San Rafael for the Petaluma group. One locomotive (no record available) and several cars were obtained and construction started. Unfortunately, the company ran out of money and the road ended in the salt marshes near Novato. Donahue, who had visions of a faster connection to San Francisco, was watching with interest, and he bought the property "as is" on October 27, 1876, for $85,000. He then started the line all over again from Petaluma by constructing a broad gauge road. The distance from Petaluma to San Rafael was 21.50 miles.

Seeing the rival North Pacific Coast advancing rapidly to the Russian River area, and planning to take a good share of the lumber business, Donahue made a deal with the lumber interests at Guerneville to build a railroad from his SF&NP at Fulton if they would furnish free bridge timbers and the right-of-way. The agreement was concluded in September, 1874, but construction, under the name of the Fulton & Guerneville Railroad, did not get under way until a year later. Some of the sections were costly to build, sometimes reaching as high as $75,000 a mile. The lumber people started to renege on the deal they had made about free timbers; consequently, when the line reached Korbel's (12 miles west of Fulton), Donahue got on his "high horse" and

SF&NP No. 99 (later NWP 99) was known as the "Coffee Grinder." This contraption hauled logging trains and river locals along the Guerneville branch.

Original Guerneville station and end of the line for many years before the branch was extended to Camp Vacation and later Cazadero.

declared, "That's as far as I'm going!" Service started to that point from Fulton on Monday, May 29, 1876; however, the lumber interests, still hauling logs and lumber by teams, forced Donahue to build to Guerneville, and the line was opened to that point on Sunday, March 25, 1877. Total distance from Fulton to Guerneville: 15.27 miles.

On July 12, 1877, a reorganization took place whereby the San Francisco & North Pacific Railroad came into being by the consolidation of The San Francisco & North Pacific Rail Road, Sonoma & Marin Railroad and the Fulton & Guerneville Railroad. The intent of the consolidation was to combine the interests of Donahue who was the controlling factor in all of the companies.

Fulton, five miles north of Santa Rosa, was a busy junction in early days. SF&NP engine No. 5 with Guerneville mixed train is at left, while at right is SF&NP No. 16 with the main-line passenger train, and a freight train can be seen in the background.

The SF&NP pushed its new broad gauge link into San Rafael and opened service on June 2, 1879, connecting with the narrow gauge SR&SQ Railroad at San Rafael for transportation to San Quentin and ferry to San Francisco - that is, almost - for a half-mile stage connection between the SF&NP station and the SR&SQ station in San Rafael was required of the traveler. With this new arrangement only one ferry connection was left to Donahue Landing which connected with a train having Cloverdale as its destination.

The transfer was not satisfactory at San Rafael because of the stage connection. The operation was therefore temporarily suspended on September 15, 1879, and the service went back to Donahue Landing for passenger trains. It was reinstated via San Rafael on June 21, 1880. To eliminate the inconvenience, dusty and "sardine can" half-mile stage ride, the SF&NP decided to extend its track about half a mile

to the North Pacific Coast San Rafael "B" Street Station. The new connecting passenger service commenced on April 3, 1882, and gave the SF&NP passengers a much better facility in their travel to San Francisco, which now could be made either via San Quentin, or the Saucelito narrow gauge train and ferry connection.

Donahue, however, was looking for a better way to transport his passengers and freight to San Francisco. On October 21, 1882, he organized The San Francisco & San Rafael Rail Road Company for the purpose of building a railroad from San Rafael to Tiburon Point on Raccoon Strait, a distance of nine miles. Three tunnels had to be built plus trestles over marsh land. The project was completed on April 28, 1884, at a cost of $677,779.50, and Tiburon became the permanent southern terminus of the SF&NP.

SF&NP engine No. 2 (later NWP 6) on a work train assignment on the Gallinas Slough trestle.

14

Tiburon became the southern rail terminal, as shown in this crisp panorama, of the SF&NP on April 28, 1884. Train sheds were added a few years later.

The facilities at Donahue Landing were moved lock, stock and barrel to Tiburon. First the railroad shop was put on a barge, then the carpenter shop, the Sonoma Hotel, the depot (still in existence at Tiburon today) and all other structures. Having a dirt floor, the roundhouse was not moveable, but it burned down anyway in the months that followed and the Landing reverted to being just another turn in Petaluma Creek. Donahue died November 26, 1885. Financial affairs of the railroad were not in good order. However, Donahue's son, James, carried on and organized The Cloverdale & Ukiah Rail Road Company on August 17, 1886, for the purpose of building 28.50 miles of line from Cloverdale to Ukiah. The line was four miles from completion when, on March 13, 1889, the property was sold to the newly formed San Francisco & North Pacific Railway Company which had come about as the result of a reorganization on December 19, 1888. Other roads included in the sale were the San Francisco & North Pacific Railroad, The San Francisco & San Rafael Rail Road, The Marin & Napa Rail Road, the Sonoma & Santa Rosa Rail Road, and the Sonoma Valley Railroad. This gave the new company a line from Tiburon to Ukiah with branch lines to Donahue, Guerneville and Glen Ellen.

In 1889 the SF&NP also organized the Santa Rosa, Sebastopol & Green Valley Railroad to build a line from Santa Rosa to Sebastopol - a distance of 6.32 miles. The road was open for traffic on February 17, 1890.

On March 3, 1890, at the age of only thirty, James Mervyn Donahue passed away. For three years the SF&NP was run for the executors of the estate and then, by court order, was sold at public auction on the steps of the courthouse at San Rafael. The highest bidder was a syndicate formed by Andrew Markham, Sydney V. Smith and A. W. Foster, so by Deed of Sale dated March 23, 1893, the properties of the SF&NP were awarded these three gentlemen.

On April 9, 1890, the tracks between Ignacio and Sears Point and Sears Point and Glen Ellen were officially changed from narrow to broad gauge. The narrow gauge trackage between Sears Point and Sonoma Landing, which had been abandoned two years before, was taken up. This made the SF&NP an entirely broad gauge road.

To extend further into the Russian River logging country, the Guerneville branch was lengthened 4.88 miles into the Meeker tract (later Bohemia) by April 1, 1892. In addition, a lumber line was laid from Guernewood Park to Finley - a distance of three miles. This was part of the Guerne & Murphy Railroad which was later taken over. In a few years this section was cut back a half mile and extended up Mission Gulch a little over two miles to more lucrative timber area.

In 1896 a temporary ferry station was constructed for the SF&NP so the present ferry building could be constructed.

15

SF&NP engines 11 and 10 on Sunday excursion train at Camp Vacation around the turn of the century.

The railroad struggled through the panic of 1893, but it was becoming very unsteady and in 1898 it was ready for the auction block once again. Its corporate entity was saved by a lease negotiated by the California Northwestern Railway Company on September 30, 1898, the day the line was, for the second time, offered for sale on the courthouse steps in San Rafael. Leading the incorporators was Arthur W. Foster of the California Northwestern Railway who had formed the new corporation on March 17, 1898. With a shot in the arm moneywise (a good chunk probably coming from the Southern Pacific which had become intensely interested because of the Santa Fe's activities in northern California) construction northward was again started. The California Northwestern reached Laughlin on March 17, 1901; Willits, March 1, 1902 and Sherwood, May 14, 1904 - a total of 39.91 miles, including mountain building of grades up to 3%.

In 1900 the CNW started an innovation, a fore-runner of today's "piggy-back." Loading ramps were constructed at San Rafael and Tiburon. Special cars, dubbed "Elephant Cars," were loaded with wagons, including the horses, through doors constructed at the car ends. When the passenger train came along, the cars would be hooked right behind the engine. At Tiburon, wagons with their full loads of merchandise, would go down the ramps and onto the ferry boat for San Francisco, or vice versa. Better roads between San Rafael and Tiburon ended the service shortly after the San Francisco earthquake of 1906.

The California Northwestern was also interested in getting some of the traffic in Napa Valley; hence, an agreement was reached with the Southern Pacific wherein it (the CNW) would have trackage rights between Ramal and Buchli and between Union and Calistoga. To make it a more direct route, the CNW incorporated the San Francisco & Napa Valley Railway on November 27, 1903, for the purpose of

building two segments: Wingo to Ramal, 2.08 miles and Buchli to Union, 8.62 miles. The line was opened for service by the CNW on May 1, 1905, with one passenger train a day between Tiburon and Calistoga via San Rafael. On July 19, 1906, the line was leased to, and on August 12, 1911, sold to the Southern Pacific Railroad. Passenger trains between Tiburon and Calistoga were discontinued on September 18, 1911.

A scene on the Sherwood branch in 1905.

SF&NP locomotive 16 at Santa Rosa, one month after earthquake of April 18, 1906 which destroyed the flour mill in the background. Directly behind locomotive is Wells Fargo Express car No. 254. The locomotive was destroyed in a head-on collision south of Ignacio four years later when it was under the NWP banner.

The greatest excitement in the life of the CNW occurred on March 1, 1905, when the Petaluma & Santa Rosa Electric Railway attempted to lay a cross-over track on the CNW main line just south of the Santa Rosa station in order to complete its line from Sebastopol to Santa Rosa. With plenty of news coverage of the bitter rivalry between the two roads, practically the entire populace of Santa Rosa

A photo of the crossing incident detailed in the text on this page.

and surrounding towns was on the side lines to watch the fight. An injunction obtained by the CNW had been dissolved and the electric line was ready to put in the cross-over. It put a big force of men to the task when all of a sudden the CNW came along with their locomotives (No. 9 and 12) and several cars loaded with gravel, and ran them back and forth across the projected crossing. Many men were hurt. The CNW men threw sand, dirt and rocks on the rails faster than the electric workers could shovel it off. Steam and hot water were also blown on the men from the CNW engines. Finally, in desperation so his men could get the crossing cut, a director threw himself over the tracks in front of the CNW engine. With the engine touching him, his men began a tug-of-war with his body; one faction trying to pull him off, the other trying to keep him on. The now "stretched" official received a lasting momento of the affair when the locomotive scalded his head with steam! It all ended when another injunction arrived permitting the electric line to proceed, and the next day the electric road was running in downtown Santa Rosa.

The incorporation of the CNW into the Northwestern Pacific will be told later in the story.

A balloon-stacked engine and train of the California Northwestern Railway are the center of this delightful photograph made at Chiquita (near Healdsburg) about the year 1901.

"SONOMA VALLEY LINES"

As early as 1865, consideration was given to the building of a railroad in the Sonoma Valley but it was ten years later, on February 18, 1875, when an experimental road called the Sonoma Valley Prismoidal Railway was finally incorporated. Its purpose was to build from the community of Sonoma to a point along Sonoma Creek or nearby San Pablo Bay for a terminus in transferring passengers to ferry boats for the journey to San Francisco. Throughout the United States there were a number of prismoidal systems in use. Their construction cost was relatively low - about $4,500 per mile including equipment. Actual construction on the Sonoma line started in the latter part of June 1876, from a point called Norfolk (now known as Wingo) on the Northwestern Pacific's Sonoma branch. By August 16, 1876, rail was being mounted along the necessary construction in this type of railroad, a cross section of which is shown in an accompanying diagram.

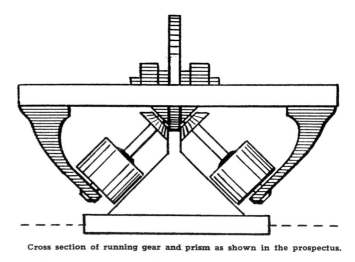

Cross section of running gear and prism as shown in the prospectus.

The locomotive used on this road, built at the Pacific Iron Works in San Francisco, was the first and only one of its type ever constructed in California. The company owned one locomotive, one box car and ten flat cars.

18

The first section of track was 3.50 miles long and started from Norfolk running to a point near Schellville (along Schell's Road). It was finished on November 24, 1876, and on that date was opened to the public for an inspection trip. The excursionists arrived on the ferry "Sonoma" from San Francisco and immediately began an inspection of the contraption. They were more eager for a ride, however, so with the one locomotive and two flat cars which had been equipped with benches on either side, they started. The train swayed a little but as it picked up speed, it ran more smoothly. At the end of the line they saw workmen putting the finishing touches on the remaining 1½ miles of the five mile road. Actually the northern terminus was to be about a mile west of Sonoma, with an extension planned to Santa Rosa and a branch to Buena Vista and still another to Sears Point. Even though the excursionists gave a grand account of the entire operation, the line lasted only six months, for on May 5, 1877, it ceased operations. Because of the peculiar construction, no satisfactory method could be devised for crossing a country road. Recent researchers have been unable to locate any trace of this line.

On July 24, 1878, the Sonoma Valley Railroad was incorporated to build a narrow gauge line in place of the prismoidal line whose properties were taken over on September 11, 1878. The new railroad changed the right-of-way slightly and built directly into Sonoma from Norfolk. The latter point, however, was not a satisfactory terminal. The line therefore was extended to a point on Petaluma Creek and given the name "Sonoma Landing." To service this point, arrangements were made with the SF&NP to have its steamers stop on their way to and from Donahue Landing for the San Francisco connection. The length of the line was 15 miles. The road had three locomotives and four passenger cars. It started service in November 1879.

On March 2, 1881, another line was organized in Sonoma Valley, that of the Sonoma & Santa Rosa Rail Road. It constructed and placed in operation on August 15, 1882, a narrow gauge line 6.53 miles in length from Sonoma to Glen Ellen. Funds for the construction were furnished by the San Francisco & North Pacific Railroad.

On August 7, 1885, the second Sonoma Valley Railroad was incorporated. By articles of consolidation dated June 30, 1885, the first company of this name and that of the Sonoma & Santa Rosa Rail Road Company conveyed their properties to the new company.

Sonoma Valley Engine 3 and mixed train at Glen Ellen station in 1887.

Another railroad to start and actually build (the last before consolidation of all Sonoma Valley lines under the San Francisco & North Pacific) was The Marin & Napa Rail Road Company. It was incorporated on August 17, 1886 and commenced construction of its narrow gauge line from Marin and Napa Junction (later Pacheco and still later Ignacio) to Sears Point on June 18, 1887. The distance was 7.67 miles. Because the line was built mainly on piles over the marshes, it was more than a year before it was placed in operation under lease to the Sonoma Valley Railroad - June 30, 1888.

Built by the Sonoma Valley Railroad in 1881, Sonoma Station, altho rebuilt at various times, was destroyed by fire, January 6, 1976.

NORTH PACIFIC COAST RAILROAD
(NORTH SHORE RAILROAD)

Much has been written about this famous line, which quietly went out of existence on Saturday, March 29, 1930. Had railfan excursions been in the prominence then as they are now, the farewell given this little "pike" would have been witnessed by hundreds, instead of the handful that came out to see its passing - a lone banner flying from the single coach with the words, "Gone, but not forgotten."

The North Pacific Coast Railroad (later the North Shore) was incorporated on December 19, 1871 with James Shafter listed as President. The nine directors included a Mr. Austin D. Moore, the ambitious gentleman of the group who promoted the venture and who was made President of the railroad just a few weeks after incorporation. He went from store to store and from farm house to farm house telling the populace to sell the railroad idea to the County Supervisors, as their help was needed in voting to issue bonds to finance the line. Moore promised to run the road through San Rafael, Tomales and up the coast to the Gualala River. On January 29, 1872 the Board voted to issue bonds in the amount of $160,000 to build the line as indicated. However, enthusiasm was short-lived, for it was not long before a Mr. George Black, Chief Engineer, resigned, saying that the building of a railroad to Gualala River was senseless, impractical and bordered on the impossible. The resultant publicity caused the people of Marin County to view the project with distrust, especially when the railroad now wanted a third of a million to finance the line, instead of the $160,000 just voted. President Moore, however, didn't stop in his efforts, and left no stone unturned. He managed to obtain 30 acres along the shore of Richardson's Bay from the Saucelito Land and Ferry Company as a gift for a rail terminal. His biggest effort, and the one that gave the road what it needed, was getting Milton S. Latham interested. Here was a man of enormous wealth, well known, a former California Congressman, Governor and appointed a United States Senator. President Moore now had the backing he needed, and construction got under way in March, 1873.

The objective was no longer Gualala River, but to get the rails to the Russian River where heavy timber felling was taking place. Three construction gangs were set-up, one near Strawberry Point, across Richardson's Bay from Saucelito, one in the hills above Fairfax, and the other at Tomales, which would work both north and south. The equipment used was a far cry from what would be available today, for then it was the Chinese coolie digging and hauling dirt and rock in dump carts. The ground breaking ceremonies, heralding the commencement of the line, took place in Saucelito on Saturday, April 12, 1873. There were, as usual, several speeches, and then a banquet where President Moore presided.

In midsummer, 1874, track layers had gone beyond Corte Madera ridge and were laying the rail into the community of Corte Madera. A newspaper report of the time stated that "the NPC had completed a little over six miles of line, with some 30 miles graded. The railroad had enough material to reach north to Tomales, had received one locomotive, expected five more any day and five passenger cars were being built. To keep construction moving some 1300 coolies were employed along with 200 white "supervisors." The rails reached San Rafael on the Junction-San Rafael branch on July 25, 1874.

The building of the line over White's Hill from Fairfax, hampered by slides, moved along slowly. However, once around the two "horns" and over the hill grading moved rapidly to Lagunitas. Along Paper Mill Creek work again crawled along as much heavy timber felling and brush cutting had to be accomplished. Past Point Reyes grading was a simple task as the line followed for the most part the curvatures of Tomales Bay. Meanwhile at the Tomales end the construction crew had received locomotive No. 1, which had been brought from Saucelito by scow via the Pacific Ocean, Tomales Bay and up Keyes Creek and unloaded just above the contemplated Ocean Roar bridge. Forging ahead, the rail-laying gangs met at a point near Millerton to complete the line through to Tomales in December, 1874. On January 7, 1875, with the ringing of cow bells and the firing of guns, the big day came with the operation of the first train from *Saucelito to Tomales.

While construction to Tomales was going on, the railroad was also seeking control of the San Rafael & San Quentin Railroad. This line was incorporated on February 25, 1869, and built as a broad gauge between title points. Ferry

* - Saucelito was once "Saucelito Bluffs" meaning "Little Willows." Name changed from Saucelito to Sausalito in 1884. In this story reference relating to period before 1884 Saucelito is thusly spelled, after 1884 - Sausalito.

In the early days passengers boarded the ferries at the foot of Market Street in San Francisco for the ride to the train terminal at Sausalito.

Sausalito Ferry Landing in 1893. The boats are the Tamalpais and San Rafael; the engine is NPC 15 (later NWP 90).

boats plied between San Francisco and San Quentin and connected with the trains. With other powerful groups not interested in this short line, the NPC was quick to grab it up, so on March 11, 1875, the road was leased for 43 years. The section was reconstructed immediately; in fact, it became narrow gauge, (three feet) in one month! Certain track alignment was also necessary at San Rafael, as the SR&SQ station and tracks were about a block over from the NPC station, and a new depot, turntable and engine shed were also built. On June 1, 1875, the main line passenger terminal was shifted from Saucelito to San Quentin. Even though it would be a longer ferry trip for passengers, it would save time because the grade north of Lyford's between Saucelito and San Rafael, slowed trains considerably plus several station stops. A few trains did, however, operate via Saucelito for local passengers. The routing via San Quentin remained until 1884.

Finishing the tunnel just north of Tomales, the NPC forged ahead. Numerous trestles were constructed between Clark Summit and Valley Ford and on to Freestone, which was the terminus for almost a half a year while working crews were grading to Howards (later Occidental), which was to be the highest point on the line, 575 feet. In September, 1876, the road reached Russian River (now Monte Rio), and was opened to Moscow Mills on October 16, 1876. A branch of a little more than a half a mile was built from Russian River station upstream to the Madrona Mill, located near the Bohemian Grove area of today.

Alexander Duncan, who operated a lumber mill just east of Jenner, near the mouth of the Russian River, entered into an agreement with the NPC specifying that if the railroad extended its trackage across the river from Moscow Mills, he would move his mill up the river to a new location, directly across from Moscow Mills, which was flat and excellent for extensive operation. Duncan had purchased some 4,000 acres of timber stand along Austin Creek, and the new site would bring his mill closer to the forest. The NPC erected a bridge across the Russian River, named the area Duncan Mills and constructed a station, roundhouse, turntable and other maintenance buildings required, for this was to be the northern terminus; the railroad had no thoughts of going any further. The first train puffed into Duncan Mills, May 5, 1877.

Instead of an air of accomplishment hanging over the executive offices of the NPC, faces were glum. Neither taxes nor interest due on the bonds had been paid. To get the road into more favorable financial light, Milton Latham took over the reins as President. The spending, which was characteristic of the road in building, continued. Passenger cars were kept immaculate in their bright yellow, locomotives were polished and buildings along the right-of-way were clean and spotless. President Latham even had built an ornate private car, the "Millwood", for use of officials, financiers and friends to show them the road.

While much attention was given the railroad proper, Latham did not forget that to go between Saucelito and San Francisco meant a six mile ferry ride. The ferry boats presently in service, the "Contra Costa," "Clinton" and "Tamalpais" (No. 1) were anything but the latest word. With

Russian River station around 1880. This later became Monte Rio. The track to the right went to the Madrona Lumber mill, a half-mile distant. The track to the left continued on to Duncan Mills.

the idea of building up the tremendous passenger potential in Marin and Sonoma Counties, Latham ordered in 1876 two elegant steamers, to be built on the east coast, the "San Rafael" and the "Saucelito." After each vessel was completed, all pieces of machinery, timbers and woodwork were carefully marked and the entire steamer dismantled. The parts were then shipped to San Francisco by rail, 239 freight cars being required for the haul! The boats were then reassembled, and the "San Rafael" made her first trip between San Francisco and San Quentin on August 11, 1877, and the "Saucelito" on October 16, 1877. The ferries won immediate approval; they were truly the "last word" with much gold trim and polished walnut; even their benches were upholstered in deep-red velvet.

With money being spent "hand over fist," and the railroad failing even to earn its operating expenses, the monied pockets of Latham were beginning to become mighty lean. To make matters worse, the inflated prices caused by heavy speculation in the Nevada Comstock collapsed and stock prices started falling. The result was financial panic, which in turn brought a business recession lasting into the 80's. Then on October 27, 1877, came the road's first marine disaster. The ferries "Clinton" and "Petaluma" collided, with the result that the "Clinton" went to the bottom of the bay.

Rumors were now flying that Latham was bankrupt, and while these rumors were squelched, it was the truth. In fact, Latham decided to take a trip to Europe to see if he could interest European capital in his railroad venture. In his absence, a friend and business associate, Joseph G. Eastland, was appointed temporary President of the NPC. On April 8, 1878, when President Eastland was returning from the Russian River in the private car "Millwood," the car left the rails in Lagunitas Canyon, plunged down the embankment and killed his infant daughter. Eastland wanted no more to do with the railroad and promptly resigned. This left the narrow gauge without a leader to guide its muddled affairs until Latham returned in the summer of 1880.

About this time a number of Tourist Guides were published in the United States to describe interesting points of railroad travel. The one published by George Crofutt probably was the best. Crofutt travelled extensively throughout the land on the many railroads to obtain his data. It is of interest to note what he said in his travel Guide of the NPC, so let us take a ride with him.

"The NPC had two southern termini, which unite at Junction (later San Anselmo) 17 miles from San Francisco. The bay was crossed by ferry from the Davis Street wharf for Saucelito and from the Market Street wharf for San Quentin. The prison of San Quentin is passed and thence San Rafael, which has a population of 3,000 and

Train time was getting near as bicyclists wheeled up to the station platform at San Anselmo in 1898.

23

two weekly papers, the Herald and Journal. At
Junction connects the track from Saucelito and
the train proceeds to Fairfax and up White's Hill
from which the scenery is beautiful. Thence at an
altitude the train plunges into a 1250 foot tunnel
and descends to San Geronimo. Passing Lagunitas,
an extensive picnic ground is seen where
thousands come on Sundays and holidays by
special trains. The train comes to Taylorville,
named in honor of a Samuel Taylor, who established the first paper mill on the Pacific
Coast at this location known as the "Pioneer
Paper Mill." After Tocoloma comes Olema (later
Point Reyes Station), an eating station, the only
one on the road, and where the train stops for
20 minutes. Leaving the timbered lands the
train soon follows along Tomales Bay where it
runs along the edge of the bay, around rocky
points, through spurs of the bluffs and across
little inlets for 16 miles passing through such
places as Millerton and Marshall. At Hamlet the
regular passenger trains meet. From here the
road follows up a little narrow valley around
rocky points, with high grass covered hills on
each side - makes one great rainbow curve, away
around the head of the valley and arrives at
Tomales where the railroad has large warehouses
for storing grain and from which large quanities
are shipped annually. Next, through a tunnel and
on to Griffins (now Fallon) and Valley Ford
station where the waters from Bodega Bay can
be seen sitting back near the station on the left.

Three miles further, Bodega Roads and another
mile Freestone. Thence a heavy grade, and
another great horse-shoe curve around the head
of a small valley. First the road bed is far above,
then far below, with a deep gorge on the left,
then the trestle bridge, 300 feet long and 137 feet
high, over a frightful gorge, beyond which is the
town of Howards (now Occidental). Redwoods
now appear on each side, as also saw mills.
Streeten Mill is passed on the left, then another
tunnel and the train decends into Tyrone Mills.
Here are extensive saw mills on the left with
side tracks running to them. The mills have a
capacity of 40,000 feet of lumber per day. Soon
Russian River (now Monte Rio) and the train
runs along the southern bank to Moscow Mills,
opposite which comes in from the north, Austin
Creek, the area abounding in the redwoods. Then
over a bridge 400 feet long and the train is at
the end of the line - Duncan Mills. Here are
many saw mills, one large hotel, the Julian - a
good station building and shops of the railroad.
Along the line of this road are located many saw
mills, which produce daily for market some
200,000 feet of redwood lumber, very profitable

24

Sausalito Terminal in 1903 during the extensive re-arrangement of track to include both gauges.

for the narrow gauge."

Crofutt says in conclusion, "the scenery along the whole line is very interesting. The rapid changes and the great variety are charming, instructive and when once made will live in pleasant memory."

It didn't take long to determine that Latham was unsuccessful in getting capital in Europe - he and the NPC were broke. On December 23, 1880, foreclosure was filed against the railroad, and it was purchased for $800,000.00 by James D. Walker of Falkner Bell & Co., who represented many of the creditors and bond holders. Walker was made President. For Latham, he had to sell his remaining holdings, art treasurers, home - everything - to pay his debts. He ended without a penny. The new President and his Board of Directors soon were out on the line making a careful inspection with an eye to a profitable operation. Walker wanted to abandon the entire line north of San Anselmo, keeping only the Saucelito - San Quentin horseshoe, but his Directors were a little hesitant in cutting off such a large section, and voted four to three to keep the line "as is." Too, more and more people were coming to Marin County and new factories were being opened and the depression was easing up, so things once again were in the optimistic light.

On December 6, 1882, the North Pacific Coast Railroad Extension Company was formed to build a more direct route from Pine (Alameda Point) to Corte Madera. This would involve the construction of one tunnel. As built in 1873 the railroad did not follow the line of later years, but at Pine circled around an inlet, angled to the right and proceeded across Richardson's Bay on a 4000 foot trestle to Strawberry Point. From this point it climbed rapidly, passing Lyford's station, thence Summit (where the present free-way goes over the hill just beyond the Tiburon turn-off), and then dropped along until opposite San Clemente, where passengers once got off to go to the race track. The line then descended along the foothills, dropping into Corte Madera.

In the spring of 1883 construction camps were set-up, and the work of boring through a new tunnel commenced. The material obtained from the tunnel was used to build a new road bed over the salt marsh from Alameda Point to just north of the Saucelito Terminal to give the road more of a straight line. The new direct line, 5.37 miles, would save time and expense, and while the first train ran over the new cut-off on February 19, 1884, the official opening was on April 26, 1884. The cost of the project came to $276,728.57. The old line of 6.10 miles was then abandoned. But all did not remain quiet, for the next item in the life of the NPC was a law suit filed by Dr. Benjamin Lyford for breach of contract. It seems that when the railroad was first constructed along Strawberry Point, the Lyford family allowed it to be built through their property with several stipulations, one of which was free passage to and from San Francisco. When the railroad opened the cut-off, the pass privileges came to an end. The Superior Court gave its decision in favor of the railroad, but the Lyfords appealed the case to the State Supreme Court, which finally upheld the lower court, and thus ended the fracas.

On the evening of February 24, 1884, the ferry "Saucelito" caught fire while she was berthed at the San Quentin wharf. Before any help could arrive the boat was a mass of flames. To save the wharf and train sheds the steamer was cut adrift and sank half a mile off shore. This disaster left the narrow gauge in a sad situation - it could not operate both from San Quentin and Saucelito with the remaining boats. It could have leased a boat from the Southern Pacific or started immediate construction of another, but the road didn't have the money to do either. So, on April 26, 1884, the railroad reluctantly discontinued the San Quentin ferry service and 0.22 mile of line that ran out on the wharf at San Quentin to the ferry slip was abandoned. However, commute service from Saucelito used San Quentin as its outer terminus for many years, even into the beginning days of the Northwestern Pacific.

President Walker resigned on January 1, 1885, and in March John W. Coleman took control as President with a new set of Directors. These men owned extensive timber areas along Austin Creek north of Duncan Mills, and their apparent interest in taking over the "slim pike" was to have their own railroad to haul their lumber. On August 19, 1885, the North Western Railroad Company of California was incorporated, and in accordance with an agreement with the North Pacific Coast Railroad, the latter was to construct along Austin Creek, a narrow gauge line of 7.41 miles in length from Duncan Mills to Ingrams (later Cazadero), lease the road and its equipment at

The hotel gardens at Duncan Mills about 1899. This area is now a barren field.

an annual rental of $2,900.00, and acquire the right to purchase the property for $58,000. A line was also built from Kidd Creek west for about half a mile to haul logs to the mill at Duncan Mills. Also from Duncan Mills construction was started on 2.8 mile branch to Markham, and another branch just short of Markham that crossed the Russian River on a trestle and went along Willow Creek for 5.14 miles. The latter operation was permitted only in the summer months, as in the winter the trestle over the river became dangerous because of high water. The NPC also constructed another short logging line to Azalea (Freezeout) across the river from Duncan Mills.

The engine "Tyrone" hauled lumber flats around Tyrone Mills, then was sold to the Duncan Mills Land & Lumber Company and hauled log cars from Kidd Creek spur to the mill at Duncan Mills on the Russian River.

Cazadero, the end of the narrow gauge line. Note the three-way stub switch.

To provide transportation to a new real estate development at the base of Mt. Tamalpais (to become the town of Mill Valley), incorporation papers were filed on September 6, 1889 for the San Francisco, Tamalpais & Bolinas Railway Company to build a branch line from Bay Junction (later Mill Valley Junction and still later Almonte) to Mill Valley. The line, 1.74 miles, was completed October 13, 1889, but regular service did not start until March 17, 1890. The cost of the line was $26,000. The road was absorbed into the NPC on April 22, 1892. "Mill Valley" had its name changed on June 29, 1892 to "Eastland" in honor of one of the real estate developers, but on March 4, 1904, it was renamed "Mill Valley."

In Fourth of July bunting stands NPC Engine 16 (later NWP 91) at San Rafael "B" Street Station.

Financially the little pike could never get itself off the ground. The minute something looked a little rosy to take care of the multitude of leases and obligations of one sort or another some disaster struck. The winter of 1889-1890 was a particularly bad one. For almost the entire month of January, 1890, it rained and stormed. The bridge across the river at Duncan Mills was partially knocked off its foundations, and many trestles along the road were washed out; in fact, service from Duncan Mills to Cazadero was not in operation for almost six months. However, there always seemed to be additional finances obtainable for improvements. In 1891 two larger locomotives were purchased, better service was offered in the suburban area, and a number of coaches that had just been delivered had the new innovation of steam heat, seats right by windows, and even the windows could be raised and lowered for ventilation to the passenger's taste.

In May, 1892, President Coleman resigned, and in his place came William Steele. He walked right into the economic depression of 1893-1894, and bond holders had given up the hope that they would receive any return on their invest-

ment. They were willing to sell their bonds for anything they could get. On May 20, 1893, Messrs. J. B. Stetson, Borel, deGuigne and J.C. Coleman of Grass Valley bought up the controlling interest in the narrow gauge. President Steele, whose term of office was short-lived, turned over the reins to J. B. Stetson.

With new blood the NPC in November, 1893, ordered a double-end ferry boat from the Fulton Iron Works to replace the worn-out "Tamalpais." It was given the name "Sausalito". The steamer was launched on May 21, 1894, and after a few quick trial runs was placed in service. It was constructed to carry narrow gauge freight cars on its lower deck. With ever-increasing passenger business, the railroad contracted in February, 1894, to build a train shed at the Sausalito terminal. It was to be 324 feet long and 80 feet wide to accommodate four trains. This would be a vast improvement, as passengers in the past had to transfer from ferry to train out in the open, which was most disagreeable in stormy weather and in the drippy fog that hit the area quite freqently. Offices and a passenger waiting room were also included under the shed.

For protection against the weather the NPC built this train shed at Sausalito in 1894. It lasted eight years.

Because the picnic cars used on the Cazadero line were of narrower body than the regular narrow gauge cars, "gauntlet" tracks were necessary at San Anselmo to accommodate both types of equipment. View is looking north.

"B" Street in San Rafael was the terminal point for the Narrow Gauge in the year 1900. From this point the trains went either to San Quentin or Sausalito.

Also in 1894, the NPC double-tracked its narrow gauge between Sausalito and Mill Valley Junction because of the increase in commute traffic. Another locomotive number 16, was purchased from Brooks Locomotive Works and delivered. In 1901, the company double tracked the section between North Portal (Corte Madera tunnel) and San Anselmo, a distance of 4.08 miles.

President Stetson, along with the communties of Marin County, did extensive advertising, pointing out why Marin County was a better place in which to live. Passenger miles increased from 15 million in 1892 to 21 million in 1901.

Elite commuters of Marin County demanded and obtained a covered station at West End, San Rafael on the suburban narrow gauge.

Each of these years except 1896 and 1898 brought a profit for the railroad. On the critical side, the freight business showed a steady decline with the falling off of lumber shipments and agricultural products. The ton-miles dropped from 4½ million in 1892 to less than three million in 1901. This was not the healthiest of situations. In 1901 the narrow gauge added the ferry "Tamalpais" (No. 2) to its fleet. The vessel was built by the Union Iron Works and was of a steel hull. The boat with its sleek operation, was the favorite with commuters for many years.

Also in 1901 an enterprising venture was going on in the mechanical department of the slim gauge. William J. Thomas, Master Mechanic, designed and built the first water tubed boiler, oil burning, cab-in-front locomotive in the United States. From the day it was outshopped the engine, Numbered 21, was quite successful in its operation, even though the crews had a hard time acquainting themselves with its new design. However, it was all too short-lived, as a fireman let the water get low, which in turn burned the tubes and finished the boiler. The engine was soon scrapped, and the idea became a memory as far as the little pike was concerned, but it was the grand-daddy of the big cab-in-front engines that were to come for the Southern Pacific for operation over the Sierra.

North Shore Engine No. 21 on San Anselmo Creek trestle. Note opening under headlight to provide draft for fire. This was an experimental engine built in the Sausalito shops by the NPC in 1901. See text above for further information.

North Shore Engine No. 18 (later NWP 145-95) at Fairfax with a picnic train about the year 1904. Bill Ritchie, Engineer, and Bob Rutherford, Fireman, on running board.

In 1899, the NPC added to its roster, steam locomotive Number 18. The giant 4-6-0, weighed 75 tons including tender, and was a product of the Brooks Locomotive Works. It was said to have been the largest narrow gauge engine built in the United States at the time. It was sleek and powerful and did away with much double-heading on the grades.

On the night of November 30, 1901, disaster once again struck the struggling narrow gauge. The ferry "San Rafael," feeling its way in the fog, was struck by the larger ferry "Sausalito." Fortunately the boats stuck together for twenty minutes, so passengers and crew could be transferred before the "San Rafael" went down. It is still unknown how many persons lost their lives in this accident, but best opinions state that there was but one along with a horse known as "Dick," who was assigned to the boat to haul carts off at either terminal. After the "San Rafael" sank, no trace of her could be found, but the North Pacific Coast was made the defendant in many law suits for presumed deaths and injuries.

At the turn of the century the railroad giants of the country were watching all sections of the land, buying up this little railroad and that little pike. In the west the Southern Pacific was watching the Santa Fe, who had designs on the railroads around Eureka, and who was making a survey for a railroad through the canyon of the south fork of the Eel River, thence through Lake, Napa and Solano counties to connect in central California with its transcontinental main line. Another survey was being made to connect the railroad on the Mendocino coast (Fort Bragg & Southeastern Railroad) with its mainline going

through Dry Creek and Anderson Valleys to Healdsburg, thence crossing Napa county to connect with the Santa Fe's main line. With all this going on, the Southern Pacific became vitally interested in the California Northwestern, which operated from Tiburon north, and even the North Pacific Coast narrow gauge. Meanwhile John Martin, known as the father of long distance high voltage electric transmission lines, having built such a line from a power house in the high Sierra to San Francisco Bay, had the thought that future surburban rail transportation should operate with electric trains. Martin, who no doubt had plenty of help from Southern Pacific financially and otherwise, prompted other capital to join him, and offered a substantial amount for the North Pacific Coast Railroad and its properties. It was accepted, so on March 7, 1902, a new company, the North Shore Railroad Company, took over. Many of the road's employees did not know what was going on, and when one would ask the other a question on the sale, the answer would invariably be "not sure" - this stuck, and the initials "N.S." became the "Not Sure" Railroad.

The property that was included in the sale consisted of 92.61 miles of narrow gauge road, viz: main line, Sausalito to Cazadero, 80.93 miles; branch lines; Mill Valley Junction to Mill Valley, 1.74 miles; San Anselmo to San Rafael, 2 miles; Duncan Mills to Markham, 2.8 miles and Bridge to Willow Creek, 5.14 miles. Operated under lease was 3.26 miles from San Rafael to San Quentin. Also included, but not operated regularly at the time, was a small section near Duncan Mills to Azalea and a 2.33 miles branch from Pedrini to Shafters Junction.

30

North Shore Engine No. 33 (later NWP 322) at Duncan Mills. The year is 1906, and all the equipment has not yet been changed from North Pacific Coast to North Shore lettering.

The management of the North Shore was headed by John Martin as President. Associated with Martin was William Rank, General Manager, who had been General Manager of the East Bay street car and interurban system. Martin and staff assembled a group of young experts to undertake to reconstruct and modernize the narrow gauge. The countryside was startled but highly pleased when Martin announced that the interurban service in Marin County would be electrified. As the new service would be broad gauge, the track would be laid with three rails, so that both the steam narrow gauge and the electric broad gauge could operate over the same section. A fourth rail, generally referred to as the "third rail," would be placed alongside the track for transmission of electric current for train propulsion. An automatic block signal system was to be provided for safety.

Work was started as quickly as possible in 1902 to ready sections in Marin County for the new service. The following was undertaken: second tracking, consisting of three rails for broad gauge and narrow gauge equipment; Main Line, Mill Valley Junction to South Portal of Corte Madera tunnel (this tunnel always stayed single tracked) 1.93 miles. Broad gauging by adding third rail: Main Line, single track, Sausalito to Fairfax; second track, Sausalito to Mill Valley Junction, 3.40 miles; second track, North Portal, Corte Madera tunnel to San Anselmo, 4.08 miles; total 19.28 miles. Branch lines, single track, Mill Valley Junction to Mill Valley, 1.74 miles; single track San Anselmo to San Rafael, "B Street", 2 miles; total branch lines 3.74 miles, making a total of 23.03 miles converted to three rail. In this construction a number of curves were straightened out, which subsequently reduced the overall mileage of the system. The operation of electric trains on the road between Sausalito and Mill Valley commenced on August 20, 1903, and on the section Mill Valley Junction and San Rafael, October 17, 1903. The portion of the road broad gauged between San Anselmo and Fairfax was not operated electrically by the North Shore.

A home-made product of the North Shore shops at Sausalito was the little electric engine, the " Electra." It was leased to the Debris Commission in San Francisco to help clean up rubble after the 1906 quake. The steam engine is Western Meat Company No. 1. The Electra is the only piece of North Shore power still in existence, being safely on display at Travel Town in Los Angeles.

In 1902 the North Shore built a freight motor to be used on its electric lines, which was named "Electra." It was to work local out of Sausalito to serve freight spurs in the electric territory. However, whenever it went out on the line, it used so much power that all other trains came to a halt. It was not rebuilt and found itself being used by the Debris Commission in San Francisco clearing earthquake damage in 1906 along with the Western Meat Company's tank engine No. 1. It then went to the United Railroads in San Francisco, thence to Southern Pacific, and in 1917 to the Pacific Electric in Los Angeles, and ended up with the final number of 1544. Today the motor rests in Traveltown, Los Angeles, for all to see.

The next step in North Shore's program of modernization was the ferry steamers. With the sinking of the "San Rafael," the line only had two boats, the "Sausalito" and the "Tamalpias," so another was ordered built, the "Cazadero." When time came for the launching, the ferry slid down the ways for 20 feet and became stuck in the cradle. It took almost a month to get the steamer in the water. After the paddle wheels were installed, horrified designers noted that the wheels did not touch the water. It was then heavily loaded with cement ballast so it would stay on an even keel and the paddle wheels would reach the proper depth in the water. Another vessel built was the car ferry "Lagunitas," which was launched without difficulty on February 1, 1903. As soon as it went into service, the "Sausalito," the only other rail car ferry of the North Shore, was taken out of service and its tracks ripped out from the lower deck and was converted to an oil burner. With passenger seats on the lower deck the capacity of the boat was increased to 3320 passengers.

The barn-looking terminal at Sausalito next came under the eyes of the new management. Even though it was only eight years old, it was ordered torn down and rebuilt. The new structure had slips that provided for both main and upper deck unloading and for use only by double ended ferry boats. The tracks, both narrow gauge and broad gauge, were rearranged for more convenient loading under modern umbrella sheds. Extensive offices were also constructed on the second floor of the new terminal along with the train dispatcher's office.

Looking north from the ferry landing at Sausalito in 1880.

The forerunner of the Southern Pacific's cab-forward articulateds is shown working at Howards (Occidental) in 1902.

In 1902 the North Shore built this new Sausalito terminal, which provided for both broad and narrow gauge track arrangements, and extensive office space on the second floor. The Pan-Pacific Exposition of 1915 donated the elephant flag poles, and the grounds became known as Elephant Park.

Bedecked with bunting, NPC Engine No. 7 handles a Fourth of July excursion train in the redwoods near Cazadero circa 1897.

North Shore Engine No. 2 and train at the San Quentin ferry landing in 1906.

Another major reconstruction project that took place under the new regime was the building of an entire new railroad between Roys, just beyond Fairfax, and Maillard on the other side of White's Hill, which included a tunnel 3190 feet long. The new line cut away heavy grades, two tunnels, and shortened the distance between the two points from 4.74 miles to 2.64 miles, or nearly half. The new section was opened for service on December 4, 1904 and the old line abandoned. The new tunnel was bored for broad gauge equipment, as Martin had plans to extend the electric line to Woodacre and even Point Reyes at some time in the future. The rock and rubble that came from the bore was used to better ballast the track between San Anselmo and Corte Madera.

A little further up the line at Keyes Creek, a long circling trestle was taken down and a straight one put in its place. However, high water damaged it quite severely in later months, so a regular bridge of two spans, each 130 feet in length, was installed.

To modernize further the steam road, some 30,000 new ties were put in place between Millerton and Duncan Mills, and all rail was replaced with the sixty pound variety.

While under the NPC management the color of the coaches had been yellow, orange, green and grayish-black. The North Shore decided to spruce up their passenger trains and painted all the passenger cars bright red. Passenger engines numbered 2, 3, 14, 15, 16, 18 and 20 were also painted red with gold leaf for lettering and numbers.

With all of these improvements the final act of the company was to speed up the trains. This proved to be disasterous, as several bad wrecks ensued. Since the narrow gauge had been plagued with rail disasters from its start, it would be of interest to list some of the major accidents as they happened.

1873

November 8th. When trestle being built over Tiburon Road (near Tiburon turn-off from present freeway) a bent collapsed by strong winds, knocking over the entire string of 15 bents like ten pins. Four men were killed and many injured.

1875

Engine #2 turned over into Tomales Bay. (It was a Mason "Bogey" type without leading trucks - this was blamed for the derailment on a sharp curve).

April 5th. During a heavy windstorm a south-bound passenger train's rear coach was literally blown off the track on a sharp curve near Lyford's station, 3½ miles north of Saucelito. The car with 19 passengers rolled down a 30 foot embankment, injuring two of the passengers.

1878

April 8th. President Eastland's private car "Millwood," left the track in Lagunitas Canyon, skidding along the right-of-way tearing out a tree, and tumbled down into Paper Mill Creek. The car's roof was crushed by a tree injuring the passengers, one of which was President Eastland's baby daughter, who died later. President Eastland resigned immediately after the wreck and forgot all about railroads.

1879

July 20th. Freight train at Clark's Summit had four box cars derailed by a stick of cordwood, which fell off the back of the tender. Brakeman died later from being thrown off the top of one of the box cars.

1882

April 17th. Passenger train between San Rafael and San Quentin derailed by a bull on the track. Engine number 9, running backwards, was turned over, but no one was injured. A crowd from San Rafael, on hearing of the wreck, crowded down the right-of-way to see it. Someone shouted, "Look out the boiler is going to blow up!" which scattered the crowd into the oozy marsh alongside the track to guffaws and laughter of the pranksters.

1886

February 21st. Engine No. 4, running backwards, left the track at Waldo Point, spun half-way around, and landed in the mud of Richardson's Bay. The coupling broke between the engine and tender, the tender going in the opposite direction from the engine and stopped in a field alongside the right-of-way fence. The coupling pin of the drawbar on the engine's pilot flew out and the two passenger cars went on by the wreck down the track and stopped just short of the Sausalito terminal. The fireman jumped to safety, but the engineer was pinned in the wreck and was drowned by the incoming tide before he could be rescued.

1894

January 14th. During a severe rainstorm which lasted several days, the conductor, engineer and fireman of the Saturday-to-Monday layover train at Cazadero decided to inspect the roadbed and trestles to see if they were intact, as the waters of Austin Creek were very high and rushing downstream at a rapid rate. Besides these men there were five others in the cab (their presence was unexplained other than they might have been on a pleasure trip to Duncan Mills). The engine stopped at a trestle just below Cazadero to allow the conductor to get off and walk across to see if the bridge was secure for the locomotive. Thinking all was okay, he signalled the engineer to come ahead (the conductor later denied this). About half way across the trestle the middle bent collapsed and Engine 9 and all on the locomotive were swept into the swirling waters. The conductor, stunned at what he saw, went for help. Another trestle washed out preventing him from reaching Duncan Mills, and as he could not recross the trestle at Austin Creek, he was caught between both washouts. Cazadero in the meantime knew nothing of the tragedy until the next morning, when there was no engine nor crew to take the train out. The conductor, after a night of terror and drenching, reached Duncan Mills by a trip around the floods through the forests and gave the alarm. The people of Cazadero set out to find the engine and crew and discovered the washed out trestle, but neither engine or any of the men were seen - the waters of Austin Creek had covered the engine, pinning and drowning all in the cab. It was the worst tragedy to hit the railroad. Eight men had vanished, the lost conductor and seven who had drowned; Engineer, Arthur Briggs; Fireman, Tom Collister; Frank Hart of San Francisco; William Bremmer, a hotel clerk at Cazadero; Thomas Gould, Postmaster at Cazadero; John Rice, engine wiper and Joseph Sabine, station agent at Cazadero. All the bodies were found in the next several days, except that of station agent Sabine who was still missing after ten days. The searchers were about to give up when an old Spanish woodchopper said he could find the body. All thought him rather on the "loco" side, but watched. A candle was lit and set on a shingle, which was then set adrift. After traveling down stream for some distance, the shingle was caught in an eddy, circled around for awhile, and then floated into some tangled brush along the bank and the candle went out. While all this was in process the old wood-

chopper was chanting some mystic "voodoo" words. When the candle went out, the old gent said, "there is where you will find him" and sure enough, there he was! The engine remained in the creek until spring when she was hauled out and sent to Sausalito to be rebuilt. That was the end of number 9, the once beautiful pride and joy of Milton Latham, for when she came out she was stencilled number 17. However, bad luck was with the engine, for in 1899 she was completely wrecked at the Corte Madera tunnel in a rear-end smash, and was scrapped.

1896

January 28th. Engine 16, backed down the apron to couple on to some cars on the ferry "Sausalito" when the apron collapsed, dropping the engine into the bay. The engineer drowned, but the fireman succeeded in getting out, but was later killed in a wreck at Tocoloma.

1903

April 5th. A northbound special pulled by Engine 31 had a "headon" collision with a gravel train pulled by Engine 33 between San Geronimo and Lagunitas. The crash could be heard for miles. The engineer and fireman on both engines jumped to safety, but the conductor of the gravel train was buried in the gravel and had to be dug out. He was badly hurt, as were two brakemen.

June 21st (Famous "Funeral Train Wreck")
A special train of one coach and Engine number 4 was chartered to carry friends of Warren Dutton, an early settler of Tomales, and one who owned large tracts of land in the area (some called him "Mr. Tomales"), from San Francisco and lower Marin County to Tomales where he was being buried. On the return trip from Tomales, after the funeral and after passing Point Reyes station, the train ran out on Trestle number 39, which crosses Paper Mill Creek. The trestle was built in a "reverse curve" or "S" shape, with curves coming on or off at either end. As the train hit the curve on the trestle, the tender and coach were snapped off, allowing the engine to go on, but catapulting the tender and car bottom-up in the creek. The roof of the car was crushed, pinning most of the passengers in the wreck. The crew started rescue operations at once. The conductor, just recovering from the proceeding wreck, ran to Point Reyes and ask for assistance. The engineer, fireman and brakeman helped getting the passengers out and tending to the injured until help arrived. Some cadets from the First Congregational Church, who were encamped by the creek, had a hospital corps and a doctor and gave valued medical aid. There were a total of 28 persons in the car of which two were killed and 25 injured. One women escaped without a scratch.

June 24th. Three days after the "Funeral Train Wreck", engine 20 with the northbound Cazadero passenger train jumped the track at a curve just south of Tocoloma. The engineer was killed and the fireman badly scalded. The rescue train almost caused another wreck when it stopped short of plowing into the wrecked passenger train. A panic did ensue in the last car when the passengers thought the rescue train would collide.

July 6th. Engine No. 4, double-heading with Engine No. 7, hit a dead cow at Keyes Creek estuary crossing below Tomales. Number 4 reared over backwards completely reversing itself, instantly killing the engineer. Engine number 7 did not leave the track.

There were other minor disasters on the narrow gauge: the Duncan Mills station burned down; there was a cave-in in the construction of the Bothin tunnel between Roys and Maillard, and the ferry "Sausalito" ran aground on Angel Island causing a panic amongst the passengers. It all added up to uncertainty and lawsuits. After two and a half years of wild spending, a forced assessment on the stockholders in July, 1903, along with just plain bad luck, President Martin was ready to throw in the towel. The Southern Pacific, which had learned that the Santa Fe had obtained an option on the narrow gauge, was now ready to obtain control of the latter road in any way that it could. A few years earlier the Southern Pacific had quietly stepped in and obtained control of the rival railroad, the California Northwestern, of which A. W. Foster was now president. When learning that the California Northwestern was completely in the hands of the Southern Pacific, the Santa Fe lost interest, so Foster purchased the North Shore. On August 4, 1904, a new Board of Directors was formed who elected Foster president. The North Shore name remained, however, and its general offices were combined with those of the California Northwestern.

Then came the morning of April 18, 1906, when Mother Nature herself played havoc with the slim gauge in the form of an earthquake. On the electric system there was little damage, other than the signal system all going "red" because of ruptured bond connections. At Irvings the bridge collapsed and fell into the creek, and at Point Reyes the morning passenger being readied for its run with engine number 14 on the head end, fell over on its side. All along Tomales Bay the damage was extensive due to the sinking of fills. Tomales, which is directly on a fault line, saw a side track turned up and placed right on the main line. The next damage point was Duncan Mills where the El Bonito Hotel had collapsed, killing four persons. Engines numbers 13 and 33, which were at Duncan Mills at the time, were hooked together and used to pull the roof and debris from the hotel, to get at the injured. Some of the cars were also turned over in the nearby yards. All tunnels survived, and in three weeks the road was partially running again, although under slow orders in many places.

In 1906, the line built a broad gauge extension, 0.58 miles between "B" Street station, San Rafael and the Union Station on Fourth Street. Electric service was then extended to the latter point.

Such, then, was the narrow gauge when the Northwestern Pacific came into being on January 8, 1907.

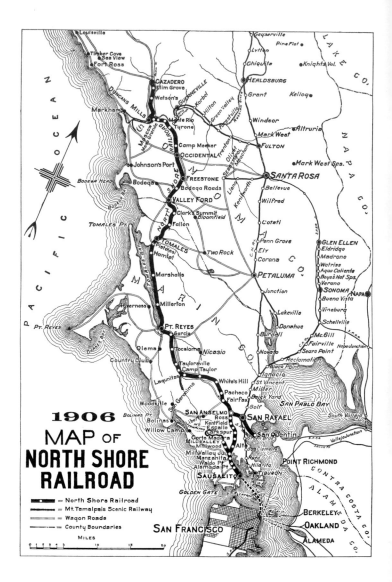

This time table became effective just a couple of hours before the famous earthquake in San Francisco.

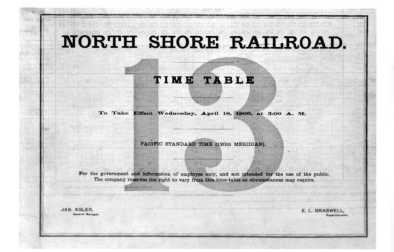

LINES AROUND EUREKA
ALBION BRANCH

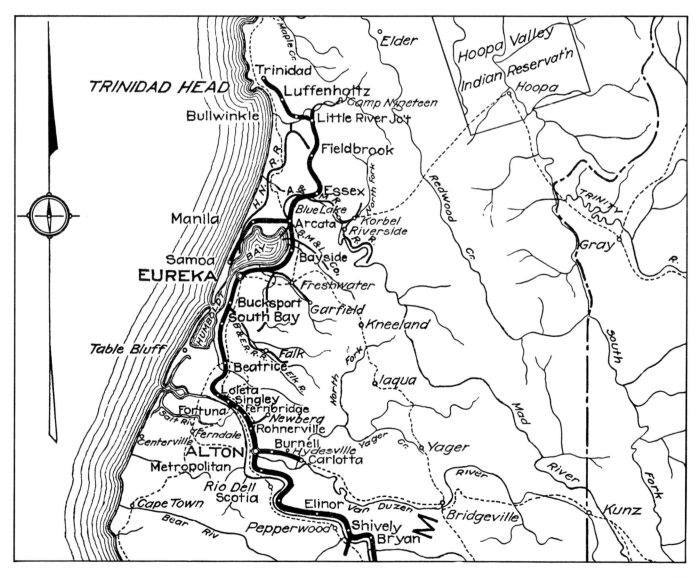

LINES AROUND EUREKA

Probably the richest area of redwood timber in the world is that in the vicinity of Eureka. Looking north, south or east, huge stands of redwoods abound. About 1875 the lumber enterpreneurs with their logging mills started in earnest. Among them was John Vance. His lumber operations were expanding, and to bring the logs to his mill from any distance was becoming a problem. It soon was solved in the form of a railroad which was given the name of Vance's Mad River Railroad. It was constructed a distance of about 12.50 miles, including small branch spurs, from Mad River Sloughs to Vance's Mill (later Essex) in 1875, and thence to Brocks in 1877. Actually it was not incorporated as a railroad, but operated as a private enterprise. On December 26, 1891, Vance transferred the railroad to Edgar and John M. Vance, his nephews. On January 6, 1892, the line was sold to the Humboldt Bay & Trinidad Lumber & Logging Company for the sum of $200,000. The new owners then entered into a ten-year contract with the Dolbeer & Carson Lumber Company to haul to tidewater their logs and manufactured products. The Humboldt Bay & Trinidad Lumber & Logging Company made plans and surveys for an extension of the line to Samoa, and the building of a new line to Essex. Rights-of-way were secured, ties and rails contracted for, but no construction work was undertaken. In order to do a general railroad business, the Vance interests incorporated the Eureka & Klamath River Railroad on January 6, 1896. The actual sale of properties took place on May 9, 1896.

The Eureka & Klamath Railroad then set about to extend the road. Its first act was to relocate about ten miles of the 12.50 miles purchased. The line was in operation from Samoa to Camp 5, a total of 17.55 miles, in 1897, and then another 2.45 miles was added to Little River in 1902 with a 1.34 mile extension on a branch at this point. During this time the ownership of the road passed to the Hammond Lumber Company. On May 18, 1903, H. E. Huntington, who at the time was the Vice President of the Southern Pacific, purchased the company's entire capital stock, 5,000 shares, from the Hammond interest, for the agreed price of $1,150,000. On the same date the railroad was leased for sole operation to the Oregon & Eureka Railroad Company. This road then constructed another 4.60 miles north to Camp 25 Junction. Shortly before coming into the realm of the Northwestern Pacific, the Oregon & Eureka did some construction work on 2.34 miles extending from 25 Junction to Trinidad (this was completed by the N.W.P.), and also did complete grading and bridging on the 3.84 miles extending from Arcata toward Eureka. (This project was abandoned in an agreement with the California & Northern.)

A passenger train on the Eureka & Klamath River pulls out of the Samoa Landing terminal for its daily run to Trinidad.

Oregon & Eureka No. 6 (later NWP No. 3) near Little
River Junction.

Oregon & Eureka No. 11. Built by the Hammond Lumber
Company at their Samoa shops in 1910. When the Northwestern Pacific took over the O&E on July 1, 1911, the
engine was transferred to the Hammond Lumber Co. Photo
taken near Fieldbrook in 1911.

The shops of the San Francisco & Northwestern at South Bay were built in 1882 by the Eel River & Eureka and taken over by the SF&NW in 1903. When the Northwestern

The road just described was in the territory north of Eureka, and it was in the firm hands of the Southern Pacific as can be seen from the stock transfer to H. E. Huntington on May 18, 1903. Ferry service was given by small craft between Eureka and Samoa to connect with the trains.

After Vance had his railroad going to the north it wasn't long before the lumber tycoons turned their efforts to the south of Eureka. Early movement of forest products from the Eel River Valley was by either boat or wagon or both. On the route was Table Bluff, about 12 miles south of Eureka, which was a ridge extending from the Coast Range to the sea and formed a barrier separating bay from river. The Eel River was only navigable for a short distance and then boats had to take to the open sea for a few miles before entering Humboldt Bay and Eureka. By wagon it was a tough pull over the winding dirt roads. So when the Eel River & Eureka Rail Road Company was incorporated on November 14, 1882, the plans included a tunnel a third of a mile long under Table Bluff, in order to give a quicker route to Eureka. Headquarters for the railroad were established at Fields Landing with yards, engine house and shops to service the equipment. Because of some litigation in obtaining rights-of-way from a gentleman named Waterman Field, the service point was soon changed from Fields Landing to South Bay. With two brand new locomotives, the "Iaqua" and "Eureka" the railroad was open for business between South Bay and Burnells (near Alton) 15.11 miles on August 24, 1884. To transport lumber and materials to Eureka from South Bay the railroad placed the stern paddle wheel steamer

"Oneatta" in service until that leg of the railroad, 6.31 miles, was open for traffic on July 6, 1885.

The Pacific Lumber Company, which had been incorporated February 27, 1869, and owned vast timber stands along the Eel River, incorporated the Humboldt Bay & Eel River Railroad on November 17, 1882, to build from Humboldt Bay to their proposed sawmill on the Eel River (known today as Scotia). However, after some grading, the lumber firm saw that the ER&E had good intentions in building their line, so concluded an agreement that the ER&E would handle their lumber shipments to Eureka from Alton and that they would construct a seven mile connecting link from their mill to Alton. The Pacific Lumber Company located its plant at Forestville in 1884 and on June 1, 1885 started the connecting rail link to Alton which was finished on August 20. Because a community by the name of Forestville already existed in California, the name was changed to Scotia in 1888 in honor of the many Nova Scotians who had settled there. Another 5.68 miles were built south to Elinor to tap more timber areas in July, 1898, and another 2.42 miles to Camp 9, by July, 1902. On February 28, 1903, the Pacific Lumber Company purchased all the property of "The Pacific Lumber Company," the control of which had shortly before been acquired by the Santa Fe Land Improvement Company.

On April 26, 1902, the California Midland Railroad was incorporated by the Eel River & Eureka Rail Road to construct a railroad from Burnells to a point 62 miles southeast. The line managed to get as far as Carlotta, 3.34 miles, in the following year, but before it could operate its newly constructed

Pacific came into being the facilities were moved to Eureka.

line it was taken over by the San Francisco & Northwestern.

Under the guidance of the Santa Fe Railway, another road was started out of Eureka to the north. This was the California & Northern Railway, incorporated on March 5, 1900, under the laws of the State of Nevada. Its intent was to construct a railroad 90 miles long from Eureka to Crescent City in Del Norte County to tap the rich timber lands in that area. At this particular time the Eureka & Klamath River was building a branch southward to Eureka from Arcata and actually had some 2.5 miles graded. The C&N offered to purchase or lease the right-of-way, but was turned down, so it started its own line which parelled the E&KR. Both railroads were soon battling to obtain a right-of-way along the Eureka waterfront, and both knew from the location of streets, sawmills, piers and other plants that there was room for only one line. To add to the confusion Andrew Hammond, owner of the E&KR and the Vance Redwood Company, incorporated the Humboldt Railroad Company on March 13, 1901, with the intent to construct a railroad 135 miles long from Dyerville to Crescent City which would practically duplicate the line planned by the C&N. While the Humboldt Railroad did have an interest in certain franchises and tracks in the city of Eureka it was more of a smokescreen than anything else. On May 18, 1903, the properties acquired were leased to the Oregon & Eureka Railroad. The battle between the C&N and the E&KR, which had both received permission to construct lines into Eureka, ended on July 12, 1901, when they agreed on a joint line along the Eureka waterfront. On October 30, 1901, the C&N completed its line to Arcata, but had no rolling stock to start operations. Meanwhile behind the scenes, the Eel River & Eureka saw the opportunity of extending its operations, so on December 3, 1901, it leased the C&N and opened the section between Eureka and Arcata for freight and passenger business on December 14. But, like many railroads of the time, money ran out, and the C&N's ambitious project to continue on to Crescent City ended at Arcata.

As mentioned earlier the railroad giants of the country left no stone unturned in their quest for expansion. Northwestern California, with no rail connection to the outside world by which its tremendous wealth of natural resources and agricultural products could move to market, was certain to fall under their scrutiny. Here was a land almost entirely isolated from the state and the nation of which it was a part - its mountains and valleys covered with the only remaining forest of redwood available for commercial exploitation. How many great railroad networks had cast their eyes on this last frontier of the west is hard to say, but two of them, the Southern Pacific and the Santa Fe, or roads respectively controlled by them, were the ones whose rails finally penetrated the territory.

The Santa Fe, which already had a large interest in the section, incorporated the San Francisco & Northwestern Railway Company on May 12, 1903, as the nucleus of its proposed acquisition and expansion program. The Eel River & Eureka sold its interest to the newly formed company on May 14, 1903, the California Midland on July 7, 1903, the California & Northern on March 22, 1904, and the Pacific Lumber on May 15, 1903. The latter company, however, retained all of its timber lands, mills and other similar property appurtenant to the lumber business. This gave the Santa Fe 50.28 miles of line in northern California. Another 1.99 miles were constructed from Camp 9 to Shively and opened for traffic in July of 1905. This section included a 1019 foot long tunnel. The SF&NW also made an agreement with the Holmes Eureka Lumber Company on June 25, 1906, in which the lumber company would build a huge trestle across the Eel River at Shively, to gain access to the timber holdings in the Shaw Tract which had been purchased by Holmes Eureka. A station was built at Holmes Flat which soon took on the name "Happy Camp." The station was destined to become well-known, as the road south was on that side of the river and passengers from the trains transferred to the Overland Auto Stage for what was to become the popular scenic ride over the mountains to Sherwood to connect with the trains of the California Northwestern.

41

Little No. 1 of the SF&NW (later NWP No. 2) takes water at Scotia.

Numbered "O" by the SF&NW, this contraption hauled passengers between Alton and Carlotta. This steam "dummy" apparently was a home-made affair.

SF&NW No. 3 (later NWP 151-351) under Santa Fe control, switches cars at Scotia.

Looking somewhat out of place in the northern California lumber country is the Santa Fe herald on the Eureka station.

The Santa Fe also had under observation a little known railroad in Mendocino County. The history of this "out-of-the-way" line begins with the Albion River Railroad Company, which was incorporated on September 24, 1885, for the purpose of operating a standard gauge section of track that had been constructed some months previously from a point near Albion (Brett), Mendocino County, eastwardly 2.25 miles for the purpose of hauling logs to a log dump. On May 26, 1891, the Albion Lumber Company was incorporated and it took over the operation of the Albion River Railroad. As log cutting was required, the line was extended to Keene's Summit, a total of 11.60 miles before the end of 1891. The railroad at the time was operated exclusively as a plant facility of the lumber company. On April 1, 1902, lumber interests headed by Robert H. Swayne purchased the Albion River Railroad from the Albion Lumber Company for a mere $67,500.00 and on May 8, incorporated the Albion & Southeastern Railroad with the intention of extending the line to Booneville, a distance of approximately 35 miles from Albion, thus setting up a general freight and passenger business. Coastal steamers would handle the traffic from San Francisco to the Albion wharfs and connection with the railroad. On March 20, 1903, another agreement was drawn up between the several logging companies of the area and the railroad for a three mile extension from Brett to where a new mill was to be built along with extensive wharfs at Albion. With the signing of the agreement construction got under way along with a branch line that was built between Clearbrook Junction and Clearbrook Gulch, one mile.

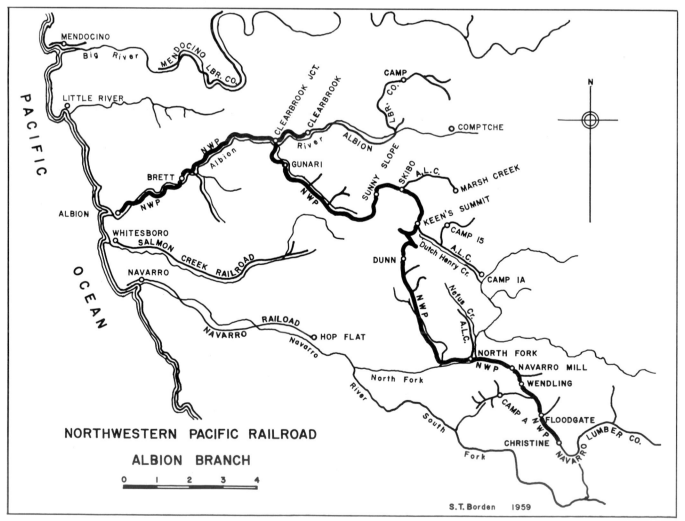

NORTHWESTERN PACIFIC RAILROAD

ALBION BRANCH

0   1   2   3   4

S. T. Borden   1959

A straight piece of track on the Albion branch. Redwood trees abound on the twenty-six mile "orphan" line, which had no rail connection with the outside world.

Upper left shows the mill at Albion in earlier times. Nothing remains today.

The Santa Fe, wanting to get a toe-hold in this area, and with ideas of extending the road to either Cloverdale or Healdsburg to connect with its planned extension from Eureka to the Bay Area, incorporated the Fort Bragg & Southeastern Railroad on March 25, 1903. The purchase price was $199,000, but for some reason it was not until January 17, 1905 that the FB&SE took over. On September 15, the railroad was completed to Wendling, 23.81 miles. Construction had been difficult beyond Keene's Summit, in fact, two switch-backs on a 3% grade had to be installed.

Shortly after the N.W.P. took over on January 8, 1907, an additional 2.90 miles were constructed to a point known as Christine. With the Southern Pacific building its line into Mexico it required a vast amount of timbers and ties and after surveying the timber potential in the area, purchased the Albion Lumber Company for one million dollars on August 31, 1907. Several logging companies that had built their lines into the woods held trackage rights over the N.W.P. to get their logs to the mills at either Navarro or Albion. For the next twenty years the Albion Branch was to see prosperous times, but the dreams of extending the "little pike" to connect up with one of the "giants" never materialized.

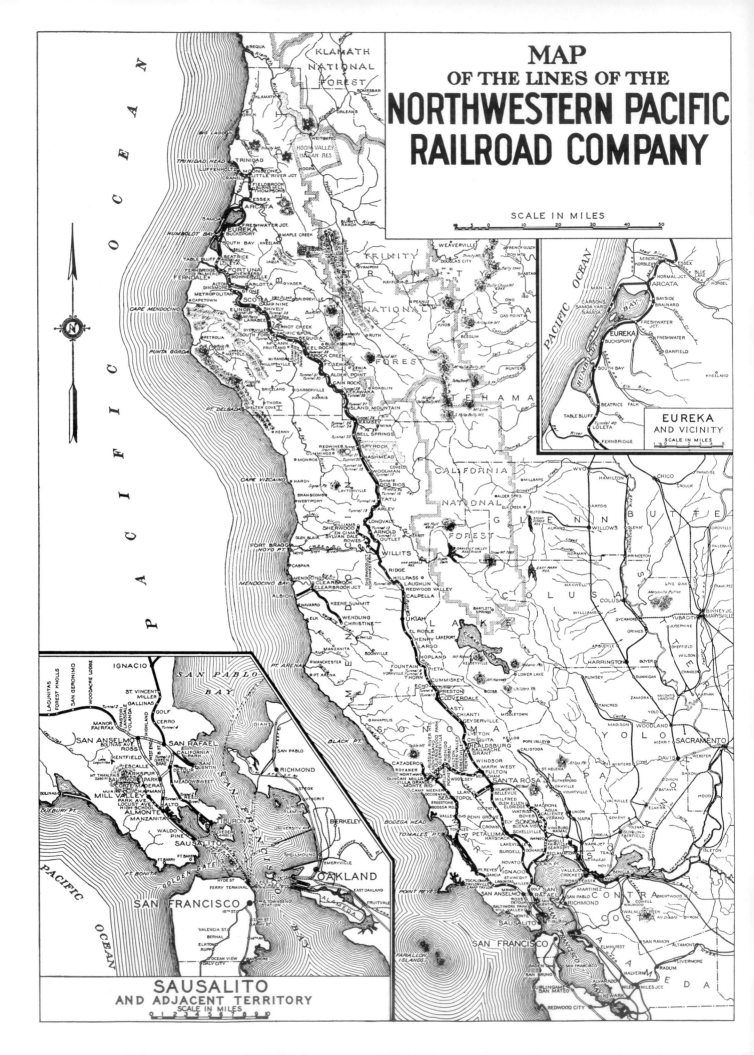

MAP
OF THE LINES OF THE
NORTHWESTERN PACIFIC RAILROAD COMPANY

SCALE IN MILES

EUREKA
AND VICINITY
SCALE IN MILES

SAUSALITO
AND ADJACENT TERRITORY
SCALE IN MILES

The Nc
sions for

WESTERN
Tiburon-Sh
Ignacio-Gle
Junction-Dc
Santa Rosa
Fulton-Boh

SHORE D
Sausalito-C
Mill Valle
San Ansel
Duncan M
Bridge-Wil
San Rafael

NORTHEF
Arcata-Shi
Samoa-Trir
Alton-Carle
Albion-We
Clearbrook

(The :
long; in
new-nam

The nc
its physic
tain A. F
Santa Fe
James A
general 1
of nine
balance
of the
William
projects,

The m
operation
between
in the n
were qui
should t
Eel Rive
Pacific I
determin
of the S
neer of
of the
addition
the past
the big
an expe
both ca
engineer
was mac
carry eq
men wa
the bett

THE

NORTHWESTERN PACIFIC

trains. On November 15, 1909, the new bridge was completed, and the broad gauge trains ran into Duncan Mills.

The construction work in the north continued, with the work from Willits being performed by the Utah Construction Company, approximately 77.10 miles, and the work done south from Shively, 23.10 miles, by Willet and Burr of San Francisco. The section from Willits to Longvale, 13 miles was completed and opened for limited traffic on August 1, 1911; Shively to South Fork, 8.3 miles, May 8, 1912; Longvale to Dos Rios, 14 miles, May 11, 1913; South Fork to McCann, 5.1 miles, May 12, 1913; McCann to Fort Seward, 15.6 miles, May 3, 1914, and from Dos Rios to Fort Seward, 50.15 miles, the task was finished on September 22, 1914.

For this event a celebration was in order. On October 23, 1914, a gold spike was driven in a tie of redwood at Cain Rock. The celebrants arrived from the north and south on special trains. The train from Sausalito was powered by Engines 136 and 114, both decorated with bunting and flags. The trains from Eureka had Engines 103 and 113 on the head end. After two hours of speech making, climaxed by the driving of the gold spike, the two groups left for Eureka for a three-day celebration. Limited traffic continued while final ballasting of track took place. The Operating Department of the Northwestern Pacific accepted the line as completed on July 1, 1915.

C A I N   R O C K

O C T.   2 3,   1 9 1 4

"Driving the Golden Spike"
NORTHWESTERN PACIFIC RAILROAD
CAIN ROCK,   OCTOBER 23RD 1914

Although the line was completed on September 22, official "gold spike" ceremonies were held on October 23, 1914. Above photo shows N.W.P. president W. S. Palmer preparing to strike the spike held by his daughter, Alice. Because of a slide, it was 3:00 AM before the three specials arrived at Eureka for further celebration.

The golden spike train (or "Spikers Special") was hauled from Sausalito to Willits by Engine 136 and from Willits to Cain Rock by Engine 114, above, gaily bedecked with festive bunting. A second and third train, powered by Engines 103 and 113, came from Eureka.

Passenger business was now the N.W.P's main objective. People were seductively attracted by the opening paragraph of the booklet "Vacation" which was published each year by the railroad.

> "In all the world there is not another recreation place like the Northwestern Pacific country, that wonderland that has in every enchanted mile a rare and wonderful charm that is all its own. It offers every variation of pleasure and recreation, every phase of beauty that the world affords, every charm of climate that the town-weary may seek."

There was no question that with the arrival of spring, and summer vacation just around the corner, the many resort and vacation spots of the Redwood Empire became most inviting. To advertise this beautiful area that stretched from Sausalito to Eureka the railroad, in addition to the "Vacation" booklet, published a variety of detailed booklets and pamphlets. Hotels, resorts, camping spots and boating areas were all included, with prices that ranged from a dollar a day. The five north bay counties - Marin, Sonoma, Lake, Mendocino and Humboldt had everything to offer the adventuresome vacationer; mountain and forest, silver streams and sun-bathed hillslopes, valleys redolent with myriad blossoms, healing springs and singing brooks, coast line and the blue reaches of the sea. The chief delight of the region was that the Northwestern Pacific Railroad made it all so easily accessible. After a pleasant trip across the bay in one of the company's big boats, built for pleasure as well as service, the traveler could board one of the many trains departing from the Sausalito terminal for the playground of America. To the Northwestern Pacific and the "out-door-loving" people of California the Redwood Empire was truly a vacationland.

Part of the information and advertising that appeared in the official time schedule that became effective August 1, 1912.

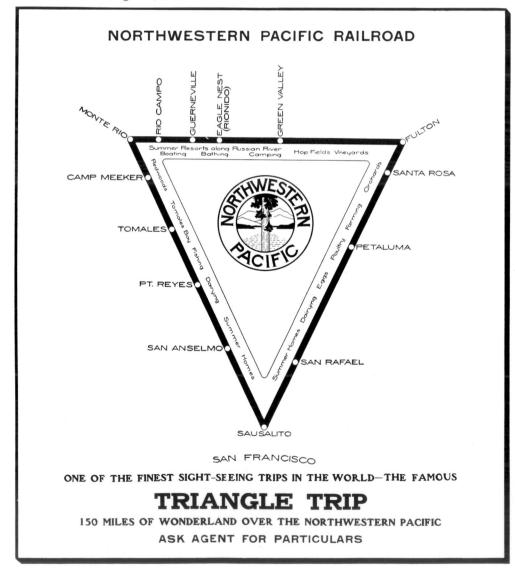

West End, San Rafael in early days of Northwestern Pacific ownership. For picture of
station at this point prior to formation of the N.W.P., see Page 29.

From 1908 to 1914, the Northwestern Pacific under-
took various construction projects and changes on
the line's southern end, the most important of
which was the building of 1.40 miles between
Baltimore Park and Detour. It was opened on April
1, 1909, and all steam passenger operations used the
new route. It made Sausalito the southern terminal.
Tiburon then became a freight-only operation with
only local passenger trains serving the district from
San Rafael. Express service to San Rafael, via the
electric interurban cars, was inaugurated over the
new section, which became known as the "cut-off."
A second track was added between Greenbrae and
San Rafael stations, and also between San Rafael
and San Anselmo, with the exception of two small
sections, one at San Anselmo and the other between
West End and "B" Street stations. Along with this,
one rail was taken up between San Rafael and San
Anselmo to end the narrow gauge operation. Between
"B" Street station and San Quentin, 3.26 miles, the
line was changed from narrow gauge to broad gauge,
and the Mill Valley branch of 1.74 miles had its
narrow gauge rail removed. This ended the necessity
of handling narrow gauge cars in the interurban
territory which, incidently, was a sight to behold
- a narrow gauge engine with a string of freight
cars of both gauges in its consist!

At the same time, consideration was given to
double-tracking Tunnel No. 1, between Alto and
Chapman (near Corte Madera). This was rejected,

however, because when it was constructed by the
North Pacific Coast in 1884, it fortunately was built
large enough to accommodate the now broad gauge
equipment. There was only one exception, and that
was when the N.W.P. leased several ex-El Paso &
Southwestern, 4-6-2 type, steam locomotives from
the Southern Pacific in 1938. Their stacks were high,
the first engine through had its stack knocked off
and it became wedged in the tunnel. The stacks
were then shortened or replaced with smaller ones
on this class of engine.

Between 1914 and 1926 the Northwestern Pacific
double tracked the cut-off between Baltimore Park
and Greenbrae and between San Anselmo and Manor.
The two small, single track sections between San
Anselmo and San Rafael were double tracked in
1930. On April 6, 1920, the narrow gauge was brought
to an end between Sausalito and Point Reyes Station,
and the section broad gauged between Manor and
Point Reyes. All transfer facilities of the narrow
gauge were moved and installed at Point Reyes. An
engine house was built to accomodate either four
broad or narrow gauge locomotives. The old narrow
gauge enginehouse south of the station was dismantled.

A statistical informataion page elsewhere in this
book gives further construction and abandonment
dates of predecessor companies and the Northwestern
Pacific to the present date.

Beginning of the end for more sections of the Northwestern Pacific was started by a disasterous fire on September 17, 1923, near Guerneville. Before the embers had died out the flames had roared to the Pacific Ocean, wiping out the entire lumber industry in the area. The Laton branch was abandoned almost immediately, and later the Markham Branch. Then the narrow gauge was cut back to Camp Meeker for passenger trains, with the last slim-gauge train leaving Cazadero on September 9, 1926. The narrow gauge was abandoned altogether on March 30, 1930, from Point Reyes to Monte Rio. It ended its famous days of old with hardly a passenger aboard or a piece of freight in its cars.

The year 1929 was another milestone in the operations of the Northwestern Pacific. In that year the Southern Pacific bought out the interest the Santa Fe had in the road, and the line became a wholly-owned subsidiary of the Southern Pacific Company. Then came the Great Depression. There were still plenty of passengers in the summer time, but nothing like the night of the glorious Fourth in 1923, when 30,000 passengers came off the trains and on to the ferries at Sausalito. Every piece of passenger equipment and all that could be borrowed had been pressed into service, and some doubled right back to the resort areas. Freight was down to a trickle, and branch lines, almost at a standstill, were becoming heavy losers. To try to make the passenger business more attractive the Northwestern Pacific did away with most of the main line open vestibule wooden cars and brought in twenty-five enclosed vestibule coaches from the Southern Pacific, along with nine modern bucket-type-seat style steel cars. For economy, on the lighter trains, gas-electric motor cars were substituted for steam trains. Fares were lowered; in fact, a "Dollar day" bargain was tried on week-ends. For example: Russian River points and return to San Francisco for only $1.25 roundtrip, or less than a cent a mile! On February 29, 1932, the Northwestern Pacific purchased the Petaluma & Santa Rosa Electric Railroad, a road which the Western Pacific had eyed for a long time and it had plans to extend its Sacramento Northern Vacaville branch to Petaluma via the electric line. The Petaluma & Santa Rosa Railroad was incorporated on June 20, 1903, and was a consolidation of the Santa Rosa Street Railway, the Union Street Railway of Santa Rosa, the Central Street Railway and the Petaluma Street Railway. The electric road was formed with great ambitions in that it planned a line from Petaluma to Sebastopol, Santa Rosa and on to Lake and Mendocino counties. It started construction at Petaluma on April 5, 1904, and built to Sebastopol, 17.07 miles, and on to Santa Rosa, 5.40 miles, with the line ready for traffic on March 2, 1905. A one-mile branch to serve the Petaluma

River section was also built. In July, 1905, a branch from Sebastopol to Forestville was in operation, and another branch from Liberty to Two Rock, 5.43 miles, was completed on July 28, 1913. The freight was handled by electric motors and the passenger business by twelve electric cars. These cars were first painted white, then a yellow-brown, then back to white. When the N.W.P. took over in 1932, the passenger service was quickly discontinued and the tracks on Fourth Street in Santa Rosa removed. On December 25, 1946, the electric motor made its last trip, and the line was completely diesel the next day. Two small diesels perform the service today with additional units from the Southern Pacific during apple season. The branch between Liberty and Two Rock was abandoned on September 29, 1952. When the Petaluma & Santa Rosa started in 1904, it also took over the river boat operation between Petaluma and San Francisco. These boats connected with the electric cars at Petaluma. The boat "Petaluma" was destroyed by fire on March 22, 1914, and a new one with the same name was ordered built and was placed in service in 1915. On November 8, 1920, the steamer "Gold" (No. 1) was also destroyed by fire. The "Fort Bragg," built in 1899, was quickly chartered and later purchased to become the second "Gold." It finally wore out in 1940 and was retired. The second "Petaluma" made its last run on August 24, 1950, its demise brought about by trucks which could haul goods faster on today's super-highways. The "Petaluma" then became a show boat at Jack London Square in Oakland. The craft came to an end when it burned and sank on Saturday, October 13, 1956.

The depression was finally easing up, but the passengers who once rode the many trains of the Northwestern Pacific were now in their autos or even riding buses. With this in mind and the road running deeply in the red, Ed Maggard, now president of the railroad, knew that the time had come to cut off the heavily losing branch lines - not just the passenger trains, but the entire line if the freight outlook was poor. The Willits-Sherwood branch was the first to go and it was followed by the Point Reyes, Donahue, Sebastopol, Russian River and San Quentin lines. The Albion Lumber Company, which had leased the orphaned Albion branch on July 1, 1921, defaulted on its $22,000 per year payment to the N.W.P. as the S.P.'s Mexico line was completed and required no more ties. Along with this the lumber market was in a distressing slump. The Navarro mill shut down on September 30, 1927, and the sprawling Albion mill ran its last log through on May 19, 1928. With a total passenger and freight revenue of less than $60 in one year, the branch ceased operation on January 16, 1930. It laid dormant until 1937 when scrap prices took an upward turn. On June 5, 1937, the scrappers moved in, fired up two ancient locomotives and started to dismantle the line. The job was finished on December 10, 1937.

For more economical operation, and ending duplicate service in Sonoma Valley, the Southern Pacific abandoned two portions of its Sonoma Valley branch: Santa Rosa to Los Guilicos, 8.3 miles, and Yulupa to Schellville, 7.2 miles, on January 15, 1934. From that date all freights to and from Southern Pacific have interchanged with the N.W.P. at Schellville instead of Santa Rosa. Also on the same date the N.W.P. abandoned the portion of its Sonoma Valley branch from Yulupa (Madrone) to Glen Ellen, 2.54 miles, installed a switch at Yulupa, and took over the line formally owned by the Southern Pacific between Yulupa and Los Guilicos. With a continued drop in freight revenues the line was cut back by the N.W.P. to Glen Ellen (S.P. Station) on October 10, 1941. The portion between Glen Ellen and Sonoma, 6.59 miles, had but little traffic and with the pressure of war this section was abandoned on September 15, 1942, and the rails used to construct the Richmond Shipyard Railway between Oakland and Richmond shipyards. On the northern end, the Trinidad branch was cut back to Korblex. Passenger trains were taken off one by one, and on May 11, 1942, the day train to Eureka was discontinued, leaving only the night trains, numbered 3 and 4. Another heavy loser was the suburban service to Marin County. A number of cuts in service were placed in effect to try to balance the books somewhere along the line, but all failed. First the Mill Valley trains were discontinued on October 1, 1940, and then on March 1, 1941, the remainder of the electric lines to San Rafael and Manor went out of the picture, as did the entire ferry boat operation.

Less than ten months later, Pearl Harbor, and the resultant four years of war brought the railroad to task. Everything that could run was placed in service, and like the other roads in the United States, there was business a-plenty for the Redwood Empire Route. When the war ended a post-war boom of prosperity hit the country, and wherever there was a stand of trees, a lumber mill sprang up. The freight business was reaching a new peace time high level.

The Eureka night trains, which had their southern terminal shifted along with the day trains from Sausalito to San Rafael on November 23, 1941, struggled along with their 40 year old chair car and Pullman. For the passenger it was inconvenient, and for the sightseeing tourist the trains ran at night, so the "Eureka Express" as it was called, went out many times with just the crew aboard. The N.W.P. applied for abandonment of the train in 1955, and in its place the company wanted to run a daily

service between Willits and South Fork. This area could not be reached by any other transportation. Hearings were held up and down the line by the State Public Utilities Commission. The result was the "Redwood," which would run three times a week between San Rafael and Eureka. The night trains were discontinued on June 2, 1956, and the new daylight operation began on the same day. The train, with its streamline modern chair cars, was given a tremendous welcome all along the line, and once again the travelers from far and wide could see the beauty of the Redwood Empire from the comforts of a train window.

While the summer traffic on week-ends was considered fair with three chair cars in the consist of the "Redwood," traffic on week days and in the winter months was sparse. On many trips not even a half dozen revenue passengers were aboard. Seeing no future in the passenger field, the Northwestern Pacific, through its parent company, Southern Pacific, knocked again on the door of the State Public Utilities Commission early in January, 1958, to request discontinuance of the train between San Rafael and Willits. After a number of hearings approval was obtained.

The last complete round trip left San Rafael at 8:35 a.m., Saturday, November 8, 1958, and left Eureka on the return the following morning at 7:45 a.m. One thousand passengers were on the train at one time or another during the two days, with a maximum of 423 passengers between Cloverdale and Santa Rosa on the return trip.

At 5:29 p.m., Sunday, November 9th, George Argall, Engineer, brought the nine car streamline train to a halt at the San Rafael station and 94 years of railroad passenger service in Sonoma County and 88 years in Marin County had come to an end.

The next morning the passenger train left for Willits never to return. One final note: just north of Ignacio, Elmer E. Pimm, brakeman, got off the train, took a glance at Conductor Ernest Sobbe, and then set the switch for the Schellville line. Hereafter the main line of the Northwestern Pacific would be between Eureka and Sonoma. The section between Ignacio and Tiburon was relegated to branch line status.

For Elmer Pimm, whose likeable personality had won many passenger friends in his thirty-six years with the N.W.P., it was back to freight service. A few weeks later, on December 22, 1958, a sad incident occured in Tiburon yard when an accident claimed the life of the genial brakeman.

The one mail express car and streamline coach powered by a lone Electro-Motive diesel unit, growled its way three times a week between Willits and Eureka until the S.P. found that further economy could be effected with a Budd-built Rail Diesel

A 1911 general view of the Russian River vacation country near Monte Rio. The scene is looking to the west, or toward Duncan Mills as the morning train from that point approaches on broad gauge rails around 7:15 AM on a summer day. The narrow gauge track was built through here in 1876-1877 and the third rail for broad gauge operation was added in 1909. The narrow gauge was abandoned in this section in 1926, and the inner rail was removed in 1930. In 1935 the entire Russian River line was abandoned.

car that had been made surplus by the discontinuance of the "Sacramento Locals." Revamping the car on one end so it could carry mail and express the unit took the place of the "train" on May 25, 1959. All went well until October 7, 1960, when the rail car smashed into a truck at Fort Seward caving in one end. It was six months before the car came back from the Sacramento shops and its new look consisted of controls completely removed from the one end and the mail and express storage area extended to include the former vestibule and control area.

While the upper end of the Northwestern Pacific was settling into a serene routine an event was about to take place on the southern end which would affect the operation of the entire railroad. On a summer day, Thursday, July 20, 1961, two boys started a fire in the railroad's Puerto Suello tunnel (north of San Rafael) which turned into a roaring holocaust. Before the blaze was out, the 1,350 foot tunnel had completely caved in from one end to the other. After hearing an estimate that three quarters of a million dollars would be required to rebuild the tunnel, the railroad applied to the ICC to abandon the section from the San Rafael station to a point on the other side of the tunnel. The railroad promised that industries from San Rafael south to Tiburon and Sausalito would be adequately served by freight car barge service into Tiburon and that freight from the north would be sent to the S.P. at their interchange point of Schellville for "beyond" destinations. After long and extended hearings the Federal body denied the application on two occasions and ordered the tunnel rebuilt. At this writing the matter is still in the Federal courts.

Shortly after the year 1963 got under way the Northwestern Pacific claimed its lone rail car service from Willits to Eureka was a money-loser and applied to drop the run to only once-a-week. Hearings were held in the latter part of May and early June at San Francisco, Willits and Eureka. Because tour groups were beginning to head to the rails along the scenic Eel River and because the service operated in an area where there were few or no auto roads, the State Public Utilities Commission denied the application on October 22, 1963.

As to the future, if the people who live in the area will support the passenger service now given and tourists find their way to take the beautiful ride, the train will remain; in fact many believe it could be just as popular as the neighboring "Skunk" train operation on the California Western Railroad, which in 1963, with its four famed motors, hauled 70,000 passengers between Willits and Fort Bragg.

The freight business, mostly lumber, has remained on a high level and it is not uncommon to see two or three, or even four 100 car freights on the line on any day. While diesels are presently assigned to the N.W.P. by the S.P., it may not be too long before this long-standing practice will end and diesels of any make or description placed on the head end at Roseville will take the freight straight through to Eureka eliminating the change of engines at Schellville, the interchange point between the N.W.P. and the S.P.

But whatever the future, with its modern diesels, push button railroading and the like, the Redwood Empire Route, as the photographs in this book portray, was at one time in its glory with electric and steam powered trains hauling commuters and vacation bound passengers. It was the day of the the thrills of seeing the diminutive 4-4-0's and the open platform passenger cars swaying to and fro along the redwood studded counties of the northern California, but like the stage coach that preceded it, the roar of the "iron horse" and the passenger car are but memories.

From the year of its construction in 1896 the Ferry Building saw millions of commuters and vacationists pass through its north end portals to the Redwood Empire, until the end of service with the departure of the ferry "Eureka" on its last run, 11:25 P.M., February 28, 1941.

The single-ended ferry "James M. Donahue" at the Sausalito slip in 1910.

Engine No. 54 on Train No. 8, the Healdsburg Passenger at Sausalito terminal in 1922 awaiting departure time, 5:45 PM.

Engine 21 on Train 4, the Ukiah Passenger, near Manzanita in 1910.

Train No. 3 with eight cars from Eureka joins main suburban line at Baltimore Park for final portion of trip to Sausalito.

Engine 108 with "Caboose Hop" at San Clemente heading for San Rafael.

Below, enroute to Russian River points, Train 222 with Engine 114, stops at Petaluma.

Engine 6 with train at Sebastopol in 1909.

No. 23, on head end of an excursion train bound for Ft. Bragg stops for water in 1938.

Hop pickers arrive at Hopland on "Hop Pickers Special" powered by 4-6-0 No. 114.

N.W.P cars sway across one of the many trestles in the redwood country.

Construction work on the California Northwestern.

Engine 201, Train 1, Longvale, 1912.

Above: One hundred eighty miles north of San Francisco is scenic Spyrock where Indian tribes of years ago guarded the Eel River gorge. Tunnel 22 is at right.

Engine 201 with construction on Island Mountain bridge. View is to the south.

Engine 13 and train at historic Fortuna station in 1911.

Extra freight with Engine 170 eases across a trestle near Eureka.

Engine 8 with train of wooden passenger equipment at South Fork in 1909.

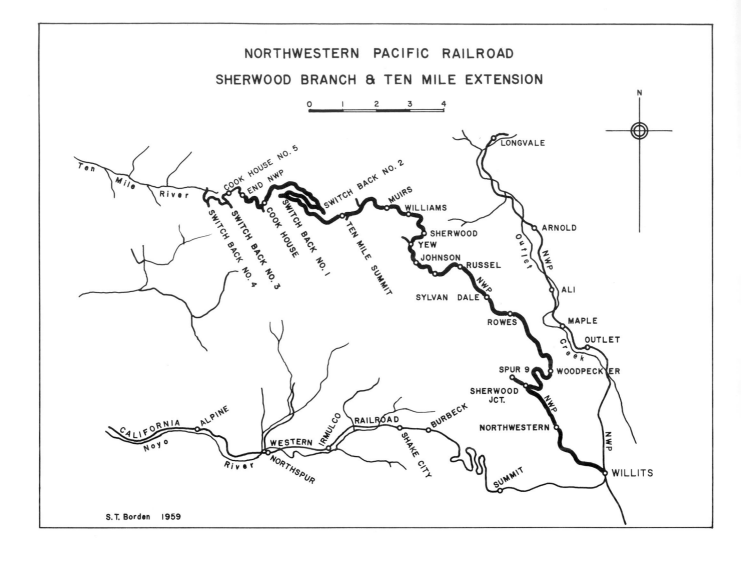

NORTHWESTERN PACIFIC RAILROAD

SHERWOOD BRANCH & TEN MILE EXTENSION

S.T. Borden 1959

No. 251, the road's only Shay, in log train service on the Sherwood branch.

Engine 202 and train along the Albion river around 1912.

Clearbrook Junction on the Albion branch. The track at left went about a mile to connect with the Albion Lumber Company's logging line into the heavy redwood forests.

Picnic train on the Albion branch, May 17, 1908. The engine is first No. 1 which later became No. 225.

Above is the track leading to Bohemian Grove, near Monte Rio; at upper right, home-bound vacationers await the train at Guernewood Park; at right is the water carnival at Monte Rio. Boat in the foreground, the Sonoma, took passengers between River Landing and Monte Rio during years 1908 and 1909 when railroad bridge was under construction after wash-out. Below: Train at Guerneville about 1908.

View of Rio Nido area on a Spring day in 1926 before summer crowds came up for vacations. At right center, daily freight train can be seen heading for Santa Rosa.

Train No. 223, the Duncan Mills Passenger, at Guerneville about 1920.

Montesano, another station nestled among the Redwoods, approximately midway between Guerneville and Monte Rio on the Russian River branch.

Engine 23 on Train 221, the morning Duncan Mills Passenger, at Guerneville.

Engine 9 and crew near Monte Rio about 1909.

The famed Monte Rio hotel. This establishment was rebuilt several times and boasted the first elevator in Sonoma County. This photo was made in 1927 but, like the railroad, nothing remains today.

A view of the Sausalito terminal of the North Pacific Coast Railroad, made about 1890. The side-wheel tug "Tiger" is at the left, the ferry "San Rafael" on the right, and Goat Island (Yerba Buena Island) in the background. This facility went into the ownership of the North Shore Railroad in 1902 and broad gauge rails were subsequently added to handle suburban electric service. The Northwestern Pacific took over in 1907 and when the Tiburon terminal was shifted to this location in 1909, it became a very busy operation, with both broad and narrow gauge passenger trains originating here. The narrow gauge trains ceased operating below Point Reyes in 1920, however the broad gauge interurban and the main and branch line steam trains continued until 1941. The area today gives little indication of its historic past.

Narrow gauge Engine No. 84 on Train No. 9, the Cazadero Passenger, nears Sausalito after a four hour run from the redwood country. The date is about 1916.

Lagunitas, about 1909.

No more passengers - no more freight; it's near the end. Engine 94 and Train 37, the daily-except-Sunday mixed from Camp Meeker to Point Reyes at Tomales station during the final days.

Down the River from Monte Rio was Sheridan. Note the dual gauge to accomodate both the broad gauge trains of the Guerneville branch, and the narrow gauge trains from down Point Reyes way.

With gloomy skies - symbolic of the occasion - passengers gather at Duncan Mills for a final photo; it is the day of the last train, November 14, 1935, and sixty years of railroading along the Russian River come to an end.

Below, a historic occasion at Cazadero: On September 10, 1926, narrow gauge service gives way to broad gauge, the photo showing the first broad gauge train into the little lumber town. Engine No. 20 is out of sight a hundred yards or so being turned on the turntable right at the end of the line. Almost exactly seven years later the broad gauge rails were removed and another California community was without railroad service.

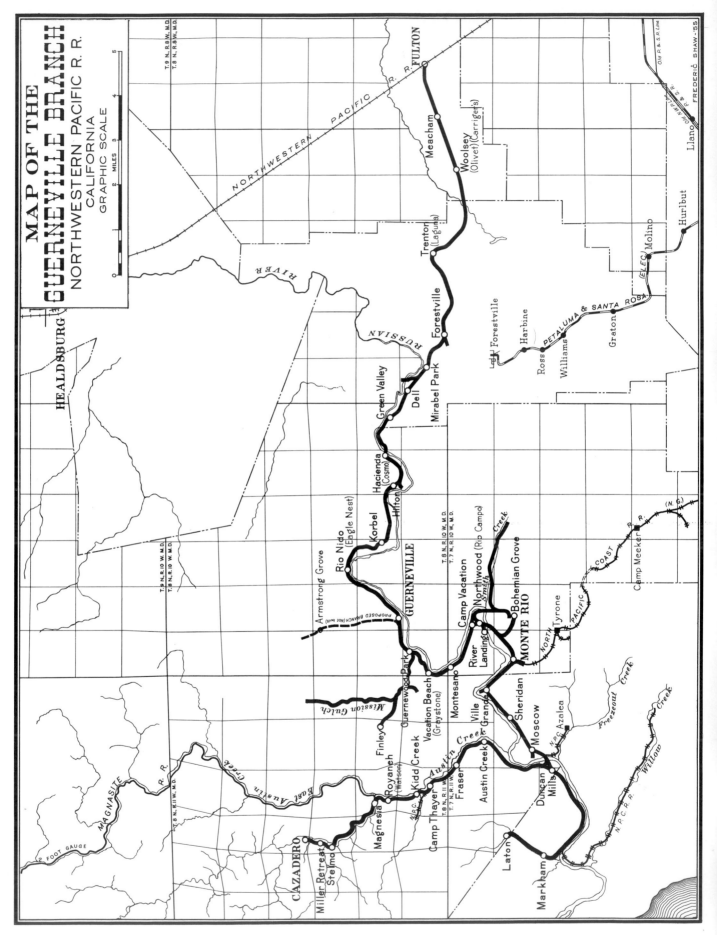

MAP OF THE
GUERNEVILLE BRANCH
NORTHWESTERN PACIFIC R. R.
CALIFORNIA
GRAPHIC SCALE

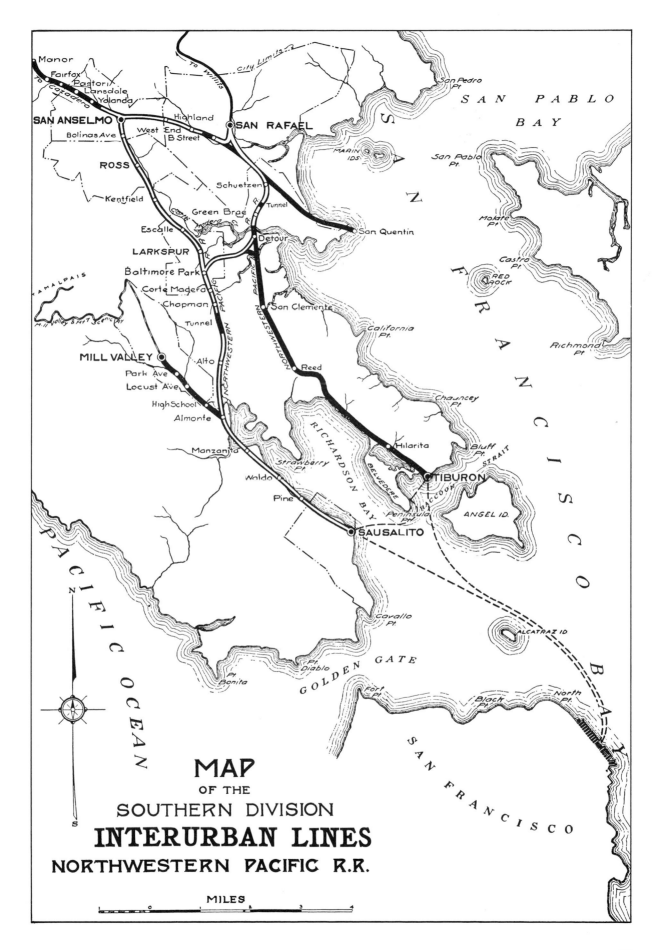

Manor
Fairfax
Pastori
Lansdale
Yolanda
To Cazadero

SAN ANSELMO
Bolinas Ave
Highland
SAN RAFAEL
West End
B Street

City Limits
To Willits

ROSS
Schuetzen
Kentfield
Tunnel
Green Brae

SAN PABLO BAY

San Pedro Pt.

San Pablo Pt.

MARIN IDS.

San Pablo Pt.

Molate Pt.

Escalle
LARKSPUR
Detour
San Quentin

Castro Pt.

RED ROCK

LARKSPUR
Baltimore Park
Corte Madera
Chopman
Tunnel
San Clemente

California Pt.

Richmond Pt.

F R A N C I S C O

TAMALPAIS

Mt. Valley & Mt. Scenic Ry.

MILL VALLEY
Park Ave
Locust Ave
High School
Almonte
Alto
Reed

Chauncey Pt.

Manzanita
Strawberry Pt.

RICHARDSON BAY

Hilarita

Bluff Pt.

STRAIT

Waldo
Pine
BELVEDERE

TIBURON

RACCOON

ANGEL ID.

Peninsula Pt.

SAUSALITO

PACIFIC OCEAN

Cavallo Pt.

ALCATRAZ ID.

Pt. Bonita
Pt. Diablo
GOLDEN GATE
Fort Pt.

Black Pt.
North Pt.

S A N   F R A N C I S C O   B A Y

N

MAP
OF THE
SOUTHERN DIVISION
INTERURBAN LINES
NORTHWESTERN PACIFIC R.R.

SAN FRANCISCO

S

MILES
0   1   2   3   4

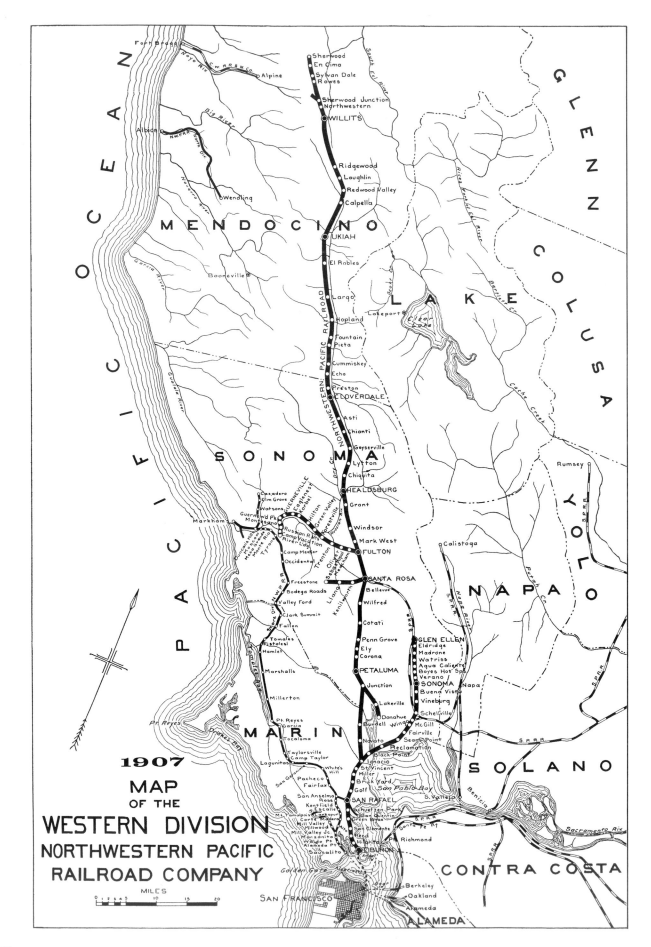

OCEAN

PACIFIC

GLENN

COLUSA

LAKE

YOLO

NAPA

MENDOCINO

SONOMA

MARIN

SOLANO

CONTRA COSTA

Fort Bragg
Sherwood
En Cima
Sylvan Dale
Rowes
Alpine
Sherwood Junction
Northwestern
WILLITS

Ridgewood
Laughlin
Redwood Valley
Calpella
Wendling

UKIAH

El Robles

Booneville

Largo
Hopland
Lakeport
Clear Lake
Fountain
Pieta
Cummiskey
Echo
Preston
CLOVERDALE
Asti
Chianti
Geyserville
Lytton
Chiquita

Rumsey

HEALDSBURG
Cazadero
Elim Grove
Watsons
Guernewood Pk
Montesano
Markham
Russian R Hts
Camp Vacation
River Lds
Camp Meeker
Occidental
GUERNEVILLE
Eaglenest
Korbel
Hilton
Green Valley
Forestville
Trenton
Freestone
Bodega Roads
Valley Ford
Clark Summit
Fallon
Tomales
Ristolesi
Hamlet
Marshalls
Millerton
Grant
Windsor
Mark West
FULTON
Sebastopol
Llano
Kenilworth
SANTA ROSA
Bellevue
Wilfred
Cotati
Penn Grove
Ely
Corona
PETALUMA
Junction
Lakeville
Donahue
Burdell
Wingo
GLEN ELLEN
Eldridge
Madrone
Watriss
Agua Caliente
Boyes Hot Spg
Verano
SONOMA
Buena Vista
Vineburg
Schellville
McGill
Fairville
Sears Point
Reclamation
Napa
Calistoga

Pt Reyes
Garcia
Tocaloma
Taylorsville
Camp Taylor
Lagunitas
San Geronimo
Pacheco
Fairfax
San Anselmo
Ross
Kentfield
Escalle
Mt Tamalpais
Larkspur
Corte Madera
Mill Valley
Millwood
Mill Valley Jc
Manzanita
Waldo Pt
Alameda Pt
Sausalito
White's Hill
Novato
Ignacio
St Vincent
Miller
Brick Yard
Golf
SAN RAFAEL
Schuetzen Park
San Quentin
Green Brae
San Clemente
Reed
Hilarita
TIBURON
Alto

Black Point
San Pablo Bay
S Vallejo
Benicia
Pt Richmond
Sacramento Riv

Santa Fe Ry

Golden Gate
SAN FRANCISCO
Berkeley
Oakland
Alameda
ALAMEDA

1907

MAP
OF THE
WESTERN DIVISION
NORTHWESTERN PACIFIC
RAILROAD COMPANY

MILES
0 1 2 3 4 5   10   15   20

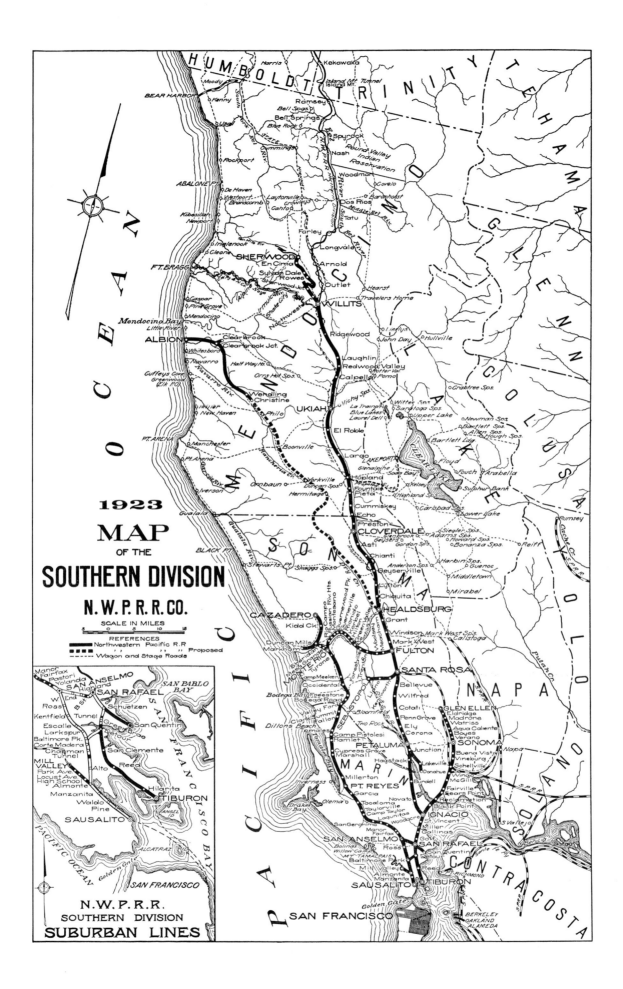

1923

MAP
OF THE
SOUTHERN DIVISION
N. W. P. R. R. CO.

SCALE IN MILES

REFERENCES
━━━ Northwestern Pacific R.R
▪▪▪▪ " " Proposed
- - - Wagon and Stage Roads

N.W.P.R.R.
SOUTHERN DIVISION
SUBURBAN LINES

LIST OF OPENING DATES FOR SERVICE OF SECTIONS OF THE NORTHWESTERN PACIFIC, SHOWING ORIGINAL ROAD, MILEAGE AND DATE

(BROAD GAUGE)

SAN FRANCISCO AND NORTH PACIFIC AREA

ORIGINAL ROAD	SECTION	MILEAGE	DATE
P&H	Petaluma - Haystack Landing	2.50	July, 1864
SF&NP	Donahue Landing - Santa Rosa	23.00	October 31, 1870
SF&NP	Santa Rosa - Windsor	9.13	March 1, 1871
SF&NP	Windsor - Grants	3.52	April 10, 1871
SF&NP	Grants - Healdsburg	1.58	July 9, 1871
SF&NP	Healdsburg - Cloverdale	17.20	April 15, 1872
F&G	Fulton - Korbel's	12.35	May 29, 1876
F&G	Korbel's - Guerneville	2.95	March 25, 1877
SF&NP	Petaluma - San Rafael	21.50	June 2, 1879
SF&NP	San Rafael - N.P.C. Junction	.40	April 3, 1882
SF&NP	San Rafael - Tiburon	8.33	April 28, 1884
C&U	Cloverdale - Ukiah	28.50	March 17, 1889
SRS&GV	Santa Rosa - Sebastopol	6.32	February 17, 1890
SF&NP	Guerneville - Bohemia	3.88	April 1, 1892
SF&NP	Guernewood Park - Finley	2.00	November 1, 1892
SF&NP	Monte Rosa - Mission Gulch	2.00	1896
SF&NP	Bohemia - Smith Creek	1.30	1896
CNW	Ukiah - Laughlin	10.11	March 17, 1901
CNW	Laughlin - Willits	15.44	March 1, 1902
CNW	Willits - Sherwood	13.75	May, 1904
SF&N	Wingo - Ramal	(1) 2.08	May 1, 1905
SF&N	Buchli - Union	(1) 8.64	May 1, 1905

(1) - operated by CNW until July 19, 1906 when leased to Southern Pacific Company and then sold to that company on August 12, 1911.

SONOMA VALLEY LINES

PRR	Norfolk - Near Schellville (Prismoidal)	3.50	November 24, 1876
SV	Sonoma Landing - Sonoma (narrow gauge)	15.00	November, 1879
S&SR	Sonoma - Glen Ellen (narrow gauge)	6.53	August 15, 1882
M&N	Sears Point - Ignacio (narrow gauge)	7.67	June 30, 1888
SF&NP	Ignacio - Glen Ellen (To Broad Gauge)	26.36	April 9, 1890

RAIL LINES AROUND EUREKA

E&KR	Samoa - Camp 5	17.55	— 1897
E&KR	Camp 5 - Little River	2.45	— 1902
E&KR	Little River Jct - end of branch	1.34	— 1902
E&KR	Little River - 25 Junction	4.60	— 1903
E&KR	25 Junction - Trinidad	2.34	— 1907

C&N	Arcata - Eureka	8.38	December 14, 1901
ER&E	Burnell's - South Bay (Field's Landing)	15.11	August, 1884
ER&E	South Bay - Eureka	6.31	July, 1885
PL	Scotia - Alton	7.01	August 20, 1885
PL	Scotia - Elinor	5.68	July, 1898
PL	Elinor - Camp Nine	2.42	July, 1902
CM	Burnell's - Carlotta	3.43	July 7, 1903
SF&NW	Camp Nine - Shively	1.99	— 1905
AL	Albion - Keene's Summit	11.60	— 1891
A&SE	In and about Albion	3.00	— 1903
A&SE	Clearbrook Jct. - Clearbrook	1.00	— 1903
FB&SE	Keene's Summit - Wendling	8.30	— 1905

NORTHWESTERN PACIFIC

NWP	Wendling - Christine	2.90	— 1908
NWP	Willits - Longvale	13.00	August 1, 1911
NWP	Longvale - Dos Rios	14.00	May 11, 1913
NWP	Dos Rios - Fort Seward	50.15	September 22, 1914
NWP	Shively - South Fork	8.30	May 8, 1912
NWP	South Fork - McCann	5.10	May 12, 1913
NWP	McCann - Fort Seward	15.60	May 3, 1914
NWP	Sherwood Extension	12.13	Between 1909 & June 5, 1923
NWP	Camp Vacation - River Landing	.28	May, 1907
NWP	Camp Vacation (Rio Campo) - Duncan Mills	4.60	November 15, 1909
NWP	Duncan Mills - Markham (Added rail for standard gauge operation)	2.80	— 1913
NWP	Markham - Laton	1.10	— 1913
NWP	Manor - Point Reyes (Added rail for standard gauge operation)	17.60	April 6, 1920
NWP	Duncan Mills - Cazadero (Added rail for standard gauge operation)	7.04	September 10, 1926
NWP	Yulupa - Los Guilicos (Taken over from Southern Pacific)	8.50	January 15, 1934
NWP	Petaluma - Sebastopol - Santa Rosa	22.47	February 29, 1932
	Sebastopol - Forestville	7.14	February 29, 1932
	Liberty - Two Rock	5.43	February 29, 1932
	Petaluma industry spur	1.00	February 29, 1932
	(Above purchased from the Petaluma & Santa Rosa electric railroad)		
NWP	Baltimore Park - Detour	1.40	April 1, 1909
NWP	San Rafael "B" Street - San Quentin (changed to broad gauge)	3.26	April 1, 1909
NWP	Started operation of electric service San Anselmo - Fairfax.	1.77	1911
NWP	Double tracked between Baltimore Park - San Rafael via Detour, except tunnel and west trestle approach, which was double-tracked in 1924.	4.00	1914
NWP	Double tracked between San Rafael and San Anselmo, except for two small sections on either end, and extended suburban operations Fairfax - Manor.	3.00	1914

| NWP | Constructed double track on new right of way, Shaver Street to "B" Street, San Rafael, and double tracked portion out of San Anselmo on the San Rafael line. | .50 | January 4, 1930 |

NORTH PACIFIC COAST - NORTH SHORE RAILROADS

SR&SQ	San Rafael - San Quentin (Broad Gauge)	3.48	March 21, 1870
NPC	Saucelito - Tomales	49.00	January 7, 1875
NPC	San Quentin - San Rafael (to Narrow gauge)	3.48	April 10, 1875 (plus 250 feet to join SR&SQ & NPC at San Rafael)
NPC	San Anselmo - San Rafael "B" Street	2.00	July 25, 1874
NPC	Tomales - Russian River (Monte Rio)	20.75	September, 1876
NPC	Monte Rio - Moscow Mills	2.75	October 16, 1876
NPC	Moscow Mills - Duncan Mills	1.00	May 5, 1877
NPC	Pedrini - Shafters	2.33	March, 1895
NPC	Duncan Mills - Markham	2.80	July, 1882
NPC	Bridge - Willow Creek	5.14	July, 1882
NPC	Azeala Spur	1.25	August, 1882
NPC	Monte Rio - Bohemia	1.00	August, 1882
NS	Alameda Point (Pine) - Corte Madera (new line)	5.37	February 19, 1884
NW	Duncan Mills - Ingrams (Cazadero)	7.20	April 11, 1886
NW	Kidd Creek Lumber spur	.60	June, 1888
SFT&B	Bay Jct. (Mill Valley Jct.)	1.74	October 13, 1889
NPC	Sausalito - Mill Valley Jct. (dbl. tracked)	3.40	— 1894
NPC	North Portal Corte Madera Tunnel - San Anselmo (double tracked)	4.08	— 1901
NS	Roys - Maillard (new line)	2.64	December 4, 1904
NS	San Rafael "B" Street - San Rafael Union Station	.58	— 1906 (both gauges)
NS	For new broad gauge electric service added third rail and fourth rail for current between Sausalito and Fairfax* 11.80 miles of which 3.40 miles were double tracked between Sausalito and Mill Valley Jct; 1.93 miles between Mill Valley Jct. and south Portal of Corte Madera tunnel; 4.08 miles between north portal of Corte Madera tunnel and San Anselmo, and single branch tracks between Mill Valley Junction and Mill Valley 1.74 miles, and San Anselmo and San Rafael 2.00 miles.		
NS	Electric service from Sausalito to Mill Valley opened - August 20, 1903.		August 20, 1903
	Electric service from Sausalito to San Rafael opened - October 17, 1903.		October 17, 1903

*Electric service between San Anselmo and Fairfax was not operated by the North Shore.

A CHRONOLOGICAL LIST OF
ABANDONMENTS OF THE NORTHWESTERN
PACIFIC OR PREDECESSOR COMPANIES
SHOWING SECTION, MILEAGE AND DATE

It is possible that in comparing the construction mileage with that of abandonment it may not agree. This is because that throughout the years changes were made in alignment that in most cases reduced, but in some increased, the overall mileage, and also, that very small sections were abandoned at some time or other with no proper notation made for record.

SECTION	MILEAGE	DATE
Prismoidal RR Norfolk - Schellville	3.50	May 5, 1877
Sears Point - Sonoma Landing	3.50	June 30, 1888
Donahue Landing - Donahue	.20	May 4, 1884
Monte Rosa - Finley	.75	— 1896
Camp Vacation - Bohemia	.66	March 19, 1907
Bohemia - Smith Creek	1.30	March 19, 1907
Guernewood Park - Mission Culch	3.50	June, 1908
Camp Vacation (Rio Campo) - River Landing	.20	November 15, 1909
Markham - Laton	1.10	March 10, 1924
Duncan Mills - Markham	2.80	August 3, 1925
Albion - Christine		
Clearbrook Jct. - Clearbrook	26.81	January 16, 1930
2nd Street, between "B" and Shaver, San Rafael	.30	— 1930
Sherwood Extension	2.71	April, 1930
Sherwood Extension	9.60	October 30, 1930
(P&SR - 4th Street - Santa Rosa)	1.07	July 1, 1932
Korblex - Trinidad	(1) 16.94	February 15, 1933
Little River Branch	(2) 1.34	February 15, 1933
Thompson's - Burn's Mill	1.10	February 15, 1933
Willits - Williams	14.52	February 15, 1933
Duncan Mills - Cazadero	7.04	August 1, 1933
Manor - Point Reyes	17.51	August 1, 1933
Madrone - Glen Ellen	2.54	January 15, 1934
Santa Rosa - Sebastopol	(3) 6.33	January 15, 1934
Petaluma (Junction switch) - Donahue	5.67	January 15, 1934
Fulton - Duncan Mills	(6) 22.99	November 15, 1935
Carlotta Extension	(5) 1.40	January 6, 1936
San Quentin - "Hill Road"	.59	— 1937
Glen Ellen - Los Guilicos	6.32	October 10, 1941
Larkspur - San Anselmo		
Fairfax - Manor	3.83	May 10, 1942
Sonoma - Glen Ellen	6.59	September 15, 1942
San Rafael "B" Street - Fairfax	4.43	December 10, 1942
"Hill Road" near San Quentin - Junction (Main line)	1.22	— 1946
Liberty - Two Rock (P&SR)	5.43	September 29, 1952
Almonte - Mill Valley	1.73	May 1, 1955
Pier to Johnson Street, Sausalito	.34	April 15, 1955
Larkspur - Baltimore Park	.51	November 15, 1959
Ross - Forestville (P&SR)	1.08	October 15, 1961

(NARROW GAUGE)

Old Line Alameda Point - Lyford's - Corte Madera	6.10	April 26, 1884
Duncan Mills - Azalea	1.25	— 1902
Old line Roys - Maillard	4.74	December 4, 1904
San Rafael "B" Street - San Quentin (changed to broad gauge)	3.26	April 1, 1909
Monte Rio - Bohemia (changed to broad gauge)	1.00	November 15, 1909
San Rafael, Union Station - San Anselmo (inner rail removed - narrow gauge discontinued)	2.54	— 1911
Mill Valley Jct - Mill Valley (inner rail removed - narrow gauge discontinued)	1.74	— 1911
Pedrini - Shafters	2.33	— 1913
Duncan Mills - Markham (changed to broad gauge)	2.80	— 1917
Bridge - Willow Creek	5.14	— 1917
Sausalito - Point Reyes	29.91	April 6, 1920
Kidd Creek extension (spur)	.60	— 1923
Duncan Mills - Cazadero (changed to broad gauge)	7.20	September 10, 1926
Monte Rio - Duncan Mills (narrow gauge abandoned)	3.30	September 10, 1926
Point Reyes - Monte Rio	(4) 37.35	March 30, 1930

(1)-6.66 miles of line sold to Hammond Lumber Co.

(2)-Little River Branch sold to Hammond Lumber Co.

(3)-Part now used by P&SR

(4)-The 4.77 miles between Camp Meeker and Monte Rio was not used between September 10, 1926, and March 30, 1930, however the track and facilities were maintained. After total abandonment in 1930, engine 90 went to Monte Rio to haul out a number of outfit cars that had been left there and also was used to dismantle the road.

(5) Sold to Hammond Lumber Co.

(6) Branch ended officially on this date, but Henry Hess Lumber Co., Guerneville, received two cars of lumber which could not be unloaded in time, so engine 112 went to Guerneville on Tuesday, November 19, 1935, to get the two empties, which was the last train movement on the branch.

ABBREVIATIONS

P&H	Petaluma & Haystack
SF&NP	San Francisco & North Pacific
C&U	Cloverdale & Ukiah
SRS&GV	Santa Rosa, Sebastopol & Green Valley
CNW	California Northwestern
SF&N	San Francisco & Napa
PRR	Prismoidal Railroad
SV	Sonoma Valley
S&SR	Sonoma & Santa Rosa
M&N	Marin & Napa
E&KR	Eureka & Klamath River
O&E	Oregon & Eureka
C&N	California & Northern
ER&E	Eel River & Eureka
PL	Pacific Lumber
CM	California Midland
AL	Albion Lumber Co.
A&SE	Albion & Southeastern
FB&SE	Fort Bragg & Southeastern
SR&SQ	San Rafael & San Quentin
NPC	North Pacific Coast
NS	North Shore
NW	North Western
SFT&B	San Francisco, Tamalpais & Bolinas
P&SR	Petaluma & Santa Rosa
NWP	Northwestern Pacific

RAIL CONNECTIONS MADE WITH NORTHWESTERN PACIFIC RAILROAD

Point	Line
Tiburon	AT&SF, Southern Pacific (by barge)
Sausalito	*AT&SF, Southern Pacific (by barge)
Mill Valley	*Mt. Tamalpias & Muir Woods Railway
Wingo	*Southern Pacific
Ramal	*Southern Pacific
Buchli	*Southern Pacific
Union	*Southern Pacific
Schellville	Southern Pacific
Petaluma	Petaluma & Santa Rosa Railroad
Santa Rosa	Petaluma & Santa Rosa Railroad
	*Southern Pacific
Guerneville	*Sonoma Land & Lumber Co.
Duncan Mills	*Duncan Mills Land & Lumber Co
Magnesia	*Sonoma Magnesite RR (2 foot gauge)
Sherwood Branch (23.8 from Willits)	*Northwestern Lumber Co.
Albion	*Albion Lumber Co.
Clearbrook	*Albion Lumber Co.
Keene's Summit	*Albion Lumber Co.
Christine	*Navarro Lumber Co.
Sequoia	*Holmes-Eureka Lumber Co.
Hammond	*Hammond Lumber Co.
Parrott Creek	Pacific Lumber Co.
Larabee	*Pacific Lumber Co.
Pacific Spur	*Pacific Lumber Co.
Shively	*Holmes-Eureka Lumber Co.

(Note - Between 1905-1912 the NWP went across Eel River at this point to Happy Camp, later Holmes Flat, to connect with scenic stages to Sherwood)

Point	Line
Elinor	*Pacific Lumber Co.
Stitz Creek	*Pacific Lumber Co.
Scotia	The Pacific Lumber Co.
Nanning Creek	*Bayside Lumber Co.
Metropolitan	*Metropolitan Lumber Co.
Dinsmore	*E. J. Dodge Lumber Co.
Baxter	*Holmes-Eureka Lumber Co.
Carlotta	*Holmes-Eureka Lumber Co.
	Pacific Lumber Co.
	*E. J. Dodge Lumber Co.
	Hammond-California Lumber Co. (Hammond Lumber Co.) (Hammond Redwood Lumber Co.) (Hammond & Little River Redwood Lumber Co.)
	*Humboldt Redwood Lumber Co. (Bayside Lumber Co.)

Point	Line
Newburg	*E. J. Dodge Lumber Co. (Eel River Valley Lumber Co)
Palmer Creek	*Holmes-Eureka Lumber Co.
South Bay	The Pacific Lumber Co.
Elk River	*Dolbeer & Carson Lumber Co.
B&ER Jct.	*Bucksport & Elk River Railroad
Press	*Bucksport & Elk River Railroad
Eureka	The Pacific Lumber Co. (Holmes-Eureka Lumber Co.)
Freshwater Jct.	*The Pacific Lumber Co. (Eureka & Freshwater Railroad)
Bayside	*Bayside Lumber Co.
Arcata	*Humboldt Northern
	*Arcata & Mad River Railroad
	*Oregon & Eureka Railroad
Korblex	Arcata & Mad River Railroad
Minor Jct.	*Warren Creek Railroad
Essex	*California Barrel Co. (Humboldt Cooperage Co.)
Fieldbrook	*Humboldt Northern Railroad
Little River	*Little River Redwood Lumber Co. (Hammond & Little River Redwood Lumber Co.)
End of Little River Branch	*Hammond Lumber Co.
25 Junction	*Hammond Lumber Co.
Carsons	*Dolbeer & Carson Lumber Co.
Samoa	Hammond-California Lumber Co. (Hammond Lumber Co.) (Hammond Redwood Lumber Co.) (Hammond & Little River Redwood Lumber Co.) Humboldt Northern Mutual Plywood Co. (Coast Redwood Lumber Co) (A. K. Wilson Timber Co.) *Little River Redwood Lumber Co.

* - Indicates connection abandoned.

STATION STOPS

Stations on the Northwestern Pacific, unlike those on many other railroads in the United States, were not all of similar overall type or pattern. Each was built according to the potential traffic of the community: some just as passenger stations, others had freight sheds built with them. Whoever had to design stations had a task on his hands indeed, and one wonders at times where the designs came from. As an example, consider the Eureka station. As originally built, it was an odd looking building with a large tower and a huge Santa Fe emblem painted on the sides. Then, on the other end of the line was the San Rafael Union Station with its block-long covered train shed. One thing certain, each station had its individuality. One of the most attractive is the station at Willits, built in 1915. It was constructed completely of redwood, significant of the great redwood forests of the area, and is still a grand building to view even today.

Many stations succumbed to fire or rot and others just became too small or outmoded, so new ones have been built in their places - San Rafael, Petaluma, Santa Rosa, Healdsburg, and Ukiah to name a few. During the later years of suburban service attractive little modern stations were built at almost every stop, a convenience to passengers that probably never again will be seen by the commuters of Marin County.

At the height of passenger operations (in 1923) stations were busy places. But today there is only one train on the road, a three-times-a-week local, and should it one day be discontinued, the use of stations for passengers will have come to an end.

In the following tables, all of the station stops are shown - even the lonely sign posts. On the main line the mileages shown are the distances from San Francisco; on the branch lines, the distance from the junction. To give the reader some idea of the many different types of stations used, a number of photographs have been included.

MAIN LINE (BROAD GAUGE)
TIBURON-SAUSALITO TO EUREKA.

Mileage from San Francisco Via Sausalito

SOUTHERN DIVISION
TIBURON-SAUSALITO TO WILLITS

Elev.	Miles	Station
	0.0	San Francisco
8	6.5	Sausalito
14	7.7	Pine (Alameda Point)
11	8.4	Waldo
8	9.2	Manzanita (Manza)
9	9.9	Almonte
30	11.0	Alto (Blithedale)
68	11.5	West Portal
81	12.2	East Portal
71	12.3	Chapman
55	12.6	Corte Madera
40	13.0	Baltimore Park
5	14.3	Detour
4	6.5	Tiburon
7	7.5	Hilarita
54	10.4	Reed
3	11.4	Meadowsweet (San Clemente)
30	14.9	Greenbrae
16	15.7	California Park (Oakmere) (Schuetzen)
5	17.0	San Rafael
105	18.1	Glenn Park (Grand Ave.)
72	18.7	Cerro
12	19.6	Forbes
4	20.0	Golf
12	21.1	Gallinas
6	21.7	Miller
8	22.0	St. Vincent
21	23.5	Hamilton Field (DeWitt)
17	24.9	Ignacio (Pacheco)
12	27.8	Novato
4	31.3	Burdell
5	33.1	San Antonio
5	36.7	Haystack
4	36.9	Crusher
5	37.1	McNear
6	37.6	Junction
9	38.5	Petaluma
12	39.2	Park Siding
28	41.0	Crown
37	42.0	Ely
64	43.3	Penn Grove (Penn's Grove)
78	43.8	Goodwin's
113	46.1	Cotati (Page's)
98	48.2	Cotate Ranch
94	48.7	Wilfred
102	50.7	Todd
112	51.3	Bellevue (Oak Grove)
150	53.8	Santa Rosa

135	54.4	Wye Siding				

135	54.4	Wye Siding				
132	58.5	Fulton		1365	139.5	Willits
123	59.8	Mark West		1339	143.7	Outlet
106	61.0	Shiloh		1326	145.3	Maple Grove
113	62.9	Windsor		1287	146.7	Ali
107	66.4	Grant		1232	148.7	Arnold
96	67.0	Bailhache		1219	148.8	Peterson
101	68.0	Healdsburg		1164	152.5	Longvale
103	69.1	Finlayson		1093	157.2	Carbon
108	69.2	Oliveto		1071	158.2	Farley
156	70.2	Chiquita		1014	161.8	Tatu
170	70.5	Simi		964	163.9	Sarnas
198	71.1	Gaddini		924	166.5	Dos Rios
183	71.9	Lytton (Littons)		886	168.0	Indian Springs
		(Litton's Springs) (Haighes)		875	169.0	Deer Lodge
213	73.9	Nervo		872	171.1	Woodman
206	75.8	Geyserville		818	174.4	Camp Rest
213	76.5	Tosca		811	175.5	Nashmead (Nash)
218	77.0	Omus		792	177.2	River Garden
238	78.8	Chianti		769	180.0	Spyrock
244	80.0	Truett's (Clairville)		704	184.3	Bell Springs
264	81.3	Asti		659	187.4	Richards
287	82.9	Icaria		620	189.3	Ramsey
315	85.2	Cloverdale		585	190.4	Two Rocks
316	86.5	McCray		550	194.5	Island Mountain
329	87.1	Preston		545	195.7	Quarry Spur
369	89.8	Echo		431	200.3	Kekawaka
423	91.8	Cummiskey		380	204.3	Hamann Gulch
436	92.6	Thorn		366	205.5	Cain Rock
472	95.3	Pieta		354	206.4	Golden Spike
477	96.8	Fountain		341	209.1	Alderpoint
488	100.1	Hopland		324	211.6	Steelhead
522	103.9	Largo		322	216.6	Fort Seward
573	105.9	Henry		265	221.5	Brock Creek
564	108.8	Clemhorst		250	222.9	Bolt
562	109.6	El Roble		235	224.0	Ladera
590	113.2	Asylum		234	225.1	Eel Rock
610	114.0	Ukiah		219	227.7	Smith
609	115.8	Presswood		217	228.3	Tanoak
634	117.0	Norlake		211	229.6	Morani
639	118.0	Pomo		196	230.1	Sequoia
673	120.1	Calpella		185	232.2	McCann
700	122.0	Holzhauer (Basil)		174	234.8	Hammond
705	122.1	Redwood Valley		169	235.5	Camp Grant
872	124.0	Laughlin		169	237.3	South Fork
1412	127.9	Hilpass		165	238.5	Perrott Creek
1913	131.4	Ridge (Ridgewood)		151	241.6	Larabee
1702	133.7	Lahm		150	242.3	P.L. Co. Spur
1450	136.8	School House		150	242.4	Larabee Ranch
1380	138.4	Muir		155	243.2	Bryan
1365	139.5	Willits		157	243.4	Bridge Creek
				149	245.6	Shively (Bluff Praire)
				130	247.0	Farnell

Elev.	Miles	Station
135	247.6	Camp Nine
125	250.0	Elinor
132	251.3	Stitz Creek
119	252.6	Perbrow
105	253.8	Glynn
101	255.6	Scotia
97	256.1	Yoder
97	256.7	Spur Track
96	257.0	Nanning Creek
89	258.7	Rio Dell (Robinson's Ferry)
85	259.0	Stone
86	259.8	Canyon Park
84	260.2	Metropolitan
85	261.0	Dinsmore
78	261.6	Baxter
65	262.7	Alton
52	263.8	Drake
48	264.5	Rohnerville
49	265.6	Newberg (Cousin's Jct.)
53	266.1	Fortuna
45	267.3	Palmer Creek
41	268.2	Worswick
35	268.7	Fernbridge (Weeott)
31	269.5	Singley
56	271.0	Loleta (Swanger)
75	272.5	Table Bluff
35	273.3	Millford
17	273.9	Beatrice (Salmon Creek)
6	275.0	Zerus
9	277.8	South Bay (Fields Landing)
9	280.7	Eureka Tallow
10	280.8	B&ER Connection (West)
10	280.9	B&ER Connection (East)
8	281.3	Associated Oil
8	281.7	Press
9	281.8	Bucksport
9	281.8	Standard Oil
7	282.0	Holmes Eureka
8	282.5	Russ
9	284.1	Eureka

STATION STOPS - NARROW GAUGE
SAUSALITO TO CAZADERO

Elev.	Miles	Station
	0.0	San Francisco
8	6.5	Sausalito (Saucelito)
14	7.7	Pine (Alameda Point)
11	8.4	Waldo
8	9.2	Manzanita (Manza)
9	9.9	Almonte (Mill Valley Jct.)
9	10.7	Power House
30	11.0	Alto (Blithedale)
68	11.5	West Portal
81	12.2	East Portal
71	12.3	Chapman
55	12.6	Corte Madera
40	13.0	Baltimore Park
18	13.4	Larkspur
9	14.0	Escalle
12	14.7	Kentfield (Kentwood) (Kent) (Tamalpais)
25	15.5	Ross
40	16.2	Bolinas Ave. (Sunny Side)
47	16.5	San Anselmo (Junction)
74	17.2	Yolanda
90	17.6	Lansdale
100	17.9	Pastori
110	18.3	Fairfax
147	18.8	Manor (Pacheco)
238	19.7	Roys
335	20.5	Bothin
419	21.4	Maillard
402	21.5	Woodacre Lodge
368	22.0	Woodacre
357	22.2	Alderney Spur
306	23.1	San Geronimo Nicasio)
250	24.5	Forest Knolls
228	25.0	Pedrini
219	25.2	Lagunitas
205	25.8	Bottini (Shafter) (Pedrini)
183	26.6	Camp Berkeley
161	27.2	Irving
138	27.9	Camp Taylor
127	29.0	Taylorville
108	29.8	Jewell
87	31.2	Tocaloma (Grove)
62	32.9	Garcia
55	34.2	North Bend
31	36.4	Point Reyes Station (Olema)
11	39.0	Bivalve (Wharf Point)
17	40.5	Millerton (Miller's Wharf)
12	43.9	Marconi (Fisherman)
7	45.4	Marshall
13	46.0	Havenwood (Cypress Grove)
12	47.4	McDonald
13	48.1	Blake's Landing
12	49.2	Pierce
7	49.4	Hamlet
9	51.2	Camp Pistolesi
115	53.1	Tomales
67	55.2	Fallon (Griffins)
154	56.8	Clark's Summit
45	59.5	Valley Ford
176	62.2	Bodega Road
222	63.7	Freestone
390	65.8	Horse Shoe Bend
570	67.6	Occidental (Howards)
402	69.0	Camp Meeker
284	70.0	Newana (Ochre)
210	70.8	Sonoma Mills (Streeten Mills)
62	72.4	Tyrone (Tyrone Mills)
41	73.8	Monte Rio (Russian River)
41	74.3	Cascade

40	74.6	Mesa Grande (Big Flat)
35	75.5	Sheridan
67	76.3	Moscow
26	77.1	Duncan Mills
31	78.2	Casini
33	78.5	Austin Creek
42	79.4	Fraser (Ferndale)
55	80.8	Kidd Creek
61	81.6	Watson
75	82.4	Magnesia
90	83.5	Cazadero Redwoods (Elim Grove)
101	83.9	Miller Retreat
106	84.3	Cazadero (Ingrams)
32	77.1	Duncan Mills
*26	79.3	Bridge
....	84.5	End of track - Willow Creek (Markham Spur)
26	79.3	Bridge
26	79.4	Doda Spur
26	79.6	Pitcher Spur
25	79.9	Markham

*—indicates bridge washed out in 1895 and never replaced.

Old Line via Strawberry Point

Elev.	Miles	Station
14	0.0	Pine (Alameda Point)
....	2.8	Lyfords
....	3.8	Collin's Summit
....	4.8	Race Track
55	6.1	Corte Madera

Old Line via White's Hill

238	0.0	Roys
565	3.0	White's Hill
400	3.8	Alderney
357	4.7	Junction with new Line

Branch - San Anselmo to San Rafael

47	0.0	San Anselmo
105	0.7	Highland
36	1.4	West End
10	2.0	"B" Street Station
5	2.5	San Rafael Union Station

Branch - San Rafael to San Quentin

10	0.0	"B" Street Station - San Rafael
8	0.4	N.P.C. Junction
12	1.2	Laurel Grove
16	1.5	Schuetzen Park
4	3.0	Wood Siding
5	3.5	San Quentin Wharf

Branch - Mill Valley

9	0.0	Almonte
9	0.4	High School
18	1.0	Locust Ave. (Millwood) (Willows)
35	1.3	Park Ave.
65	1.8	Mill Valley

Additional Branches

Shafter's Wood Spur	2.33 Miles
Azalea (Freezeout)	1.25 Miles
Kidd Creek Spur	.60 Miles

The sections between Sausalito-Point Reyes, Monte Rio-Cazadero, Duncan Mills-Markham, and branches between San Anselmo and San Rafael, San Rafael and San Quentin, and Almonte and Mill Valley, were all broad-gauged in later years.

BROAD GAUGE BRANCH LINES
SONOMA VALLEY

17	0.0	Ignacio
4	2.0	Homefarm
8	3.6	Black Point
1	4.6	Rose
1	5.7	Serena
1	5.9	Reclamation
1	6.5	Greenwood
8	8.5	Sears Point
4	10.3	Fairville
2	11.1	Quarries
1	11.8	McGill
6	12.9	Wingo
10	15.5	Schellville
49	17.3	Vineburg
60	18.1	Batto
105	18.6	Bonilla (Buena Vista)
106	19.0	Stando
100	19.4	Sebastiani (Milani)
97	19.9	Sonoma
116	21.2	Verano
125	21.5	Coney Island
126	21.7	Pioneer Grove
129	21.9	Boyes Springs
126	22.5	Fetters Springs
131	22.8	Aqua Caliente
149	23.6	Watriss
169	24.2	Madrone (Yulupa) (Whitman's)
191	24.9	Eldridge
221	25.6	Pagani (Chauvet)
228	26.3	Glen Ellen
169	24.2	Yulupa (Madrone) (Whitman's)
212	24.9	Eldridge (Hills)
279	26.4	Glen Ellen
305	27.0	Warfield

371	28.4	Beltane
403	28.7	Felice
416	30.1	Wildwood
405	30.8	Kenwood
424	31.5	Hillview
427	32.3	Lawndale
465	33.0	Los Guilicos

ADDITIONAL SONOMA VALLEY LINES

Elev.	Miles	Station
8	0.0	Sears Point
5	3.5	Sonoma Landing

Above was under narrow gauge operation only between November, 1879 and June 30, 1888.

6	0.0	Wingo
18	2.0	Ramal
15	5.5	Buchli
13	7.1	Caneros
13	8.7	Stanley
43	12.1	West Napa
78	14.1	Union

The sections between Wingo and Ramal, and Buchli and Union were built by the California Northwestern but were sold to Southern Pacific on August 12, 1911.

DONAHUE BRANCH

Elev.	Miles	Station
6	0.0	Junction
5	1.1	Campbell
6	4.0	Rotto
4	4.8	Lakeville
5	5.6	Donahue
4	6.0	Donahue Landing

SEBASTOPOL BRANCH

150	0.0	Santa Rosa
120	1.4	Osborne
96	2.4	Kenilworth
90	3.2	Wright
74	4.8	Llano
63	6.3	Sebastopol

GUERNEVILLE BRANCH

Elev.	Miles	Station
132	0.0	Fulton
87	2.1	Meacham (Meacham's)
81	2.9	Woolsey (Olivet) (Carriger) (Carriger's)
63	5.4	Trenton (Laguna)
61	5.6	Elpa
62	7.3	Forestville
61	7.9	Mirabel Park
61	8.2	Dell

64	9.0	Green Valley
73	10.2	Hacienda (Cosmo)
69	10.9	Hilton
69	11.4	Odd Fellow
58	11.9	Pocket
67	12.4	Korbel (Korbel's)
57	13.7	Rio Nido (Eagle Nest)
41	14.9	Riverside Resort
46	15.0	Shellard
52	15.4	Guerneville
48	16.2	Guernewood Park
52	16.7	Vacation Beach (Graystone)
52	17.1	Montesano
52	17.4	Russian River Heights
48	18.3	Northwood (Rio Campo) (Camp Vacation)
47	18.6	River Landing
40	19.0	Bohemia (Via old Route)
38	19.1	Bohemia (Via new Route)
41	19.7	Monte Rio
41	20.2	Fern Cove (Cascade)
40	20.5	Villa Grande (Mesa Grande)
35	21.4	Sheridan
67	22.2	Moscow
26	23.0	Duncan Mills
33	24.4	Austin Creek
42	25.3	Fraser
50	26.2	Camp Thayer
55	26.7	Kidd Creek
61	27.5	Royaneh (Watson)
75	28.3	Magnesia
90	29.4	Cazadero Redwoods
95	29.6	Stelmo
101	29.8	Miller Retreat
106	30.2	Cazadero
26	23.0	Duncan Mills
25	25.8	Markham
....	26.9	Laton

This branch had two other small branches: (1) Guernewood Park - Mission Canyon, approximately 4 miles, and (2) Smith Creek 1.3 miles from Bohemia. Both were taken up by 1908.

SHERWOOD BRANCH

Elev.	Miles	Station
1365	0.0	Willits
1495	2.7	Northwestern
1600	4.4	Sherwood Junction
1636	4.8	Spur 9 Goat Creek Landing
	5.3	Dutch Henry
1966	5.6	Woodpecker
2175	8.3	Walkers
2187	8.8	Rowes
2231	9.6	Craft
2235	9.9	Sylvan Dale
2271	10.5	Swamp

Elev.	Miles	Station
2289	11.1	Russell
2394	12.0	En Cima
2338	12.6	Johnson
2339	13.2	Yew
2264	13.9	Sherwood
2289	14.4	Williams
2246	15.1	Muirs
2275	16.2	Old Cook House Spur
2325	16.6	Bull Donkey Spur
2370	16.8	Ten Mile Summit
2285	17.3	Water Tank
2072	19.0	Switch Back #1
1896	20.3	Switch Back #2
1812	20.7	Water Tank
1432	22.8	Cook House Spur
1257	23.8	End of N.W.P. Track — Start Northwestern Redwood Co.
1198	24.1	End of Track 5-15-1919
1121	24.5	Cook House #5
1052	24.9	End of Track 10-27-1920
1050	25.0	Water Tank
1055	25.1	Switch Back #3
937	25.6	Switch Back #4
883	26.0	End of track 6-5-1923.

Roadbed graded 400 ft. beyond with trestle under construction, but road was never extended.

ALBION BRANCH
(Had no Physical connection)

Elev.	Miles	Station
174	0.0	Albion (Wharf)
175	3.25	Brett
204	7.32	Clearbrook Jct.
225	1.00	Clearbrook branch
227	8.30	Gunari
404	12.37	Sunny Slope
456	13.05	Skibo
547	14.65	Start of switch back
611	15.44	Keene Summit
453	15.65	End of switch back
488	16.54	Dunn
355	22.15	Navarro Mill (Stearn's Mill)
430	22.87	Wendling
445	25.65	Christine
447	25.81	End of track

BROAD GAUGE BRANCH LINES

CARLOTTA BRANCH

Elev.	Miles	Station
65	0.0	Alton
86	0.9	Newell
110	1.4	Burnell
88	1.8	Williams
125	4.4	Kniss
135	4.9	Carlotta

SAMOA BRANCH

17	0.0	Arcata
10	0.7	Daniels
8	3.1	Manila
9	5.5	H. N. RR Crossing
9	5.9	Carsons
8	6.6	Samoa Yard
10	7.1	Samoa

TRINIDAD BRANCH

9	0.0	Eureka
10	1.0	Foundry
10	1.1	Langford
9	1.3	Haughey Mill
9	2.6	Freshwater
9	3.4	Brainard
10	5.1	Bracut
12	5.4	Brainard (old location)
9	5.7	Bayside
9	6.5	Bayside Junction
8	7.7	A&MR Crossing
17	8.4	Arcata
20	8.8	A&MR Crossing
21	8.9	Gannon
59	9.5	Normal Junction
41	11.1	Korblex
50	11.7	A&MR Crossing
58	11.9	Minor Junction
61	12.5	McCloskey
63	12.8	Englehart
60	13.3	Essex (Mad River)
68	13.5	Shingle Mill
73	14.9	Dairy
59	15.5	Brocks
90	15.7	Thompsons
97	1.1	Burns Mill
71	16.3	Carson's #2
157	17.8	Fieldbrook
168	21.3	Little River Junction
217	1.3	Little River Branch Camp 9
247	22.5	Crannell (Bullwinkle)
356	24.3	Moonstone
353	24.6	Camp 10
332	25.3	Luffenholtz
326	26.1	25 Junction
331	27.2	Culbert
326	28.2	Trinidad

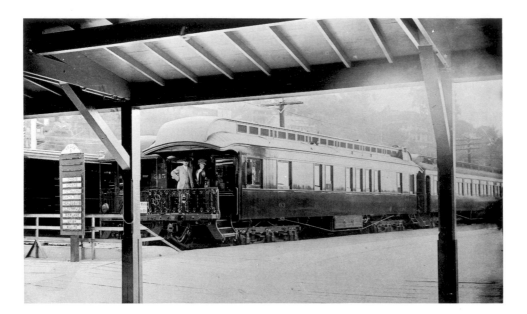

The railroad President's private car ready to leave Sausalito. Car was built in 1876 for Peter Donahue.

The Ukiah passenger ready to leave Tiburon terminal in 1908. Southern Pacific Calistoga train is at right.

Clear board at the little station of Reed, between Tiburon and San Rafael.

Schuetzen Park, not far from San Rafael, was a popular picnic area in the days when the Northwestern Pacific was young. This point was re-named California Park after World War I.

San Rafael Station looking north. The block long structure saw a continuous parade of steam and electric operations during the height of the North-western Pacific's passenger activities.

Ignacio was once the junction with the narrow gauge lines in Sonoma Valley.

The mission type station at Petaluma was built to replace an old wood structure that had been condemned.

Penn Grove was in the heart of the world's "egg basket."

Northwestern Pacific Engine No. 12 on local freight pulls into the Santa Rosa station. The old wooden depot was destroyed by fire about 1904 and was replaced with this stone structure.

Cloverdale was fairly typical of the stations built during construction of the line.

Preston and Largo were stations built by the CNW, located on the main line between Cloverdale and Ukiah. Note the white letters on black background in station names. One of the NWP's worst wrecks occured at Largo in February, 1929 — a main-line meet between a freight and passenger train.

"Made of California Redwood" is inscribed on the unique Willets station.

NORTHERN DIVISION
(BROAD GAUGE)
WILLITS-EUREKA

Deep in the Eel River country are the adjoining stations of Alderpoint and Ft. Seward, the latter one of the most attractive stations on the line, built in 1914. Train No. 71, southbound freight approaches on the main line.

Alton Junction. To the right is the main line from Sausalito to Eureka; at the left is the Carlotta branch.

Fortuna, left, and Beatrice exemplify the inconsistency of station design.

South Bay is the second station below Eureka. Here Engine 13 and train receive clear board about the year 1909.

Arcata is the first important station north of Eureka, and serves a large lumber area. Passenger service ended on this section in the Spring of 1932.

Nestled alongside a large rocky hill is Trinidad station, the northermost point of the broad gauge.

ALBION BRANCH
(Had no Physical connection)

At left is the sign post indicating the location of Wendling, near the southern end of the Albion branch. While it says 130.39 miles to San Francisco, the line through to a connection with main line was never constructed, but ended a few miles further up the canyon at Christine. Below is the Albion station.

100

GUERNEVILLE BRANCH

Rio Nido, one of the most popular resorts on the Russian River, handled thousands of train passengers each summer.

After a day at the beach picnickers await the train at Guernewood Park on an August Sunday in 1935.

Narrow gauge Engine 92 arrives with Passenger Train No. 60 at Monte Rio, junction point between the broad and narrow gauge on the Guerneville branch.

The San Geronimo station, built for the narrow gauge, served broad gauge trains after the narrow gauge was removed in April, 1920.

Typical of the little stations built for summer travel was Camp Pistolesi on the narrow gauge, 51 miles from San Francisco.

NARROW GAUGE
SAUSALITO TO CAZADERO

Tomales was the only flat-top station building on the narrow gauge.

The station at Bodega Road was located in the dairy section of Sonoma County as attested by the milk cans to be put aboard the afternoon passenger.

Because the station was destroyed by fire, Duncan Mills used a narrow gauge coach and box car for a station around 1908.

Watson was located on the Cazadero line 4.5 miles above Duncan Mills.

Cazadero - the end of the narrow gauge, 84 miles from San Francisco.

TRESTLES
(over 300 feet)

While the construction problems overcome by the Northwestern Pacific and predecessor companies were not as severe as those encountered by the legendary Central Pacific, Rio Grande, or South Park, they were by no means of small proportions as evidenced by the cuts and fills, the forty-five tunnels, and the hundreds of bridges and trestles that have existed on the line.

The building of the N.W.P. was done, of course, without the advanced machinery that is available now, and where today a mountain would be removed and gorges filled, the early builders tunneled the mountains and bridged the ravines and sloughs. An example of the latter can still be seen in the remains of the narrow gauge between Point Reyes and Marshall, and Clark Summit and Valley Ford - where the road was literally built on trestles.

Tunnels are expensive to maintain. The wooden lining often has to be replaced, and there is the constant threat of fire, even from today's diesel locomotives. The longest tunnel on the line, No. 27 at Island Mountain, is watered down once a week,

and there are fire curtains on each end. Some tunnels have been "daylighted," others partially or fully lined with concrete, and still others abandoned.

This chapter provides photographs of some of the more interesting structures, and statistical information on all the tunnels, and all the bridges and trestles of 300 feet or more in length. The basic figures are as of the year 1916, and brought up to date with as much accuracy as possible.

MAIN LINE TIBURON—EUREKA

Struct. No.	Location or Nearest To	Length (ft)	Type	Mean Height	Built
9.25	Reed	752.8	Open Deck	38	1931
11.11	Meadowsweet	344.0	Open Deck	12	....
14.61	South approach Corte Madera Creek	1252.0	Open Deck	15	1923
14.61	N. Approach Corte Madera Creek	489.6	Open Deck	25	1923
37.00	N. approach Petaluma Creek	848.0	Open Deck	20	1916
67.40	Grant	285.0	Open Deck	10	1918
88.34	Tunnel No. 6	389.9	Open Deck	32	1915
99.69	Feliz Creek	374.7	Open Deck	14	1932
115.93	Ackeman Creek	357.0	Ballast Deck	14	1918-40
217.38	Fort Seward	304.0	Conical Arch	85	1911
219.00	Mud Creek	315.0	Open Deck	82	1936
221.73	Brock Creek	329.0	Ballast Deck	64	1941
256.77	Scotia Bluffs	932.0	Open Deck	36	1938-55
257.04	Nanning Creek	1399.0	Open Deck	40	1940-55
257.24	French Gulch	376.0	Open Deck	32	1930
257.35	Scotia Bluffs	335.0	Open Deck	22	1924-55
257.84	Scotia Bluffs	360.0	Open Deck	16	1918-55
270.68	Swauger Creek & Highway	602.6	Open Deck	38	1924

SONOMA BRANCH

Struct. No.	Location or Nearest To	Length (ft)	Type	Mean Height	Built
26.33	Novato Creek	372.7	Open Deck	8	1927
28.79	Petaluma Creek—S. Approach	492.0	Open Deck	10	1920
28.79	Petaluma Creek—N. Approach	1594.0	Open Deck	10	1922-27

SEBASTOPOL BRANCH

Struct. No.	Location or Nearest To	Length (ft)	Type	Mean Height	Built
59-E	Gravenstein	598.0	Open Deck	10	1916

GUERNEVILLE BRANCH

Struct. No.	Location or Nearest To	Length (ft)	Type	Mean Height	Built
61-J	Woolsey	320.0	Open Deck	13	1931
62-I	Laguna Creek	1251.7	Open Deck	13	1916
64-C	Elpa	320.0	Open Deck	9	1931
68-A	South approach—Russian River (1st crossing)	1465.0	Open Deck	15	1918
77-A	South approach—Russian River (2nd crossing)	418.0	Open Deck	32	1909
81-C	North approach—Russian River (2nd crossing)	400.6	Open Deck	25	1921

ALBION BRANCH

Struct. No.	Location or Nearest To	Length (ft)	Type	Mean Height	Built
130.0	Floodgate Creek	525.0	Open Deck	70	1905
150.8	Brett	455.0	Ballast Deck	14	1891
151.0	Brett	601.0	Open Deck	10	1891
154.0	Albion River	342.0	Open Deck	14	1903
154.0	Albion River	418.0	Open Deck	14	1903

CARLOTTA BRANCH

Struct. No.	Location or Nearest To	Length (ft)	Type	Mean Height	Built
267-C	South approach—Yager Creek	486.0	Open Deck	30	1918

SAMOA BRANCH

Struct. No.	Location or Nearest To	Length (ft)	Type	Mean Height	Built
269-C	South approach—Mad River Slough	314.0	Open Deck	25	1916

Out of a tunnel almost a mile long on to a 620 foot bridge at Island Mountain steams Engine 181 with an excursion train.

Engine 182 and passenger train creep along Scotia Bluffs.

TRINIDAD BRANCH

285.64	East approach—Eureka Slough	382.9	Open Deck	18	1916
305-D	Hammond & Little River RR Crossing				
	Little River Junction	699.0	Open Deck	106	1903
306-K	Crannell	345.0	Open Deck	75	1916
307-A	Crannell	428.0	Open Deck	68	1916
307-B	Crannell	462.0	Open Deck	70	1916
310-D	25 Junction	537.0	Open Deck	84	1922
311-A	Culbert	716.0	Open Deck	70	1922
311-E	Trinidad	477.0	Open Deck	66	1926
312-A	Trinidad	639.0	Open Deck	70	1924

NARROW GAUGE — SAUSALITO-CAZADERO

7-D	Pine	556.0	Redwood Box	6	1874
7-E	Pine	400.0	Redwood Box	4	1874
20-B	Roys	480.5	Open Deck	30	1928
20-D	Roys-Highway Undergrade	491.2	Open Deck	36	1928
35.6	Arroyo San Geronimo	601.6	Open Deck	18	1929
54.9	Tomales Creek (Stempel Creek)	623.0	Open Deck	32	1876
58.8	Estero Americano Creek	704.0	Open Deck	26	1876
61.9	Ebabias Creek	380.5	Open Deck	23	1876
62.7	Salmon Creek	605.9	Open Deck	11	1876
65.2	Salmon Creek	430.5	Open Deck	25	1876
66.9	Brown Creek	504.7	Open Deck	130	1876
68.7	Maquire Creek	393.0	Open Deck	24	1876
70.5	Larry Creek	430.5	Open Deck	67	1876

NOTE - Although not listed above, the longest trestle was the 4000 foot structure of the North Pacific Coast that was in existence between 1872 and 1884 across Richardson's Bay. The trestle with the greatest depth and reported to be the largest of its kind in the United States when built was the trestle over Brown's Creek on the narrow gauge - 142 feet in height.

The narrow gauge had another long trestle across the Russian River at Markham's. No data is available as to its length. It was washed out in 1895.

The Guerneville branch had a 404 foot combination and two span Howe Truss over the Russian River into Bohemia near Mile Post 77. It was washed out in a flood, March 19, 1907.

Branch lines with no bridges, tunnels or trestles over 300 feet are not shown. The Petaluma and Santa Rosa railroad's longest trestle is at Mile Post 1.17, 2nd Petaluma Creek crossing - 161'2", open deck, 25' in height, built in 1936.

North Shore narrow gauge passenger heading south over the 430-foot Larry Creek trestle north of Camp Meeker.

Narrow Gauge train drifts over Brown's canyon trestle. When
built this was the tallest trestle in the U.S.—142 feet in height.

P & S R excursion train rumbles over Santa Rosa Creek.

Double-header narrow gauge
passenger blasts up grade and
over trestle at Horseshoe Bend
between Freestone and Occidental.

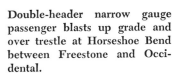

Near Reed station, Engine 114,
deadheads Passenger train from
San Rafael to Tiburon.

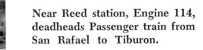

BRIDGES

(Main Line Tiburon—Eureka)

Name	Struct. No.	Location	East or West	Type Superstructure and Length	Year Built
Highway Undergrade	9.25	Tiburon	E	1 - 50' Deck Girder	1937
Corte Madera Creek	14.61	Greenbrae	E	1 - 51'6" Bascule Span	1924
Gallinas Creek	20.91	Gallinas	E	1 - 40' Bascule Span	1911
Novato Creek	26.95	Novato	E	1 - 30' Deck Girder	1917
Petaluma Creek	37.16	McNear	W	1 - 180' Thru Swing Truss	1909
Highway Undergrade	65.10	Grant	E	1 - 50' Thru Girder	1915
Russian River	67.62	Healdsburg	W	1 - 198' Thru Truss	1901
				2 - 97'6" Thru Trusses	1921
Russian River (2nd Crossing)	120.50	Calpella	E	2 - 50' Thru Girders	1928
Highway Undergrade	135.61	Willits	W	1 - 30' Thru Girder	1921
Outlet Creek (1st Crossing)	141.07	Outlet	W	3 - 60' Deck Girders	1910
Outlet Creek (2nd Crossing)	145.69	Outlet	E	2 - 100' Thru Rivited Trusses	1911
Outlet Creek (3rd Crossing)	147.26	Ali	E	2 - 70' Deck Girders	1910
Outlet Creek (4th Crossing)	147.75	Ali	E	2 - 80' Deck Girders	1910
Outlet Creek (5th Crossing)	148.17	Ali	E	3 - 80' Deck Girders	1910
Outlet Creek (6th Crossing)	149.25	Arnold	E	3 - 70' Thru Girders	1911
Outlet Crossing (7th Crossing)	151.14	Peterson	E	3 - 60' Deck Girders	1911
Highway Undergrade	151.20	Peterson	E	1 - 35' Thru Girder	1921
Outlet Creek (8th Crossing)	152.07	Peterson	E	4 - 70' Deck Girders	
				2 - 60' Deck Girders	1911
Outlet Creek (9th Crossing)	156.12	Longvale	E	5 - 60' Deck Girders	1911
Outlet Creek (10th Crossing)	157.17	Farley	W	4 - 70' Deck Girders	1911
Outlet Creek (11th Crossing)	157.32	Farley	W	1 - 70' Deck Girder	
				3 - 60' Deck Girders	1911
Outlet Creek (12th Crossing)	159.60	Farley	E	4 - 70' Deck Girders	1911
				1 - 60' Deck Girder	1911
Berger Creek	167.39	Dos Rios	E	1 - 100' Deck Girder	1911
Woodman Creek	171.49	Woodman	E	1 - 50' Deck Girder	1913
Shell Rock Creek	178.29	Spyrock	W	3 - 50' Deck Girders	1913
Blue Rock Creek	182.90	Spyrock	E	2 - 60' Deck Girders	1913
				2 - 50' Deck Girders	1913
Bell Springs	185.01	Bell Springs	E	3 - 60' Deck Girders	1913
Eel River (1st Crossing)	194.68	Island Mountain	E	2 - 200' Deck Trusses	
				1 - 100' Deck Girder	
				2 - 60' Deck Girders	1913
Kekawaka Creek	200.01	Kekawaka	W	3 - 80' Deck Girders	1914
Eel River (2nd Crossing)	206.51	Cain Rock	E	3 - 200' Thru Trusses	
				3 - 70' Deck Girders	
				5 - 60' Deck Girders	1913
Fort Seward Creek	211.68	Steelhead	W	3 - 80' Deck Girders	
				2 - 60' Deck Girders	1914
Over Slide	228.02	Tanoak	W	2 - 50' Deck Girders	1914

112

State Highway (Undergrade)	236.26	Camp Grant	E	1 - 23' I Beam Span	1911
Eel River (3rd Crossing)	237.75	South Fork	E	2 - 200' Thru Pin Trusses 2 - 180' Thru Pin Trusses	1910
Larabee Creek	241.97	Larabee	E	2 - 150' Thru Pin Trusses	1910
Van Duzen River	261.77	Alton	W	3 - 160' Thru Pin Trusses	1913
State Highway (undergrade)	270.80	Loleta	E	1 - 61'3" Deck Girder	1930
Elk River	280.41	Bucksport	W	1 - 40' Thru Girder	1914

BRIDGES ON BRANCH LINES

SONOMA BRANCH

Name	Struct. No.	Location	East or West	Type Superstructure and Length	Year Built
Novato Creek	26.33	Ignacio	E	1 - 34' Deck Girder	1917
Petaluma Creek	28.79	Black Point	E	1 - 250' Thru Swing Truss	1911
Sonoma Creek	37.79	Wingo	....	1 - 61' Bascule Span	1921
Calababeza Creek	53.00	Beltane	W	2 - 38' Deck Girders	....
Sonoma Creek	56.55	Hilview	....	1 - 80' Deck Girder	....

GUERNEVILLE BRANCH

Russian River (1st Crossing)	68 A	Hacienda	W	1 - 200 Thru Pin Span	1914
Russian River (2nd Crossing)	77-A	Northwood	E	3 - 130' Thru Phoenix Spans	1909
Russian River (3rd Crossing)	81.4	Duncan Mills	W	8 - 60' Deck Girders	1917

ALBION BRANCH

N. Fork Navarro River	133.6	Navarro Mill	E	1 - 75' Howe Truss	1905
Albion River (1st Crossing)	147.3	Clearbrook Jct.	E	1 - 52' Howe Truss	1891
Albion River (2nd Crossing)	151.6	Brett	E	1 - 100' Howe Truss 1 - 90' Howe Truss	1891
Albion River (3rd Crossing)	154.0	Albion	....	1 - 35' "A" Truss	1903

CARLOTTA BRANCH

Yager Creek	267.0	Carlotta	....	1 - 90' Thru Truss	1939

SAMOA BRANCH

Mad River Slough	296-C	Manila	W	1 - 39' Bascule Lift Span	1927

TRINIDAD BRANCH

Eureka Slough	285.67	Eureka -	E	1 - 188' Thru Swing Truss	1916
Highway Overgrade	294-B	Normal Jct.	E	1 - 48' Deck Girder	1931
Mad River	296-A	Minor Jct.	E	2 - 143' Howe Truss Spans	1912

NARROW GAUGE - SAUSALITO TO CAZADERO

Paper Mill Creek and Highway Overgrade	27-C	Camp Taylor	W	1 - 130' Thru Phoenix Col. Span	1930
Keyes Creek	50.5	Camp Pistolesi	W	2 - 130' Thru Spans	1906
Dutch Bill Creek	70.8	Newana	E	1 - 153' Steel Deck Bridge	....
Dutch Bill Creek	71.6	Tyrone	W	1 - 61' Howe Truss	....
Highway Overgrade	71.7	Tyrone	W	1 - 30' Deck Girder	1926
Austin Creek	82.1	Magnesia	W	1 - 160' Thru Truss	....

BRIDGES

Broad gauge Engine 22 on Train 225 heads east over bridge at Duncan Mills. The bridge was rebuilt in 1917 with eight 60-foot deck girders.

Narrow gauge engines 13 and 16 doublehead a passenger train over the bridge into the lumber community of Duncan Mills.

Bohemia bridge looking west from "Flaherty Pool."

Main line crosses Eel River just north of South Fork on 760 foot bridge.

Two-span bridge into Bohemia on the Russian River near Monte Rio. High waters collapsed the bridge March 19, 1907. A new bridge was built half mile down-river.

North Shore Engine No. 3 heads south over the Ocean Roar bridge over Keyes Creek on the narrow gauge in 1906.

A passenger train powered by a ten-wheeler is southbound on the bridge over Russian River at Healdsburg.

South of Alton the main line crosses Van Duzen River with Engine 9 on the "business end" of a passenger train.

Narrow Gauge passenger approaching Duncan Mills on the 512 foot bridge over Russian River.

Petaluma Creek bridge on Tiburon-Eureka main line.

Broad gauge passenger train crossing Russian River between Monte Rio and Rio Campo heading toward San Francisco.

TUNNELS
(Main Line Tiburon—Eureka)

No	Mile Post West Portal	Between Stations		Length	Tunnel Lining Concrete	Timber	Portal West	East	Year Built
1	9.47	Tiburon	— Reed	566.2	....	566.2	Timber	Timber	1884
2	10.29	Reed	— Meadowsweet	1848.8	38.1	1810.7	Concrete	Concrete	1884
3	15.17	Green Brae	— San Rafael	1104.6	24.0	1080.6	Concrete	Concrete	1884
4	18.16	San Rafael	— Cerro	1350.5	18.0	1332.5	Timber	Concrete	1879
5	85.62	Cloverdale	— Preston	349.5	27.0	322.5	Timber	Timber	1889
6	87.79	Preston	— Echo	1762.2	....	*1015.4	Timber	Timber	1889
7	89.12	Preston	— Echo	261.2	25.7	235.5	Concrete	Timber	1889
8	93.90	Echo	— Pieta	1269.5	....	* 50.5	Rock	Timber	1889
9	94.85	Echo	— Pieta	445.8	40.5	405.3	Timber	Timber	1889
10	126.10	Laughlin	— Ridge	180.1	....	180.1	Timber	Timber	1902
11	145.49	Outlet	— Arnold	651.3	....	651.3	Timber	Timber	1910
12	149.94	Arnold	— Longvale	881.2	12.4	868.8	Timber	Concrete	1911
13	156.00	Longvale	— Farley	227.8	57.0	170.8	Concrete	Concrete	1911
14	160.92	Farley	— Dos Rios	382.5	322.5	60.0	Concrete	Timber	1911
15	163.61	Farley	— Dos Rios	339.0	105.3	233.7	Concrete	Concrete	1911
16	166.95	Dos Rios	— Indian Springs	374.4	69.6	304.8	Timber	Concrete	1911
17	169.64	Deer Lodge	— Woodman	173.5	60.0	113.5	Timber	Timber	1912
18	171.42	Woodman	— Camp Rest	194.6	22.0	172.6	Timber	Concrete	1912
19	172.59	Woodman	— Camp Rest	656.0	176.2	479.8	Timber	Concrete	1912
20	175.24	Camp Rest	— Nashmead	467.2	12.2	455.0	Timber	Concrete	1913
21	175.94	Nashmead	— River Garden	333.5	100.2	233.3	Concrete	Timber	1913
22	179.18	River Garden	— Spyrock	128.7	12.0	166.7	Concrete	Timber	1913
23	183.33	Spyrock	— Bell Springs	106.5	....	106.5	Timber	Timber	1913
24	188.07	Bell Springs	— Ramsey	463.9	170.0	293.9	Concrete	Timber	1913
25	188.61	Bell Springs	— Ramsey	265.2	41.3	223.9	Concrete	Timber	1913
26	189.58	Ramsey	— Island Mountain	182.8	....	182.8	Timber	Timber	1913
27	194.80	Island Mountain	— Kekawaka	4313.1	619.4	3693.7	Concrete	Concrete	1913
28	199.79	Island Mountain	— Kekawaka	263.8	58.1	205.7	Concrete	Concrete	1914
29	200.90	Kekawaka	— Cain Rock	280.5	125.6	154.9	Timber	Concrete	1914
30	209.54	Alderpoint	— Fort Seward	348.2	348.2	....	Concrete	Concrete	1914
31	212.45	Alderpoint	— Fort Seward	471.0	350.0	121.0	Concrete	Concrete	1914
32	223.32	Brock Creek	— Eel Rock	311.9	....	311.9	Timber	Timber	1912
33	225.52	Eel Rock	— Smith	664.1	195.9	468.2	Concrete	Concrete	1912
34	226.95	Eel Rock	— Smith	368.1	27.0	341.1	Concrete	Concrete	1911
35	227.96	Smith	— Tanoak	251.7	12.0	239.7	Timber	Concrete	1911
36	228.82	Tanoak	— Sequoia	246.8	39.6	207.2	Concrete	Concrete	1912
37	234.00	McCann	— Camp Grant	269.6	23.0	246.6	Timber	Concrete	1911
38	243.59	Bryan	— Shively	1124.2	13.4	1110.8	Timber	Concrete	1910
39	246.93	Shively	— Elinor	1019.4	20.0	999.4	Concrete	Timber	1904
40	271.95	Loleta	—. Beatrice	1946.7	15.0	1931.7	Timber	Concrete	1884

* - Tunnel 6 unlined 746.8' and Tunnel 8 unlined 1219.0'

(NARROW GAUGE - MAIN LINE - SAUSALITO TO CAZADERO)

No	Mile Post West Portal	Between Stations		Length	Tunnel Lining Concrete	Timber	Portal West	East	Year Built
1	11.69	Alto	— Chapman	2182.9	....	2182.9	Timber	Timber	1884
*2	20.26	Roys	— Whites Hill	370.0	....	370.0	Timber	Timber	1874
*3	22.31	Roys	— Whites Hill	1250.0	....	1250.0	Timber	Timber	1874
2	20.74	Bothin	— Mailliard	3190.2	....	3190.2	Timber	Timber	1904
3	51.85	Camp Pistolesi	— Tomales	98.4	(Rock - 98.4)		Rock	Rock	1874
4	53.67	Tomales	— Fallon	1706.4	....	1706.4	Timber	Timber	1875
5	71.02	Camp Meeker	— Tyrone	426.3	(Rock-326.3)	100.0	Timber	Timber	1876

Tunnel 1 still in use on broad Guage Sausalito Branch.
* - indicates old route around Whites Hill.

Under the original system adopted by the Company, the letters "N.W.P." were painted under the cab windows, and the engine numbers were placed in large numerals on the sides of tenders. While all the available numbers were not used, the broad (standard) gauge engines were placed in the following blocks: 1-100 for the 4-4-0's (with a 0-4-0 being numbered 99); 101-150 for the 4-6-0's; 151-200 for the 2-6-0's; and the 200 series for various types - 2-6-2's, a 2-4-2, 0-6-0's, a Shay and a Heisler, for a total of 46 engines on hand at the close of the year 1908. This total included 38 obtained with acquired lines, plus the Company's first new rolling stock - eight new engines purchased in 1908 from Alco: 4-4-0's No. 22 and 23; 4-6-0's No. 111-114, and 2-6-0's No. 153-154.

With increasing freight and passenger traffic, and progress being made in the construction of a physical connection between the north and the south ends, the N.W.P. found need for more motive power, so in the years 1910-1912 and 1914, twenty-three more engines were purchased, all from Alco: 4-4-0's 51-54; 4-6-0's 130-141 and 160-161; and 0-6-0's 227-231. In 1917 and 1918, due principally to World War I, the road could not buy any more new locomotives, but upon hearing of two lines in Nevada, the Bullfrog Goldfield and the Las Vegas Tonopah, that were suspending operations, the N.W.P. bought five engines that were available there - one from the BFG and four from the LV&T. Three of the LV&T engines were given N.W.P. numbers 170-172, and the other was assigned the number 129. The BFG engine became N.W.P. 178.

In 1914 2-6-0's 151-154 were renumbered to 351-354 in order to clear the 151-200 block for more 4-6-0's; in 1918 4-6-0's 160-161 were changed to 180-181; and No. 129 became 179.

In 1922 the Northwestern Pacific purchased its last new steam locomotives - 4-6-0's No. 182-184 and 142-143, both groups coming from Baldwin. Rounding out the broad (standard) gauge roster were two second-hand 2-6-0's acquired from the Southern Pacific in 1929, becoming N.W.P. 300 and 301. Though they did not all exist at the same time, the N.W.P. had a total of eighty-three engines in its regular standard gauge roster. Over the years quite a few locomotives were borrowed or leased (see Pages 174 and 175) including SP No. 2248, a 4-6-0 built by Cooke in 1896. No. 2248 was the last steam engine to run under its own power on the Northwestern Pacific. It was leased from the Southern Pacific on November 20, 1955 - for that day only - on the occasion of the running of a special train from Tiburon to Healdsburg and return in honor of Willis A. Silverthorn, veteran engineer, who retired that day after forty-five years of service. Bill himself ran the engine, and

the five-car train was crowded with his friends and well-wishers. Truly an era came to a close that evening of November 20, 1955, when Engineer Silverthorn descended from that venerable 4-6-0.

— — —

Over on the Narrow Gauge in 1907 there were sixteen engines of the former North Shore Railroad sitting around, scattered between the numbers 2 and 40. Most, but not all of these were eventually re-lettered to N.W.P. without change of number. In addition, also in 1907, the N.W.P. acquired four engines from the South Pacific Coast Railway, another Southern Pacific subsidiary, which was being changed from narrow to standard gauge. They were assigned N.W.P. numbers 10, 17, 19 and 21. However, things were due for another change. Because the narrow gauge numbers to a large degree duplicated the broad (standard) gauge engine numbers, it was decided that the narrow gauge engines should be renumbered, so in 1908 the following reassignments took place.

No. 11 became No. 82	14 became No. 92
3	83	21	144
20	84	18	145
17	85	13	195
19	86	40	321
10	87	33	322
15	90	31	323
16	91		

A tentative assignment of Engines 2, 4, 7 and 8 to new numbers 89, 81, 80 and 88 was made, but the engines never were actually re-stenciled, so despite references in other publications to such numbers, the N. W. P. narrow gauge did not have engines with these numbers.

In 1924 some other renumberings took place on the Narrow Gauge. By this time there were only six engines left. No. 85 was changed to 93, and 144 and 145 were renumbered to 94 and 95. This placed the entire remaining narrow gauge roster of engines in one group of numbers - 90-95.

— — —

In the 1920's an attractive new paint scheme was tried on some of the broad gauge passenger engines which won immediate approval of the traveling public. A two-tone green was applied to the engine and tender, with the jacket over the boiler a metallic blue-grey; the cab roof was painted red, and the N.W.P. insignia was placed on the tender, and the number and lettering were done in gold with red border trim. Engines 21, 22, 52 and 53 received this treatment and they emerged from the paint shop at Tiburon a pleasing sight to behold. Engine crews and roundhouse forces took pride in the locomotives and for a few years they were kept in immaculate condition, but because of cost no further engines were painted in this manner. Also in the 'twenties' there was a system-wide change of engine numbers from the tender to the cab, and the letters "N.W.P." from the cab to the tender. With this the N.W.P. herald in gold lettering was added to the tenders of a number of locomotives.

— — —

In the transportation medium the railroads are unchallenged in their inherent ability to handle goods and passengers safely. Nevertheless, the Northwestern Pacific, like every railroad, had wrecks. There were numerous minor mishaps but there were also some real disasters. The first major incident occurred on the night of August 8, 1910, near Ignacio. Train No. 6, the Santa Rosa passenger, consisting of a baggage car and five coaches hauled by Engine No. 20, collided head-on with an extra freight powered by Engine No. 18. The 4-4-0's hit with such force that they fused themselves together and stood straight up in the air. Both engine crews and fourteen passengers were killed, and many passengers injured. Engine 20 eventually was repaired, but No. 18 was hauled away in a gondola with not enough left to rebuild. The second disaster took place on February 28, 1929, when 4-6-0 No. 184 heading a freight train, and another 4-6-0, No. 141 on No. 2, the Eureka passenger, met head-on at a point about an eighth of a mile north of Largo. Three crew members were killed and thirty-two passengers injured. Both locomotives were badly wrecked but were later repaired at Tiburon.

On July 3, 1908, No. 154 (later 354), a 2-6-0 just outshopped from American Locomotive Works, left the rails and turned over with a three-car train near Novato. On May 16, 1910, Engines 113 and 21 had a "cornfield" meet at the small community of Ely - just north of Petaluma, but damage was minor. On an Autumn day in October, 1911, at a point about a mile and a half south of Hopland, Engine 23 turned over after hitting a cow. Several cars of the train, the Ukiah passenger, No. 4, went off the track, but no passengers were hurt. On July 4, 1911, Engine 105, through a signal error in switching, sailed off the freight apron at Tiburon into the Bay. A similar incident happened to No. 112 on June 29, 1913, near the same location - Schooner Wharf - when piling gave way. Both locomotives were hauled out of the salty waters and repaired. On August 6, 1937, near Elinor, some hobos had a small fire going under one of the trestles which got out of hand and burned the structure. With supports weakened, Engine 182 plunged through and turned over, sustaining serious damage. It was, however, also repaired at the Tiburon shops. Of minor note, but nonetheless contributing to the demise of another steam engine, was a head-on collision between SP 2801, a heavy 2-8-0, and N.W.P. No. 114 near Dos Rios on September 30, 1946. The 114 came out second best and was soon scrapped. And finally, while other proud engines throughout the country were dying of diesel cancer, No. 184 fell victim of the elements. On January 17, 1953, she was swept off the tracks by a slide near Scotia and buried in 45 feet of water in the Eel River. Three good railroad men went with her, and a monument to their memory has been emplaced at Eureka. The engine was hauled out and scrapped on the spot. The worst wreck on the Narrow Gauge occurred on September 24, 1909, when a fast-moving freight derailed at Freestone, destroying six box and seven flat cars.

— — —

The first ominous portents appeared on the horizon in the mid 1930's when the Southern Pacific acquired its first diesel. Even by this time the Northwestern Pacific was beginning to lose its autonomy, and more and more of its own engines were rusting away in the boneyard at Tiburon while increasing numbers of engines were being leased from the mother company. But at least the N.W.P. was still all steam. World War II was the tragic instrument that delayed the steamers' disappearance into the western sunset by a few years, but the diesel seeds had been sown and there was no stopping the virulent growth, and by ten years after the close of the War the great change-over had been almost completed. The Northwestern Pacific was one of the first sections of the entire Southern Pacific to become fully dieselized. By August, 1953, the last of the leased S.P. steamers had been returned, and there were only eight N.W.P. engines on the road, of which just five were active. The final day was September 20, 1953 - Engine No. 182 in charge of Engineer Armand Demuelle on an extra freight from Willits to Tiburon. Today leased Southern Pacific diesels power all Northwestern Pacific trains, and the distinctive and attractive Northwestern Pacific herald no longer adorns any active railroad rolling stock in the Redwood Empire.

The accompanying roster lists the basic date for all ninety-eight operating Northwestern Pacific locomotives, which were comprised of the types shown in the table below. Complete historical information is published in connection with the individual pictures.

	Broad Gauge	Narrow Gauge
4-4-0	27	9
0-4-0	1	--
4-6-0	38	2
2-6-2	2	--
2-4-2	1	--
0-6-0	6	--
2-6-0	6	1
2-8-0	--	3
Shay	1	--
Heisler	1	--
Total	83	15

N.W.P. LOCOMOTIVE ROSTER
(Broad Gauge)

No.	Class	Built By	Builder's Number	Date	Drivers	Cylinders	Total Engine Weight	T.F.	Off Roster
				4-4-0					
1	....	Baldwin	7400	1884	47"	12x22	51,100	7,317	12-4-1916
2	....	Baldwin	7013	1883	50"	12x22	54,600	7,317	7-15-1920
3	....	Baldwin	8947	1887	57"	14x24	64,400	10,000	8-1-1923
4	....	R. Norris	1009	1862	57"	13x22	52,900	7,760	7-15-1920
5	....	Booth	17	1873	63"	14x22	56,500	8,276	6-30-1911
6	....	Booth	14	1870	63"	14x22	60,500	8,145	7-31-1915
7	....	Booth	15	1870	64"	14x24	64,400	8,740	4-17-1920
8	....	Baldwin	5485	1881	63"	15x24	71,000	9,470	5-1-1925
9	E-43	Grant	1664	1883	59"	16x24	86,300	12,390	5-15-1938
10	E-44	Grant	1665	1883	59"	16x24	84,200	12,390	6-10-1937
11	....	Grant	....	1878	63"	16x24	70,250	11,600	5-15-1912
12	....	Grant	....	1878	63"	16x24	70,250	11,600	11-11-1926
13	....	Baldwin	3831	1875	57"	16x24	74,300	13,280	4-8-1929
14	E-45	Grant	....	1888	62"	16x24	88,550	12,630	9-26-1936
15	....	Baldwin	4416	1878	61"	17x24	79,240	12,535	10-21-1930
16	....	Penn RR	1031	1886	59"	17x24	83,600	13,990	10-21-1930
17	E-46	Rogers	4155	1889	63"	17x24	87,300	13,100	9-21-1935
18	....	Rogers	4154	1889	63"	17x24	87,300	13,000	10-31-1910
19	E-47	Rogers	3305	1884	61"	18x24	93,800	17,880	7-13-1937
20	E-47	Rogers	3306	1884	61"	18x24	91,300	17,880	9-26-1936
21	E-48	Baldwin	24035	1904	69"	18x24	117,350	17,240	6-10-1937
22	E-49	American	44959	1908	69"	18x24	128,500	17,240	10-1-1938
23	E-49	American	44960	1908	69"	18x24	128,500	17,240	3-14-1949
51	E-50	American	54580	1914	63"	19x26	158,500	25,330	2-28-1938
52	E-50	American	54581	1914	63"	19x26	158,500	25,330	2-28-1938
53	E-50	American	54582	1914	63"	19x26	158,500	25,330	5-6-1938
54	E-50	American	54583	1914	63"	19x26	158,500	25,330	4-30-1938
				0-4-0 TANK TYPE					
99	....	E. Jardine	....	1887		6x12	11,000	1,468	2-18-1910
				4-6-0					
101	....	Rogers	4212	1889	57"	16x24	94,400	12,330	9-30-1928
102	....	Grant	....	1888	55"	18x24	102,000	16,820	5-31-1929
103	T-43	Richmond	3304	1901	57"	18x24	120,260	19,710	12-15-1935
104	T-43	Richmond	3303	1901	57"	18x24	120,260	20,870	9-26-1936
105	T-44	American	25620	1902	57"	19x26	134,000	25,200	7-17-1934
106	T-44	American	25621	1902	57"	19x26	134,000	25,200	3-10-1934
107	T-44	Baldwin	23933	1904	57"	19x26	136,300	25,200	4-10-1937
108	T-44	Baldwin	23951	1904	57"	19x26	136,300	25,200	10-21-1948
109	T-45	Baldwin	18179	1900	57"	19x26	130,300	25,200	10-14-1948
110	T-45	Baldwin	17759	1900	57"	19x26	130,300	25,200	4-10-1937
111	T-46	American	44955	1908	57"	19x26	137,800	25,200	10-31-1949
112	T-46	American	44956	1908	57"	19x26	137,800	25,200	8-31-1952
113	T-46	American	44957	1908	57"	19x26	137,800	25,200	10-3-1947
114	T-46	American	44958	1908	57"	19x26	137,800	25,200	2-6-1947
130	T-47	American	49089	1910	63"	20x28	173,000	30,200	7-18-1938
131	T-47	American	49090	1910	63"	20x28	173,000	30,200	7-18-1938
132	T-47	American	49091	1910	63"	20x28	173,000	30,200	10-1-1938
133	T-47	American	49092	1910	63"	20x28	173,000	30,200	10-31-1938
134	T-48	American	51536	1912	63"	20x28	175,500	30,200	12-31-1940
135	T-48	American	51537	1912	63"	20x28	175,500	30,200	11-30-1940

136	T-49	American	54578	1914	63"	20x28	180,000	30,222	10-31-1940
137	T-49	American	54579	1914	63"	20x28	180,000	30,222	12-31-1940
138	T-49	American	54975	1914	63"	20x28	180,000	30,222	12-31-1940
139	T-50	American	54976	1914	63"	20x28	180,000	30,220	3-27-1947
140	T-50	American	54977	1914	63"	20x28	180,000	30,220	2-21-1957
141	T-50	American	54978	1914	63"	20x28	180,000	31,020	3-31-1954
142	T-51	Baldwin	55356	1922	63"	20x28	181,670	30,220	8-7-1953
143	T-51	Baldwin	55473	1922	63"	20x28	181,670	30,220	12-28-1953
170	T-52	Baldwin	30105	1907	57"	21x26	186,750	32,490	12-21-1950
171	T-52	Baldwin	30106	1907	57"	21x26	186,750	32,490	12-14-1946
172	T-52	Baldwin	31094	1907	57"	21x26	186,750	32,490	11-18-1948
178	T-53	Baldwin	29726	1906	63"	21x28	169,800	33,320	1-21-1954
179	T-54	American	44753	1907	63"	21x28	189,280	30,220	8-4-1952
180	T-55	American	54979	1914	57"	21x28	196,500	36,830	9-21-1952
181	T-55	American	54980	1914	57"	21x28	196,500	36,830	7-1-1955
182	T-59	Baldwin	55351	1922	57"	21x28	196,980	36,830	11-21-1955
183	T-59	Baldwin	55470	1922	57"	21x28	196,980	36,830	5-6-1955
184	T-59	Baldwin	55471	1922	57"	21x28	196,980	36,830	11-23-1953

2-6-2 TANK TYPE

| 201 | .... | Baldwin | 22446 | 1903 | 47" | 17x22 | 117,100 | 18,400 | 10-21-1930 |
| 202 | PR-3 | Baldwin | 22474 | 1903 | 47" | 17x22 | 117,100 | 18,400 | 10-31-1937 |

2-4-2 TANK TYPE

| 225 | CO-1 | Porter | 905 | 1887 | 41" | 12x18 | 52,070 | 6,717 | 10-31-1937 |

0-6-0

226	....	Hinkley	....	1880	52"	16x24	70,900	14,450	1910
227	S-20	American	48037	1910	50"	19x24	124,500	23,560	11-5-1948
228	S-20	American	48038	1910	50"	19x24	124,500	23,560	1-27-1949
229	S-21	American	54981	1914	50"	19x24	138,800	26,510	10-14-1948
230	S-21	American	54982	1914	50"	19x24	138,800	26,510	11-30-1948
231	S-21	American	54983	1914	50"	19x24	138,800	26,510	6-21-1950

SHAY TYPE

| 251 | SH-1 | Lima | 909 | 1904 | 40" | 13½x15 | 213,500 | 27,630 | 1-1-1935 |

HEISLER TYPE

| 255 | .... | Heisler | 1254 | 1912 | 40" | 16½x14 | 145,900 | 24,800 | 2-27-1924 |

2-6-0

300	M-4	Cooke	2624	1901	63"	20x28	146,000	28,710	11-18-1936
301	M-4	Cooke	2626	1901	63"	20x28	146,000	28,710	11-18-1936
351	....	Baldwin	8776	1887	39"	13x22	51,800	10,530	9-20-1916
352	....	Baldwin	8092	1886	55"	17x24	86,800	16,078	5-31-1929
353	M-22	American	45284	1908	57"	18x24	114,500	20,300	12-15-1935
354	M-22	American	45285	1908	57"	18x24	114,500	20,300	9-12-1935

LOCOMOTIVES OF THE SAN FRANCISCO & NORTH PACIFIC
THAT DID NOT REACH THE NORTHWESTERN PACIFIC NUMBERING

4	"Geyser"	Un	Booth	16	1873	64"	14x24	64,400
11	"Ukiah"	Un	Booth	30	1874	63"	16x24	70,000
131	CP 131, "Greyhound"	Un	Rhode Island	76	1868	56"	15x22	60,000
133	CP 132, "Deerhound"	Un	Rhode Island	77	1868	56"	15x22	60,000

(3) This was second No. 3. It was built by Baldwin in 1887 as No. 3, the "Cahuenga" of the Los Angeles County Railroad. It became Eureka & Klamath River 6 in 1900, Oregon & Eureka 6 in 1903, and NWP second No. 3 in 1911 (when the NWP took over the O&E), replacing first No. 3 which had become second No. 1. This photo was made near McCann in 1914. Engine was in stationary boiler service at Willits for a time before being retired in 1923.

(4) No. 4 was the North-western Pacific's oldest engine. It was built by R. Norris in 1862 as No. 2, the "San Jose," of the San Francisco & San Jose Railroad, and in 1871 became the first engine, No. 1, of the San Francisco & North Pacific Rail Road, re-taining the name San Jose. The engine was retired in 1920. This photo was taken at Sausalito about 1909.

(5) Formerly SF&NP 5, the "Santa Rosa," this engine was about worn out when it went into the NWP roster in 1907. It was built by Booth in 1873 and was scrapped in 1911. Photo at Tiburon about 1909.

(6) Formerly SF&NP 2, the "J. G. Downey." It was built by Booth in 1870, and blew up in 1915 and was scrapped. Picture at Tiburon about 1914.

(7) Formerly SF&NP 3, the "W J. Ralston." Frequently assigned to the San Quentin locals, this engine was involved in a collision with an electric train at the Corte Madera tunnel in 1914. It was built by Booth in 1870 and was retired in 1920. Photo: Sausalito, 1912.

After the tunnel crash in 1914, a new steel cab was applied and the engine was re-assigned to the San Quentin run. This photo was made at San Rafael in 1917.

(8) Formerly SF&NP 8, the "San Rafael." Known as the "Bullet," it was a favorite on the Sonoma Valley branch. It was used in the motion picture "Iron Horse" filmed in 1923. It was built by Baldwin in 1881 and was retired in 1925. Photo at Tiburon about 1915.

(9) Formerly SF&NP 9, the "Marin." Originally a twin to No. 10, below, No. 9 was built by Grant in 1883, but this picture shows the engine with a new boiler put on when it was partially rebuilt in 1917. Engine's last service was as a stationary boiler at Sausalito and Eureka. This photo shows it, however, in active duty on the afternoon train from the Russian River in August, 1935.

(10) Formerly SF&NP 10, the "Healdsburg." On ready track at Sausalito in 1916.
Looks a little different with the new boiler that was applied in 1917. Originally No. 9 and No. 10 looked quite alike. No. 10 was used mainly for relief passenger runs, and was scrapped in 1937. Photo at Sausalito in 1920.

(11) Formerly SF&NP 6, the "Cloverdale." No. 11 and No. 12 were twin products of the Grant works in 1878, but No. 11 was relatively short-lived on the NWP, being scrapped in 1912. Photo at Sebastopol in 1909.

(12) Formerly SF&NP 7, the "Petaluma." Used on the Russian River freights in the early days, and also took part in the film "Iron Horse," in 1923. It lasted quite a bit longer than No. 11, not being retired until 1926. Picture at Tiburon in 1914.

(13) This engine was built by Baldwin in 1875 for the Santa Fe as No. 07. It was named "Colorado Springs," and also bore the numbers 25 and 45 while on the Santa Fe. It was sold to the SF&NW in 1905 and became NWP 13 in 1907. Retired in 1929. Photo taken near Holmes Flat, 1908.

(14) Formerly SF&NP 14, the "Tiburon." Always ready to go, the engineers called her "steady and reliable."

A later view of No. 14 after being rebuilt with a new boiler. Sausalito, 1915.

(15) Of Santa Fe parentage was this little kettle. It was built by Baldwin in 1878 for the New Mexico & Southern Pacific, a Santa Fe predecessor, originally numbered 203 and named "C. C. Jackson." It was subsequently renumbered to NM&SP 503, Santa Fe 103, Santa Fe 049 and SF&NW 7. In 1908 the lettering on the engine was changed to NWP, but communications then not being what they are today, it was not realized that on the southern end of the NWP (the road was not yet complete) there was also a No. 7, an engine which had been renumbered from one of the SF&NP engines. When this fact was discovered, this engine was renumbered to 15. Photo was made at Sausalito in 1916 when the locomotive was assigned to the Sonoma Valley trains. Scrapped in 1930.

(19) Formerly SF&NP 12, the "Peter Donahue." It was built by Rogers in 1884, and rebuilt in 1917 with a new boiler, and was used extensively to Point Reyes when that branch was broad gauge. Engine was dismantled in 1937. Photo at Point Reyes in 1926.

(20) Formerly SF&NP 13, the "Tom Rogers," originally an exact twin of No. 19. In the picture above, No. 19 is shown with a new boiler, while at left the photo of SF&NP 13 shows the engines as they looked when new, taken at Santa Rosa in 1900. NWP 20 was photographed at Manor around the year 1923 waiting for the electric train connection before departing on the Saturday-only run to Lagunitas. No. 20 was scrapped in 1936 after sitting in the "boneyard" at Tiburon for four or five years.

(21) Formerly SF&NP 24, that road's newest 4-4-0. Not named. It was built by Baldwin in 1904, and referred to as "The Flying Jackrabbit" by many engineers. Scrapped in 1937. Photo at Sausalito in 1936.

(22) Numbers 22 and 23, cast from the same die at Alco in 1908, were among the first eight new engines acquired by the NWP. The picture illustrates No. 22 on Train No. 224, the Duncan Mills Passenger, at Santa Rosa in 1931, when there were still two scheduled trains daily each way on the Guerneville (Russian River) branch. The engine was broken up in 1938. Other new engines received in 1908 were 4-6-0's 111-114 and 2-6-0's 153-154, later renumbered to 353-354.

(23) Builder photo, 1908. This engine was used on several excursions during the last days of its existence, and was the last 4-4-0 on the NWP, outlasting by eleven years Numbers 51-54 which were built six years later. Scrapped in 1949.

(99) This outlandish looking affair was purchased by the SF&NP in 1898. It was dubbed the "Coffee Grinder," and spent its entire life on the Russian River branch hauling logs or River passenger locals. The mechanism on front was sort of a portable donkey engine used for dragging logs. The engine was sold in 1910 to the North Bend Lumber Company and thus matched, at three years, No. 18 and No. 226 for briefness of existence on the NWP. Photo near Guerneville in 1904.

(101) Formerly SF&NP 18, the "Skaggs." It was the only Rogers-built (1889) 4-6-0 on the NWP, and as rail was made heavier on the Russian River branch after 1909, it was in more or less regular service on the Santa Rosa-Duncan Mills freight. It was scrapped in 1928. Photo at Duncan Mills in 1920.

(102) Formerly SF&NP 15, the "Eureka." The oldest broad gauge ten-wheel type on the NWP, built by Grant in 1888. Retired in 1929. Shown here at Santa Rosa in 1917 on the Sebastopol passenger.

(103) Formerly SF&NP 20 (above), No. 103 was built by Richmond in 1901 to the same specifications as No. 104. Photo taken at San Anselmo in 1927 waiting to take "mixed" to Point Reyes before returning to Sausalito with the afternoon passenger.

(104) Though an exact duplicate, when built, of No. 103, No. 104's first number was California Northwestern 31, being restenciled to NWP in 1908. Photo at Tiburon in 1909. Scrapped in 1936.

(105) Formerly SF&NP 21. Numbers 105 and 106 were another pair that were just alike, built by American in 1902. No. 105 saw service mostly on the northern end of the line handling log trains, but once, in July 1911, when working on the south end, it ran off of the freight apron at Tiburon into the bay, but was fished out and repaired. Dismantled in 1934.

(106) Formerly SF&NP 25 and CNW 32. Twin of 105. (Wish someone would turn up with a full view of this engine.) Shown here on the Sherwood-Willits passenger about 1911. Handled the first work train north of Willits in construction days. Broken up in 1934.

(107) Left.

(108) Above, right.

These two, still another pair of twins, were built by Baldwin in 1904 as SF&NP 22 and 23. No. 107, pictured at Santa Rosa in 1908, worked under the NWP banner for thirty years and was scrapped in 1937. No. 108 lasted until 1948. It was used on freights during the week and in passenger service on Sundays and holidays, and hauled the last scheduled train on the Russian River branch, November 14, 1935. Photo was taken at Santa Rosa in 1936.

144

(109-Above)

(110-Right)

Both of these locomotives were built by Baldwin in 1900. No. 109's prior numbers were CNW 1 and 30; No. 110 was originally SF&NP 19. The records show that 110 spent most of its time in logging service around Eureka, while 109 was used in "horseshoe" freight service on the southern district - Sausalito-San Rafael-Tiburon. Also, in its last years this engine frequently powered railfan excursions. Photo at Kenwood in 1936.

(111-114) The Northwestern Pacific was but one year old when it acquired its first new locomotives: The four pictured on these pages, plus Numbers 22 and 23 mentioned earlier, and 2-6-0's Numbers 153 and 154. These four were constructed from the same plans by Alco in 1908, and were used in both freight and passenger assignments.

No. 111 - Left: Builder photo, 1908. Engine scrapped in 1949.

No. 112 - Below: This is the only NWP locomotive remaining in existence, and is the property of the Pacific Coast Chapter, Railway & Locomotive Historical Society. Photo at Tiburon in the summer of 1955 shows the engine as it was repainted in two-tone green for exhibition at the Southern Pacific Centennial display at Sacramento in August of that year.

No. 113 - Above: At Kenwood (on Sonoma Valley branch) in 1936. Scrapped in 1947.

No. 114 - Left: Photo at Arcata in 1938. Engine was in head-on collision with SP 2801 near Dos Rios on September 30, 1946, and was badly wrecked. It was cut up in 1947.

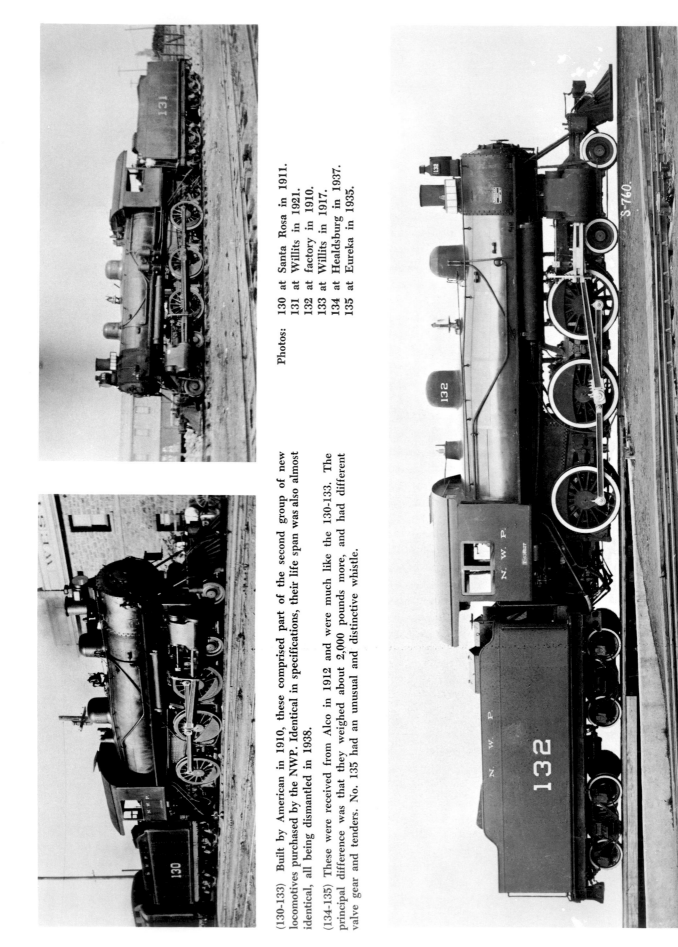

(130-133) Built by American in 1910, these comprised part of the second group of new locomotives purchased by the NWP. Identical in specifications, their life span was also almost identical, all being dismantled in 1938.

(134-135) These were received from Alco in 1912 and were much like the 130-133. The principal difference was that they weighed about 2,000 pounds more, and had different valve gear and tenders. No. 135 had an unusual and distinctive whistle.

Photos: 130 at Santa Rosa in 1911.
131 at Willits in 1921.
132 at factory in 1910.
133 at Willits in 1917.
134 at Healdsburg in 1937.
135 at Eureka in 1935.

(136-141) The engines of this group were practically the same as those in the preceding order except they were slightly heavier. They were constructed by American in 1914. No. 136 hauled the first train through to Willits for the last-spike ceremonies at Cain Rock. No. 140 with special train, on April 10, 1938, made the fastest time recorded from Willits to Sausalito - three hours. No. 141, in 1937, made the fastest freight train run - six hours from Willits to Tiburon.

Photos: 136 at Factory in 1914. Engine scrapped in 1940.
137 at Santa Rosa with southbound "Eureka Express" in 1935. Engine scrapped 1940.
138 at Willits on local freight in 1938. Engine scrapped in 1940.
139 at Sausalito in 1939. Engine scrapped in 1947.
140 at factory in 1914. Engine scrapped in 1914.
141 at Eureka in 1948. Engine scrapped in 1954. Last NWP engine on property.

(142) At Santa Rosa in 1922 awaiting the Sunday-only scheduled departure of Train No. 11. Numbers 142 and 143 were among the last new engines acquired by the NWP. Both were scrapped in 1953. The simple changing of the location of the headlight considerably alters the appearance of these identical engines, constructed by Alco in 1922.

(143) At San Rafael in the summer of 1935 on the night train from Eureka.

(170) Formerly Las Vegas & Tonopah No. 4. Photo at Eureka in 1941.

(171) Formerly Las Vegas & Tonopah No. 5. Photo at Petaluma in 1940.

(172) Formerly Las Vegas & Tonopah No. 8. Photo at Petaluma in 1935.

These three were all built in 1907 for the LV&T and were purchased by the NWP on June 30, 1918. No. 170 was scrapped in 1950; 171 in 1946; and 172 in 1948.

(178) This engine was built by Baldwin in 1906 as Bullfrog Goldfield No. 13, later No. 11, and was purchased by the NWP in 1917, and was dismantled in 1954. The upper picture was taken at Santa Rosa in 1935; the lower in the desert, probably around 1912.

(179) Built for the Las Vegas & Tonopah in 1907 as that road's No. 12, this engine was sold to the NWP in 1917, becoming No. 129. In 1918, to better fit into the numbering plan, it was renumbered to 179. Scrapped in 1952. Upper photo at Cloverdale in 1934; the lower at Tiburon in 1917.

(180-181) These were acquired from Alco in 1914 and were originally numbered 160-161, changed in 1918. The above is a factory photo taken in 1914; the print of 180 shows the engine's appearance on the line; and 181 was photographed at Madera, California, on the Southern Pacific's Western Division in 1954. No. 180 was scrapped in 1952, No. 181 in 1955.

(182-184) Puchased from Baldwin in 1922, these were the heaviest, and along with Numbers 142 and 143, were the last new engines acquired by the NWP. No. 182, right, was used on several railfan excursions. No. 183, in its last days was used on the Southern Pacific. No. 184 was the "jinx" engine of the road, and met its end on January 17, 1953, when it was swept by a slide into 45 feet of water at Scotia Bluffs and scrapped on the spot after being recovered from the river. Photo of 182 was taken at Petaluma in 1940; of 183 at Lathrop in 1954; of 184 at Detour in 1924.

(201) Built for use on the Sherwood Branch with its switchbacks and sharp turns, this engine came from Baldwin in 1903 as California Northwestern No. 33, and was renumbered to NWP in 1908. Originally it was a 2-6-2 tank engine but the tender was put on in 1910. Photo at Tiburon in 1929. Engine was scrapped in 1930.

(202) An exact duplicate of No. 201, 202 was originally numbered CNW 34 and saw most of its service on the Albion Branch. It was assigned to the "orphaned" line in 1912 and was unbelieveably changed from oil to wood burning as cordwood was abundant in the area. Changed back to oil in 1923. Photo on Albion Branch in 1913. 201 and 202 were the only 2-6-2 types on the road. No. 202 was scrapped in 1937.

(225) This was the only 2-4-2 on the road. It was built by Porter in 1887 as a 0-4-2T. Purchased from National City & Otay (#5) in 1906 by the Ft. Bragg & Southeastern and numbered 1. Became NWP first No. 1 in 1907 and renumbered to 225 in January 1909. It, like the 202, worked principally on the Albion branch, although this photo was made at Tiburon in 1917 when the engine was in for shopping, having been brought from Albion by steamer. Dismantled in 1937.

(226) The first of NWP's half dozen 0-6-0's. It was built by Hinkley in 1880 as Santa Fe 122, later becoming Santa Fe 2232. In 1906 it became FB&SE #2 and was renumbered NWP 210 in 1907 and to NWP 226 in 1908. Photo was taken in 1909 at Albion and engine was scrapped in 1910.

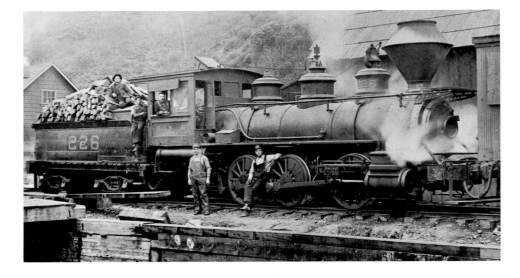

(227-228) These were the first new switch engines received by the NWP, coming from Alco in 1910. For many years switching passenger cars at Sausalito was the regular duty of 227, but during World War II it was leased to the San Diego & Arizona Eastern, the photo at right having been taken at San Diego in 1946. No. 228 was leased to the Southern Pacific in 1941 and the picture below was made at an industrial track in San Francisco that year. 227 was scrapped in 1948; 228 in 1949.

(229-231) The year 1914 must have been a good one for the NWP, for in addition to four 4-4-0's (51-54) and eight 4-6-0's (136-141, 180-181), the road purchased these three switch engines from Alco, the last of this type acquired. No. 231 was the only switcher to have the herald on the tender. Numbers 229 and 230 were broken up in 1948, No. 231 in 1950. Photos: 229 at Petaluma in 1939; 230 at Tiburon in 1936; and 231 at Petaluma in 1941.

(251) The NWP's only Shay was built by Lima in 1904 as Northwestern Redwood Company No. 1. It became California Northwestern second No. 32 on January 1, 1905, and was stenciled to NWP 251 on March 13, 1908. Photo was taken on the Sherwood branch about 1910. The engine was a woodburner while on the NWR and CNW.

(255) The only Heisler on the road. It was built in 1912 for the Jordan River Lumber Company as No. 7, became Horseshoe Lumber Co. 7, and was purchased by the NWP in 1922 for service on the Sherwood branch. It was too light for that work expected of it, however, and was sold in 1924 to the Shaw Bertram Lumber Company, Klamath Falls, Oregon.

(300-301) Except for an SP ten-wheeler (2248) leased for one day, these were the last engines acquired by the NWP. This pair was leased from the SP in 1929 to bolster motive power needs, but they were not of much help, spending practically as much time awaiting repairs as they did in working. They were built by Cooke in 1901 as SP 2140 and 2142, becoming SP 1714 and 1716 the same year. They were retired by the NWP in 1934 and were scrapped in 1936.

(351) This engine was built by Baldwin in 1887 as Eel River & Eureka No. 3, the "Defender." It became San Francisco & Northwestern No. 3 in 1903; NWP 151 in 1908, and 351 in 1914. The photo as 151 was taken at Eureka about 1910. We have been unable to locate a picture of this engine as No. 351. Engine scrapped in 1916.

(352) Much traveled was this little kettle. It was built by Baldwin in 1886 as Gulf, Colorado & Santa Fe No. 65, later becoming GC&SF 314 and Santa Fe 0179. It was sold in 1903 to the SF&NW where it became that road's No. 5. It was renumbered to NWP 152 in 1908, and to NWP 352 in 1914. Upper photo was taken at Arcata in 1910, the lower at South Bay in 1920.

(353-354) The Northwestern Pacific was a new company in 1907, and in 1908 it bought eight new locomotives - 4-4-0's No. 22 and 23, 4-6-0's No. 111-114, and these two 2-6-0's originally numbered 153 and 154. The latter two were renumbered in 1914 to 353 and 354, becoming the highest numbered engines on the road. The above builder photo shows the engines as they looked when new; the other pictures illustrate the engines on the line. Both were scrapped in 1935.

On March 30, 1930, silence descended on the enginehouse at Point Reyes. The Narrow Gauge was finished, and Engine 90 had made her final run. The engine remained at Point Reyes until 1933 when it was loaded on a standard gauge flat car and hauled to the shops at Tiburon where it was placed, along with Numbers 94 and 95, on a specially constructed narrow gauge track, to be held for disposition. But there was no longer any need for narrow gauge steam locomotives, and all three were scrapped in December, 1935.

(82) Formerly NPC 11, "Marin," and NS 11, the Baldwin built engine of 1876 was relettered NWP 82 in 1907, but it was worn out and never did get a chance to turn-a-wheel on the NWP. Scrapped in 1911.

(83) Formerly NPC 3, "Tomales," and NS 3, this engine out-shopped by Baldwin in 1875, was given the number 83 on the NWP in July, 1908. "Little Buttercup" was the affectionate name given this locomotive. It was used as an extra in local passenger service. Photo taken at Sausalito in 1911. Scrapped in 1913.

(84) A homemade product - built in the NPC shops at Sausalito in 1900 and given the number 20. Later NS 20. Became NWP 84 in 1908. Photo at Point Reyes in 1917. This weedburner was used on the Manor-Point Reyes passenger trains most of the time. Retired in 1920.

(85) This engine, a product of Baldwin, 1884, started its career on the South Pacific Coast Railroad between Alameda and Santa Cruz as their Number 14. Joined the NWP in July, 1907 and numbered 85. Photo taken at Lagunitas in 1915. (See comments of No. 93.)

(86) Formerly SPC 15. Built by Brooks in 1884. Acquired by the NWP in July 1907 and renumbered to 86 in January, 1908. Photo taken at Point Reyes in 1916. Was assigned to passenger locals on the slim gauge between Manor and Point Reyes. Sold to Duncan Mills Land & Lumber Company in 1920. Scrapped at Duncan Mills in 1926.

(87) Formerly SPC 10. Built by Baldwin in 1880. Acquired by the NWP in December, 1907, and took the number 87 in March, 1908. The engine was scrapped in November, 1917. Photo taken at Sausalito in 1913. The engine was used mainly in stand-by service for passenger trains.

(90) Built by Brooks in 1891. Formerly NPC 15 and NS 15. The favorite among narrow gauge hoggers. Kept as neat as a pin. Only narrow gauge engine that received the NWP herald on its tender. Was used on the last day of operation, March 29, 1930. Also used in tearing up what was left of the narrow gauge line in December, 1930. Photo taken at Point Reyes, 1925.

(91) Formerly NPC 16 (above) and NS 16. The engine became 91 on the NWP in July 1908. "She ran as slick as a whistle," but cutting back the narrow gauge to Camp Meeker in 1926 sent the engine into retirement. Photo taken at Point Reyes in 1927. When renumbered from 16 to NWP 91 in 1908, the number plate on the smoke box door was just turned upside down!

(92) Formerly NPC (below) 14 and NS 14. Built by Brooks in 1891, this engine became NWP 92 in January, 1908. Photo taken at San Anselmo in 1916 - steamed up for the run of the Camp Meeker freight. In addition to regular passenger service, passengers could ride this train between Manor and Camp Meeker - a three hour trip. The engine made its last trip on September 19, 1926. Scrapped in October, 1934 at Point Reyes, after having sat in the "bone-pile" for eight years.

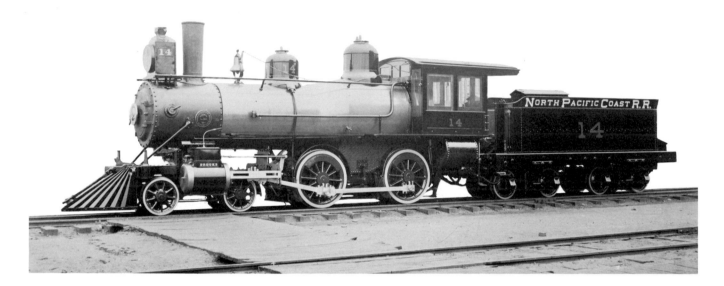

(93) (See comments of Engine 85) On June 11, 1924, this engine emerged from the paint shop as No. 93. On the first trip it stalled with passenger train on the Tyrone-Occidental hill. Placed in dead-line at Point Reyes, where it stayed until scrapped ten years later in 1934. Photo taken of engine in dead-line at Point Reyes in 1928.

(144) This Baldwin built engine, out-shopped in 1887, was number 20 on the South Pacific Coast Railroad. Sold to NWP in January, 1908, and numbered 144. Picture taken at Lagunitas where crew and friends pause for photo.

(144) Left, on Occidental freight at San Anselmo in the summer of 1915. After switching, the engine returns to Occidental in the afternoon.

(94) Number changed from 144 to 94 on February 12, 1924. Photo taken at Point Reyes in 1925. The "Rocking Horse," as engineers dubbed the engine, was used in freight and mixed train service right up until the day before abandonment of the narrow gauge line in March, 1930. Engine was taken to Tiburon on a flat car for storage and future sale along with engines 90 and 95. However, there were no buyers, so the engines were scrapped.

NPC 18 It was reported to be the largest narrow gauge locomotive when built in 1899 by the Brooks Locomotive Works.

(145) Formerly NPC 18 (above) and NS 18. Retained the number 18 on the NWP until February, 1908, when it was restenciled 145. Filled with water and oil, the engine was ready for some heavy duty freight work - photo taken at Sausalito in 1916.

(95) Renumbered from 145 to 95 on April 11, 1924, the engine had already steamed her last when it was hauled out of the Point Reyes engine house for pictures in 1927.

(195) Formerly NPC 13 and NS 13. Built by Baldwin in 1883. The little 2-6-0 was renumbered 195 when the NWP took over the NS in 1907, but the engine had seen its day and never turned a wheel for the NWP It sat in the weeds at Sausalito until scrapped in 1910.

(NS 40) Built by Baldwin in 1880 for the Denver & Rio Grande as their No. 44, "Texas Creek." Purchased by the North Shore in December, 1903, and given the number 40. When the NWP took over, the engine became 321 in March, 1908, but the "pot" had seen her day and was retired one year later. Note— this photo shows the engine as No. 40 - we have been unable to locate a photo as 321. Can any reader help?

(322) Formerly Hancock & Calumet No. 2, "Tamarack," and Duluth, South Shore & Atlantic No. 33. Purchased by the North Shore in 1903 and retained the number 33. The locomotive, built by Baldwin in 1885, was taken over by the NWP in 1907 and given the number 322. Photo at Sausalito in 1911.
Engine retired a few months later in 1911.

(323) Formerly Hancock & Calumet No. 3 "Osceola" and Duluth, South Shore & Atlantic No. 31. Purchased by the North Shore in 1903 and retained the number 31. The locomotive, built by Baldwin in 1885, was taken over by the NWP in 1907 and given the number 323. Photo at Sausalito in 1915. Engine scrapped in 1915.

LEASED ENGINES

From the year of its organization until around 1930 the Northwestern Pacific with its substantial passenger traffic was particularly busy during the summer seasons and frequently it was necessary for the road to turn to the Southern Pacific for additional motive power. It is unknown whether this power was formally leased or just merely borrowed, but shop records indicate the presence, at one time or another, of the following Southern Pacific locomotives: 1306, 1309, 1332, 1347, 1356, 1359, 1380, 1394, 1413, 1418, 1424, 1425, 1474, 1475, 1478, all 4-4-0's; 1627, 1717, 2-6-0's; 2040, 2098, 2099, 2115, 2153, 2158, 4-6-0's; and 2505, a 2-8-0. Additionally, in the summer of 1913, Santa Fe engine No. 127, a 4-4-0, saw service on the Northwestern Pacific.

From 1930, with the drastic curtailment of passenger trains, and abandonment of various segments of the line, the N.W.P. was able to chug along with its own stable of horses until 1934 when, on August 10, SP Engine No. 2566 was leased. The succeeding years saw the rather rapid removal from service and eventual scrapping of owned locomotives - five in 1935, five in 1936, seven in 1937, ten in 1938, and finally, by 1957 the last (except No. 112) N.W.P. locomotive had been broken up. To take the places of these engines, more and more Southern Pacific engines were leased. The accompanying table lists such locomotives, giving not only the dates to the N.W.P., but the dates the engines were returned to their parent company. (In several instances the same engine was leased twice, and both dates are given.)

As pointed out above, 2566 was the first SP engine leased after 1930; No. 2937 had the latest lease date; No. 2819 was leased for the longest period; 2750 for the shortest period; and on August 31, 1953, the last S.P. steam engines remaining on the N.W.P. were returned. They were 2345, 2356, 2564, 2582, 2810 and 2842. One other SP engine, No. 2248, a 1896-built 4-6-0, was the last steam engine to run on the N.W.P. It was leased for one day - November 20, 1955 - to honor the retirement of veteran engineer W. A. Silverthorn, contributor of many pictures and much information found in this book.

NO.	TYPE	LEASED	RETURNED	NO.	TYPE	LEASED	RETURNED
1131	0-6-0	7-23-1948	6-8-1949	2580	2-8-0	6-10-1939	4-19-1946
1500	4-4-0	8-10-1948	2-17-1949	2582	2-8-0	6-12-1946	8-31-1953
1644	2-6-0	4-1-1947	1-29-1950	2593	2-8-0	10-27-1947	5-13-1950
1654	2-6-0	3-31-1947	7-19-1949	2612	2-8-0	10-8-1947	1-6-1950
1703	2-6-0	11-17-1946	12-4-1947	2625	2-8-0	9-2-1948	2-27-1950
1734	2-6-0	8-23-1948	2-25-1942	2656	2-8-0	5-13-1950	4-1-1952
1763	2-6-0	9-12-1947	10-5-1950	2688	2-8-0	8-13-1942	4-20-1950
1772	2-6-0	8-24-1948	6-2-1952	2690	2-8-0	8-9-1942	3-1-1950
1795	2-6-0	6-8-1949	10-1-1951	2708	2-8-0	7-10-1934	10-25-1951
1814	2-6-0	6-8-1949	10-3-1950	2732	2-8-0	3-25-1950	12-17-1952
1825	2-6-0	5-13-1949	1-30-1952	2736	2-8-0	2-23-1947	7-22-1949
1829	2-6-0	1-6-1950	3-1-1950	2750	2-8-0	10-3-1949	10-26-1949
2267	4-6-0	3-9-1947	10-7-1947	2751	2-8-0	6-25-1951	10-29-1951
2271	4-6-0	11-25-1947	3-23-1949	2755	2-8-0	7-23-1947	8-11-1953
2283	4-6-0	9-14-1947	10-21-1949	2759	2-8-0	8-10-1937	5-14-1953
2289	4-6-0	6-7-1946	11-30-1947	2762	2-8-0	7-15-1950	3-3-1953
2296	4-6-0	3-9-1947	4-6-1948	2786	2-8-0	5-28-1948	7-2-1948
2296	4-6-0	8-30-1948	9-25-1948	2793	2-8-0	8-6-1936	8-14-1953
2297	4-6-0	11-1-1946	10-7-1947	2801	2-8-0	7-31-1944	10-15-1950
2298	4-6-0	9-18-1947	1-14-1948	2806	2-8-0	1-18-1947	7-10-1950
2298	4-6-0	9-1-1948	7-9-1949	2810	2-8-0	1-3-1948	8-31-1953
2303	4-6-0	10-30-1945	1-19-1946	2812	2-8-0	2-20-1947	8-18-1950
2303	4-6-0	7-14-1946	1-18-1947	2813	2-8-0	2-25-1950	3-31-1953
2304	4-6-0	10-28-1945	12-4-1945	2819	2-8-0	7-25-1934	11-13-1951
2307	4-6-0	6-14-1946	7-8-1947	2836	2-8-0	6-18-1943	9-28-1943
2318	4-6-0	6-10-1940	9-1-1943	2842	2-8-0	3-24-1950	8-31-1953
2318	4-6-0	4-7-1949	9-13-1950	2855	2-8-0	10-5-1947	11-30-1952
2320	4-6-0	6-8-1942	11-15-1951	2913	4-8-0	3-28-1950	12-8-1950
2321	4-6-0	1-29-1950	8-16-1953	2937	4-8-0	8-24-1952	5-26-1953
2332	4-6-0	11-18-1949	9-23-1950	2943	4-8-0	7-1-1949	9-6-1949
2336	4-6-0	6-14-1940	9-20-1951	2951	4-8-0	7-1-1949	1-10-1952
2339	4-6-0	12-2-1940	9-16-1950	3100	4-6-2	7-28-1938	5-13-1941
2345	4-6-0	5-29-1952	8-31-1953	3101	4-6-2	6-18-1939	5-7-1941
2348	4-6-0	7-28-1952	6-3-1953	3102	4-6-2	6-18-1938	5-14-1941
2356	4-6-0	9-20-1951	8-31-1953	3102	4-6-2	7-26-1945	10-28-1945
2358	4-6-0	5-18-1950	8-19-1953	3104	4-6-2	6-17-1938	6-19-1942
2459	4-6-2	6-13-1948	8-30-1948	3105	4-6-2	7-30-1938	7-1-1940
2500	2-8-0	11-5-1946	12-1947	3106	4-6-2	6-20-1938	11-15-1941
2513	2-8-0	10-31-1949	5-16-1953	3106	4-6-2	8-9-1945	10-30-1945
2514	2-8-0	8-5-1936	11-19-1951	3108	4-6-2	6-19-1938	5-28-1942
2517	2-8-0	2-5-1950	11-21-1952	3109	4-6-2	7-30-1938	6-1-1941
2523	2-8-0	6-8-1948	7-11-1948	3203	2-8-2	8-2-1949	10-6-1950
2524	2-8-0	2-27-1950	6-13-1953	3211	2-8-2	4-23-1948	8-2-1949
2525	2-8-0	7-17-1952	8-8-1953	3214	2-8-2	12-21-1947	4-23-1948
2527	2-8-0	2-27-1950	12-13-1951	3224	2-8-2	7-29-1948	9-2-1948
2530	2-8-0	8-19-1937	8-10-1953	3227	2-8-2	4-2-1949	6-25-1949
2531	2-8-0	6-5-1946	2-26-1952	3227	2-8-2	2-9-1950	9-30-1950
2535	2-8-0	7-24-1934	10-6-1951	3236	2-8-2	12-22-1947	12-28-1948
2541	2-8-0	7-30-1952	7-30-1953	3236	2-8-2	6-25-1949	10-2-1950
2542	2-8-0	12-7-1947	2-25-1950				
2551	2-8-0	12-11-1949	11-3-1950				
2556	2-8-0	2-17-1950	6-25-1951				
2561	2-8-0	8-6-1936	9-27-1950				
2564	2-8-0	8-6-1950	8-31-1953				
2566	2-8-0	7-10-1934	11-10-1935				
2571	2-8-0	2-25-1950	9-24-1951				
2573	2-8-0	8-18-1937	11-9-1950				

Across the page we have a photo of an engine that was not on the roster: Northwestern Pacific No. 50. How come? During World War II engines were shifted from one area to another and NWP 228 and SD&AE 50 were involved in a collision which damaged the NWP engine and the tender of the Arizona engine. To keep one engine going while repairs were being made, tenders were switched. Photo at Los Angeles in May, 1945.

175

Engine 154 (later 354) had been in service only about ninety days when it was wrecked north of Novato on July 3, 1908.

The North Shore's Train No. 7, the 6:10 A.M. daily passenger from Point Reyes to San Francisco did not make the trip on April 18, 1906. It was turned over by the famous San Francisco earthquake of that date.

Monument at Eureka station placed in memory of the three crewmen who died on January 17, 1953 when their engine, No. 184, was swept by a slide into 45 feet of water at Scotia Bluffs.

Picnic-bound passengers got no further than this point on White's Hill, west of Fairfax, when the North Shore's train jumped the track and turned over. The year - 1903.

Above, engines 18 and 20, both 4-4-0's, had a head-on collision on August 8, 1910 at a point now known as Hamilton Field. This was the NWP's worst wreck, and while Engine 20 was subsequently repaired, No. 18 was totally demolished.

Engine No. 114 came out second-best in a head-on collision with leased SP Engine 2801 near Dos Rios on September 30, 1946. No. 114 was not repaired after this wreck.

Always maintained, but with the hope that it will never be used, is this wrecker stationed at Eureka.

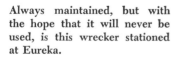

On a section that had originally been narrow gauge, broad gauge Engine No. 10 derails and almost turns over near Lagunitas in 1922.

In the road's second most serious wreck, Engine No. 184 on a freight train, and Engine No. 141 on the Eureka Passenger, met on a main line near Largo (ten miles south of Ukiah) on February 28, 1929. Both engines were fixed up. No. 184 was destroyed in a slide at Scotia Bluffs in 1953.

Rotten piling caused Engine No. 112 to go into the Bay at Tiburon on June 29, 1913.

High water west of Scotia in 1916 causes considerable damage.

Trains were annulled along the Guerneville branch on February 3, 1915, as Russian River goes over its banks at Guerneville.

The heavy rains of the coastal areas of northern California caused this slide on the N.W.P. west of Scotia in 1912.

Engine 23 hit a stray cow and was wrecked near Hopland in October, 1911.

Heavy rains caused slides which sent track into the Eel River at Nanning Creek along Scotia Bluffs, February 12, 1947.

Derrick 55 cleaning out debris along a trestle. Note wheels lifting off the track!

On the evening of October 16, 1947, the steamer "Petaluma" hit a submerged log in Petaluma Creek and promptly sank. The craft was refloated and repaired, however, three years later the service came to an end.

Leased engine, SP No. 2913 meets with misfortune on the northern end of the N.W.P. during the year 1950.

Each year, Old Man Winter plays havoc with the northern end of the Northwestern Pacific. Here equipment digs out a slide south of Scotia along the Eel River in January, 1946.

Fire at Tunnel No. 4, just north of San Rafael. See Page 58 for details.

Wrecker No. 040 fishes Engine 53 back up the hill after being swept off the rails by a mud slide just across the river from Duncan Mills in December, 1920, on its first and only trip on the Russian River branch.

ENGINE OR ROUNDHOUSES ON THE NORTHWESTERN PACIFIC & PREDECESSOR COMPANIES

BROAD GAUGE

Location	*Stalls	Built by	Date	Remarks
Sausalito	4	N.P.C.	1875	Dismantled 1942
Tiburon	11	SF&NP	1884	Dismantled 1958
San Rafael	1	SF&NP	1879	Destroyed 1905 by fire
Glen Ellen	2	S&SR	1882	Dismantled 1934
Donahue	2	SF&NP	1870	Dismantled 1884
Petaluma	2	SF&NP	1870	Dismantled 1908
Ukiah	5	SF&NP	1889	Dismantled 1942
Willits	5	CNW	1902	Still in Service
Shively	2	SF&NW	1905	Dismantled about 1912
South Bay	2	ER&E	1890	Dismantled 1931
Eureka	8	NWP	1920-1929	Still in Service
Arcata	1	CN	1901	Dismantled 1911
Essex	4	E&KR	1898	Dismantled 1920
Luffenholtz	2	O&E	1904	Destroyed 1906 by fire
Trinidad	2	NWP	1913	Dismantled 1924
Albion	2	A. Lbr. Co.	1891	Dismantled 1937
Navarro	1	FB&SE	1905	Dismantled 1937

NARROW GAUGE

Location	*Stalls	Built by	Date	Remarks
Sausalito	4	NPC	1875	Dismantled 1920
Mill Valley	1	NPC	1889	Dismantled about 1908
San Rafael "B" Street	2	NPC	1875	Dismantled 1903
Point Reyes	4	NWP	1920	Sold to M. Vonsen after narrow gauge aband. 1930
Tomales	3	NPC	1889	Destroyed by fire about 1900
Duncan Mills	2	NPC	1877	Dismantled before 1900
Cazadero	1	NPC	1886	Dismantled around 1908

The rails are gone and locomotive facilities at Glen Ellen await scrapper after N.W.P. shifted over to S.P.'s Sonoma Valley line, Yulupa to Los Guilicos, January 15, 1934. — Louis Stein collection

Engine facilities at the busy Sausalito terminal in 1915. The narrow gauge engine house is at the left, the broad gauge in the center.

Above, enginemen turn No. 90 at the turntable at Point
Reyes in 1928. The enginehouse had two stalls that could
accomodate two engines each.

Right is the ramshackle engine shop at Albion which was
dismantled in 1937.

Tiburon roundhouse in 1930.

Willits roundhouse, midpoint on the N.W.P. main line to
Eureka, 1914.

Armstrong turntable and two-stall enginehouse at Petaluma
in 1914.

"Little Josie," SF&NP No. 1, in right stall at Ukiah round-house in 1905, with C&NW 21, 20 and 32 in others.

Eight-stall roundhouse at Eureka with newly-emplaced steel turntable.

Sausalito engine terminal, 1931, with 4-4-0's 23 and 53 in foreground.

TURNTABLES - NORTHWESTERN PACIFIC
AND PREDECESSOR COMPANIES

BROAD GAUGE

Location	Remarks
Sausalito	Dismantled 1942
Tiburon	Dismantled 1963
San Rafael	Dismantled 1905
Ignacio	Dismantled 1934
Glen Ellen	Dismantled 1934
Kenwood	Dismantled 1941
Donahue	Dismantled 1884
Santa Rosa	Dismantled before 1925
Fulton	Dismantled 1908
Healdsburg	Still in Service
Cloverdale	Dismantled 1941
Ukiah	Dismantled 1953
Ridge	Dismantled 1953
Willits	Still in Service
Island Mountain	Dismantled 1953
Fort Seward	Dismantled 1941
Scotia	Dismantled 1931
South Bay	Dismantled 1931
Eureka	Still in Service
Arcata	Dismantled 1911
Essex	Dismantled 1920
Trinidad	Dismantled 1924
Sebastopol	Dismantled before 1910
Cazadero	Dismantled 1933
Guerneville	Dismantled 1910
Duncan Mills	Dismantled 1916

NARROW GAUGE

Location	Remarks
Sausalito	Dismantled 1920
San Rafael	Dismantled 1903
Point Reyes (old)	Dismantled 1920
Point Reyes (later)	Dismantled 1933
Tomales	Dismantled 1930
Occidental	Dismantled 1930
Cazadero	Rebuilt to Broad Gauge 1926

Narrow gauge turntable at the end of the line at Cazadero about 1919.

NWP No. 105 on the old "Armstrong" table at Eureka.

187

WATER AND FUEL STATIONS
NORTHWESTERN PACIFIC

BROAD GAUGE
MAIN LINE
SAUSALITO - TIBURON TO EUREKA

Location	Remarks
Sausalito	Water & Fuel
Tiburon	Water & Fuel
Hilarita	Water
San Rafael	Water
Ignacio	Water & Fuel
Novato	Water
Burdell	Water
Petaluma	Water & Fuel
Cotati	Water
Santa Rosa	Water & Fuel
Fulton	Water & Fuel
Healdsburg	Water
Cloverdale	Water & Fuel
Hopland	Water
Ukiah	Water & Fuel
Redwood Valley	Water
Ridge	Water
Willits	Water & Fuel
Longvale	Water
Tatu	Water
Dos Rios	Water & Fuel
Stony Creek	Water
Spyrock	Water
Bell Springs	Water & Fuel
Two Rocks	Water
Island Mountain	Water & Fuel
Kekawaka	Water
Hamann Gulch	Water
Steelhead	Water
Fort Seward	Water & Fuel
Eel Rock	Water
McCann	Water
South Fork	Water
Camp Nine	Water
Elinor	Water
Scotia	Water & Fuel
Alton	Water & Fuel
Table Bluff	Water
Millford	Water
South Bay	Water & Fuel
Eureka	Water & Fuel

SONOMA BRANCH

Location	Remarks
Schellville	Water
Sonoma	Water
Glen Ellen	Water & Fuel
Kenwood	Water

GUERNEVILLE BRANCH

Korbel	Water
Rio Nido	Water
Duncan Mills	Water & Fuel
Fraser	Water

SEBASTOPOL BRANCH

Sebastopol	Fuel

SHERWOOD BRANCH

Northwestern	Water
Rowes	Water
En Cima	Water
M.P. 17.3	Water
M.P. 20.7	Water
M.P. 25.0	Water

TRINIDAD BRANCH

Samoa	Water & Fuel
Arcata	Fuel
McCloskey	Water
Essex	Water
Little River Jct.	Water
25 Junction	Water
Trinidad	Fuel

ALBION BRANCH

Albion	Water & Fuel
Skibo	Water
Dunn	Water
Navarro Mill	Water & Fuel

NARROW GAUGE

Sausalito	Water & Fuel
Mill Valley	Water
Larkspur	Water
Ross	Water
San Anselmo	Water & Fuel
San Rafael "B" Street	Water & Fuel
Bothin	Water
Lagunitas	Water
Point Reyes	Water & Fuel
Marshall	Water
Tomales	Water & Fuel
Fallon	Water
Freestone	Water
Occidental	Fuel
Tyrone	Water
Sheridan	Water
Duncan Mills	Water & Fuel
Ferndale	Water
Cazadero	Water & Fuel

With the advent of total dieselization water tanks were no longer required and have been dismantled.

Sausalito, 1922.

Narrow gauge Engine No. 91 and train at Fallon in 1925. Water to this tank came from a spring located in the center of a tunnel one mile west.

Freestone tank on the narrow gauge was of high capacity to fill the needs of thirsty engines for the grades ahead.

Sheridan tank, on the Russian River two miles west of Monte Rio in the days of the narrow gauge.

Two crude box affairs made up the water tank on the Albion branch about the year 1915.

Tiburon tank was always in heavy demand for water to keep the many steam freight and switch engines moving.

Above, another water supply on the Albion branch.

Right, Fraser tank on the Duncan Mills-Cazadero line. Served narrow gauge trains first, then later broad line engines.

Below, Engine No. 11 takes water at Santa Rosa in 1908. Though not seen clearly in the picture, the ornament on top of the water spout is an eagle.

Engine 109 on First Section of Train 224 to Russian River, stops opposite tank and spout at Santa Rosa in 1930.

Engine No. 53 of the Eureka-San Francisco passenger, takes water at Willits in 1924.

Hopland tank was one of the largest on the line.

PASSENGER TRAIN CARS

Narrow Gauge Engine No. 92 with daily passenger at Camp Meeker on southbound trip in summer of 1909.

PASSENGER
TRAIN
CARS

MAIN LINE

NARROW GAUGE

ELECTRIC

AND

FERRY BOATS

- - - they're here in history and photo - still and action.

PASSENGER CARS
NORTHWESTERN PACIFIC

If the locomotives were many and varied, the passenger cars were even more so, and the Car Department of the newly-formed Northwestern Pacific was faced with the task of unifying and standardizing the rolling stock from the several consolidated companies. The cars were of the open-end platform type and were lighted by oil or kerosene lamps, none being electrically lighted in those days; there were cars with flat tops, and with clerestory and arch roofs; there were coaches, combinations, smokers, second-class, picnic, and even hunters' cars. They came from many of the famous builders of the time: Carter, Kimball, Barney & Smith, Wason, Pullman, and others. The first order of business was to apply standard olive green paint to all equipment, including the narrow gauge and electric coaches which, under the North Shore, were a Tuscan red. The name "Northwestern Pacific" was placed on the letterboards, and a numbering system was established. Generally speaking, the block from Number 1 up was for main line cars; the 200, 300 and 500 series were for electrics; 600 for head-end cars, and the narrow gauge equipment was placed in the 700, 800 and 900 series.

To modernize the main line trains, thirteen closed-vestibule coaches were ordered in 1907 and were delivered in 1908 from the St. Louis Car Company, and in 1914 the road ordered thirty steel coaches and chair cars with closed vestibules, all from Pullman, which was the last purchase of new main line cars. Nine steel and fifteen wooden were obtained from the Southern Pacific, however, in 1930, and numbered into the N.W.P. system.

The Northwestern Pacific always had a big vacation business, so to supplement their own cars a number were always borrowed from the Southern Pacific during the summer months and were used extensively on the Sonoma and Guerneville branches.

With the depression of 1929 business rapidly diminished. A gas electric car had been purchased from the Visalia Electric and was proving successful on light runs, so four more were leased from the S.P., two built by Pullman and two by Brill. They were tried on the branches, but with not much success because of their weight and lack of pulling power. With declining patronage they were assigned to runs on the main line through to Eureka. To make the schedule their hauling capacity on the level stretches was limited to one coach and one baggage car.

With three types of service—suburban, broad and narrow gauge, the ingenuity of N.W.P. shop force was ever present in obtaining maximum use of all the cars. A number of narrow gauge cars were made into broad gauge passenger coaches and several into electric trailers. Others went from suburban motors to trailers and many of the main line passenger cars were converted into suburban electric trailers.

With the depression in full swing in the early thirties and the narrow gauge abandoned, a great number of passenger cars were retired. The remaining cars were sent through the shops to be made more attractive to the rider. Each car came out with a different interior paint job and the ends were painted "Never Without Public Regard". But as the depression eased, the many people who had used the trains were now in their own autos and the passenger business went from bad to worse, and finally shortly after the start of World War II only the night trains from San Rafael to Eureka remained. When these trains ended, arriving at either terminal on the morning of June 2, 1956, the identity of the Northwestern Pacific passenger car came to an end for on that day, with the inauguration of the "Redwood", only the modern, air-conditioned equipment of the Southern Pacific remained in service on the Redwood Empire route.

195

BROAD GAUGE

OPEN PLATFORM WOODEN COACHES

NWP NO.	FORMER NUMBER	BUILDER	DATE	SEATS	WEIGHT	DISPOSITION
1	No Number issued					
2	Ex O & E	....	....	58	36,400	To Bunk Car MW 0214 6-30-1916
* 3	SF&NP 3	Wason	1884	56	40,500	Retired 10-21-1930
4	SF&NP 4	Wason	1884	56	40,500	Retired 10-21-1928
5	SF&NP 5	Cal. Pac	1868	59	40,000	Hunter's Car To MW 902 2-12-1908
6	No Number issued					
7	SF&NP 7	Cummings	1874	54	41,000	Retired 12-31-1929
8	No Number issued					
9	SF&NP 9	Cummings	1874	53	41,000	Retired 12-28-1929
10	SF&NP 10	SF&NP	1876	54	42,000	Retired 12-28-1929
11	SF&NP 11	SF&NP	1876	54	42,000	Retired 10-21-1930
12	SF&NP 12	SF&NP	1876	54	42,000	Retired 10-21-1930
13	SF&NP 13	SF&NP	1876	54	42,000	Retired 10-21-1930
14	SF&NP 14	SF&NP	1882	60	42,000	Retired 10-21-1930
15	SF&NP 15	SF&NP	1882	60	42,000	Retired 10-21-1930
16	SF&NP 16	Wason	1884	58	40,500	To Air Brake Instruction Car #09 1-31-1924. Retired 10-21-1930
17	SF&NP 17	Wason	1884	60	40,500	To Electric Trailer #238 2-17-1912
18	SF&NP 18	Wason	1884	60	40,500	To Electric Trailer #237 1-30-1912
19	SF&NP 19	Wason	1885	60	40,500	To Electric Trailer #236 1-29-1912
20	SF&NP 20	Wason	1885	60	40,500	To Electric Trailer #239 2-17-1912
21	SF&NP 21	Wason	1885	60	40,500	To Electric Trailer #235 1-26-1912
22	SF&NP 22	Wason	1885	60	40,500	To Electric Trailer #234 11-18-1911
*23	SF&NP 23	Harlan	1887	56	41,000	Retired 10-21-1930
24	SF&NP 24	Harlan	1887	54	41,000	Retired 10-21-1930

OPEN WOODEN PICNIC CARS

NWP NO.	FORMER NUMBER	BUILDER	DATE	SEATS	WEIGHT	DISPOSITION
25	SF&NP 25	SF&NP	1881	56	35,000	To MW 0209 1-21-1915
26	SF&NP 26	SF&NP	1885	68	37,000	To MW 900 5-8-1908
27	SF&NP 27	SF&NP	1885	68	37,000	To Caboose 6021 6-20-1913
28	SF&NP 28	SF&NP	1885	68	37,000	To Caboose 6014 12-16-1908
29	SF&NP 29	SF&NP	1885	68	37,000	To MW 901 5-8-1908
1st 30	SF&NP 30	SF&NP	1885	68	37,000	TO MW 929 5-4-1910
1st 31	SF&NP 31	SF&NP	1885	68	37,000	To MW 945 2-18-1911

Note * - Denotes "smoker"

NWP NO.	FORMER NUMBER	BUILDER	DATE	SEATS	WEIGHT	DISPOSITION
2nd 30	Ex O & E	O & E	1905	64	48,600	Retired 1-1-1934
2nd 31	Ex O & E	O & E	1905	64	48,600	Retired 5-31-1932
32	SF&NP 32	Harlan	1887	54	41,000	Retired 10-21-1930
33	SF&NP 33	Harlan	1887	54	41,000	Retired 10-21-1930
*34	SF&NP 34	Harlan	1888	54	41,000	Retired 10-21-1930
35	SF&NP 35	Harlan	1888	54	41,000	Retired 10-21-1930
*36	SF&NP 36	Harlan	1888	54	41,000	Retired 10-21-1930
37	SF&NP 37	Harlan	1888	54	41,000	To SP 6-12-1936. Sold to Selznick Studios 1-31-1939.
38	SF&NP 38	Harlan	1888	54	41,000	Today still in use by R.K.O. Studios owners - Desilu Studios
39	SF&NP 44	Carter	1889	62	40,000	To Electric Trailer #230 4-15-1911
40	SF&NP 46	Carter	1889	62	40,000	To Electric Trailer #231 4-20-1911
41	SF&NP 48	Carter	1889	62	40,000	To Electric Trailer #232 4-15-1911
42	SF&NP 47	Carter	1889	62	40,000	To Electric Trailer #233 4-16-1911
43	No Number issued					
44	CNW 100	Pullman	1902	66	56,500	To Electric Motor #331 12-19-1924
45	CNW 101	Pullman	1902	66	56,500	To Electric Trailer #240 12-11-1914
46	CNW 102	Pullman	1902	66	56,500	To Electric Trailer #241 12-15-1914
47	CNW 103	Pullman	1902	66	56,500	To Electric Trailer #242 11-23-1914
48	CNW 104	Pullman	1902	66	56,500	To Electric Trailer #243 11-23-1914
49	CNW 105	Pullman	1902	66	56,500	To Electric Trailer #244 3-10-1915
*50	SF&NP 50	Barney & Smith	1899	68	56,500	To MW 232 3-21-1934
*51	SF&NP 51	Barney & Smith	1899	68	56,500	To MW 233 3-21-1934
*52	SF&NP 52	Barney & Smith	1899	68	56,500	To MW 234 3-21-1934
53	SF&NP 53	Barney & Smith	1899	68	56,500	To MW 248 9-21-1937
54	SF&NP 54	Pullman	1902	67	56,500	To Electric Motor #332 12-29-1924
55	SF&NP 55	Pullman	1902	67	56,500	Retired 1-1-1934
56	SF&NP 56	Pullman	1902	67	56,500	To MW 249 9-21-1937
57	SF&NP 57	Pullman	1902	67	56,500	Retired 10-15-1940
58	SF&NP 58	Barney & Smith	1903	67	56,500	To MW 239 7-26-1934
59	SF&NP 59	Barney & Smith	1903	67	56,500	Retired 1-1-1934
60	SF&NP 60	Barney & Smith	1903	65	56,500	To MW 235 3-21-1934
61	SF&NP 61	Barney & Smith	1903	67	56,500	Retired 10-15-1940
62	No Number Issued					
*63	SF&NP 63	Barney & Smith	1903	66	56,500	Retired 1-1-1934
*64	SF&NP 64	Barney & Smith	1904	65	56,500	To MW 236 3-21-1934
65	SF&NP 65	Barney & Smith	1904	67	56,500	Retired 3-1-1941
66	SF&NP 66	Barney & Smith	1904	67	56,500	Retired 3-1-1941
67	SF&NP 67	Barney & Smith	1904	67	57,900	Retired 10-15-1940
*68	SF&NP 68	Barney & Smith	1904	67	56,500	To MW 237 3-21-1934

Note * - Denotes "smoker"

Cars 2-42, except picnic cars 25-31: oil lamps for lighting; Cars 44-68 Pintsch gas for lighting. Picnic cars 25-31 - no lights. Cars 53, 55, 56, 57, 58, 59, 61, 65, 66 and 67 were converted to electric suburban trailer service in 1923 and electric lighting installed. Disposition as indicated above.

Vacation is over, time to go home, as passengers board afternoon broad gauge train with its open platform cars at Monte Rio. Year 1922.

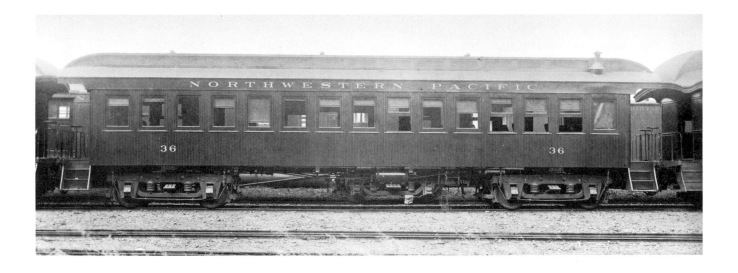

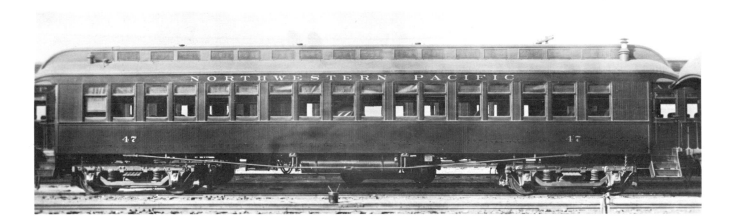

NWP NO.	FORMER NO.	BUILDER	DATE	SEATS	WEIGHT	DISPOSITION
69		American Car & Foundry	1908	73	86,000	To Business Car "Sequoia" #04 3-15-1916
*70		American Car & Foundry	1908	70	86,000	To MW 261 8-16-1941
71		American Car & Foundry	1908	73	86,000	To MW 260 12-10-1940
72		American Car & Foundry	1908	73	86,000	To MW 258 6-21-1940
*73		American Car & Foundry	1908	70	86,000	Retired 1946
74		American Car & Foundry	1908	73	86,000	To MW 254 1-29-1940
*75		American Car & Foundry	1908	70	86,000	Sold 6-10-1941 for scrap
76		American Car & Foundry	1908	73	86,000	To MW 270 8-27-1942
77		American Car & Foundry	1908	73	86,000	To MW 253 6-3-1938
78		American Car & Foundry	1908	73	86,000	To MW 255 1-29-1940
79		American Car & Foundry	1908	73	86,000	To MW 259 10-8-1940
80		American Car & Foundry	1908	73	86,000	To MW 256 1-31-1940
81		American Car & Foundry	1908	73	86,000	To MW 257 1-29-1940
82	SP 1250	St. Louis Car Co.	1907	72	84,600	Returned to SP 5-25-1936
83	SP 1993	Barney & Smith	1903	70	82,000	Returned to SP 4-1-1935
84	SP 1990	Barney & Smith	1903	70	82,300	Returned to SP 4-1-1935
85	SP 1660	St. Louis Car Co.	1907	72	82,900	Returned to SP 5-25-1936
86	SP 1635	St. Louis Car Co.	1907	70	84,800	Returned to SP 5-25-1936
87	SP 1325	Barney & Smith	1900	62	69,300	Returned to SP 4-1-1935
88	SP 1494	Barney & Smith	1903	70	88,200	Returned to SP 4-1-1935
89	SP 1498	Pullman	1902	70	81,300	Returned to SP 4-1-1935
90	SP 1669	St. Louis Car Co.	1907	72	83,000	Returned to SP 4-1-1935
91	SP 1653	St. Louis Car Co.	1907	72	82,900	Returned to SP 4-1-1935
92	SP 1662	St. Louis Car Co.	1907	70	82,900	Returned to SP 4-1-1935
93	SP 1982	Barney & Smith	1903	70	81,000	Returned to SP 4-1-1935
98	SP 1811	American Car & Foundry	1906	60	84,600	Returned to SP 4-1-1935
104	SP 1460	Pullman	1903	59	80,900	Returned to SP 4-1-1935
106	SP 1926	Pullman	1903	59	82,200	Returned to SP 4-1-1935

NOTE: On March 25, 1930, the N.W.P. acquired 25 passenger cars from the Southern Pacific, 12 coaches and 13 chair cars. The 12 coaches were renumbered as above (82-93), but only three chair cars (98-104-106) were renumbered, the rest were returned to the Southern Pacific in 1932 and 1933. Coaches 69-93 and Chair Cars 104 and 106 used Pintsch Gas for lighting. Chair Car No. 98 was electric lighted.

* - indicates "smoker"

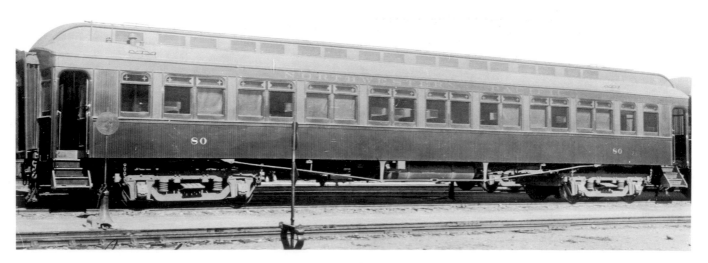

NO.	FORMER NUMBER	BUILDER	DATE	SEATS	WEIGHT	DISPOSITION
110	SF&NW 1	Pac. Lbr.	....	56	54,400	Retired 3-19-1919
111	SF&NW 2	Pac. Lbr.	....	56	41,000	Retired 10-21-1930
112	Ex Combo SF&NW 3	Pac. Lbr.	....	56	41,000	Retired 10-21-1930
113	SF&NW 4	Carter	....	52	36,500	Retired 12-15-1927
114	SF&NW 5	Carter	....	52	36,700	Retired 10-21-1930
115	SF&NW 6	Carter	....	52	35,800	Retired 4-21-1928
116	SF&NW 7	Carter	....	54	35,800	Retired 4-21-1928
117	SF&NW 8	Carter	....	54	35,800	Retired 4-21-1928
118	SF&NW 9; ER&E 4	....	....	54	37,100	To MW 0212 4-27-1916
119	SF&NW 10; ER&E 5	....	....	54	36,900	To MW 0213 4-27-1916
120	SP 1101 - 3	Wason	1869	54	46,000	To Caboose 6200 3-27-1919
121	CP 1105 - 11	C.P. RR	1873	54	46,000	Retired 4-21-1928
122	CP 1110 - 16	Wason	1869	54	46,000	To MW 240 1-4-1936
123	CP 1121 - 29	Wason	1861	54	46,000	To MW 241 1-4-1936
124	CP 1125 - 33	Wason	1868	54	46,000	To MW 242 1-4-1936
125	CP 1158 - 68	Gilbert & Bush	1869	54	46,000	Retired 5-31-1932
150	NWP 720; NS 30; NPC 30	Carter	1893	50	32,000	Retired 2-28-1930
151	NWP 721; NS 31; NPC 31	Carter	1893	50	32,000	Retired 2-28-1930
152	NWP 722; NS 32; NPC 32	Carter	1893	50	32,000	Retired 2-28-1930
153	NWP 723; NS 33; NPC 33	Carter	1893	50	32,000	Retired 2-28-1930
154	NWP 724; NS 34; NPC 34	Carter	1893	50	32,000	Retired 2-20-1930
155	NWP 727; NS 37; NPC 37	Carter	1893	50	32,000	Retired 2-20-1930

NOTE: 110-125; 150-155 had oil lamps for lighting. 150-155 were converted from narrow gauge to broad gauge service in May, 1920, except car No. 151, which was on 9-30-1920.

176	SF&NP 1	Wason	1884	32	40,500	Retired 9-21-1926
177	SF&NP 2	SF&NP	1879	36	42,000	To MW 078 12-31-1930
178	SF&NP 6	Cummings	1874	34	41,000	Retired 5-31-1932
179	SF&NP 39	SF&NP	1889	36	42,000	Retired 5-31-1932
180	SF&NP 41	Carter	1889	34	40,000	Retired 6-15-1936
181	SF&NP 45	Carter	1889	34	40,000	Retired 5-31-1932
182	SF&NP 49	Barney & Smith	1899	40	56,300	Retired 12-23-1927
183	SF&NP 62	Barney & Smith	1903	40	56,500	To Electric Baggage Motor No. 370 4-1923
184	O&E 1	O & E	1907	28	40,800	To Caboose 6201 4-16-1923
185	NWP 359-511; NS 202, NPC 38	Pullman	1897	32	56,500	From Motor 359 6-11-1920 Retired 1-13-1930

NOTE - Numbers 175 - 185 had Oil Lamps for Lighting

203

210	PE&E	478	Pullman	1913	58	70,600	Received from S.P. 1-17-1931
211	PE&E	479	Pullman	1913	58	70,600	Received from S.P. 1-24-1931
212	PE&E	480	Pullman	1913	58	70,600	Received from S.P. 1-23-1931
213	PE&E	481	Pullman	1913	58	73,800	Received from S.P. 12-10-1930
214	PE&E	482	Pullman	1913	58	77,400	Received from S.P. 11-24-1930
215	PE&E	484	Pullman	1913	58	73,100	Received from S.P. 11-24-1930
216	PE&E	485	Pullman	1913	58	73,400	Received from S.P. 10-3-1930
217	PE&E	486	Pullman	1913	58	73,400	Received from S.P. 10-1-1930
218	PE&E	483	Pullman	1913	58	72,800	Received from S.P. 9-26-1930

NOTE: When the Southern Pacific abandoned the Portland, Eugene & Eastern electric service in 1928, these nine cars found their way to the NWP, having been converted to main line passenger service (210-213 at Sacramento shops and 214-218 at Tiburon shops). They were to be used as trailers for the gas-electrics, but after a short time they were assigned to the regular steam-hauled trains to Russian River and Sonoma Valley. These cars were electrically lighted and were dubbed "Kitten Cars" as their ends had the appearance of a kitten. All were returned to the SP on November 1, 1936.

CLOSED VESTIBULE STEEL SMOKING CARS

NO.	BUILDER	DATE	SEATS	WEIGHT	DISPOSITION
400	Pullman	1914	73	101,900	To SP #1004 8-30-1935 To Crew Car 2835 7-26-1956 Sold to Nat. Metals for Scrap 7-3-1957
401	Pullman	1914	73	101,900	To SP #1005 8-30-1935 To Cab 998 4-30-1940 Restored 12-31-1943 To Coach Cab 953 6-17-1954
402	Pullman	1914	73	101,900	To SP #1006 8-30-1935 To Caboose 999 4-30-1940 Restored 1-5-1944 Retired SPdeM 3-24-1947
403	Pullman	1914	73	104,300	To SP #1007 5-25-1935 To FdelP 3-5-1958
404	Pullman	1914	73	104,300	To SP #1008 8-30-1935 To Com. Met. Scrap 7-23-1958
405	Pullman	1914	73	104,300	To SP #1009 5-25-1925 Sold, 1960

NOTE: 400-405 had Pintsch gas for lighting, but were changed to electric after being sold to Southern Pacific.

ABBREVIATIONS: Cab.—Caboose; FdelP—Ferrocarril del Pacific. (Mexico)

CLOSED VESTIBULE STEEL COACHES

NO.	BUILDER	DATE	SEATS	WEIGHT	DISPOSITION
450	Pullman	1914	72	102,400	To SP #1979 7-1-1942 To FdelP 12-21-1951
451	Pullman	1914	72	102,400	To SP #1980 7-1-1942 To FdelP 12-21-1951
452	Pullman	1914	72	102,400	To SP #1981 7-1-1942 Broken Up 4-21-1949
453	Pullman	1914	72	102,400	To MW 6091 9-18-1948; To MW 279 9-29-1952
454	Pullman	1914	72	102,600	To SP 1010 5-24-1935 To Crew Car #2848 6-12-57
455	Pullman	1914	72	102,600	To SP #1011 8-30-1935 Retired 4-1962 - Scrapped
456	Pullman	1914	72	102,600	To SP #1982 7-1-1942 To Safety Inst. Car #147 12-4-1951
457	Pullman	1914	72	102,600	To SP #1983 7-1-1942 To FdelP 12-21-1951
458	Pullman	1914	72	102,600	To SP #1012 8-30-1935 To Ry. & Loco. Hist. Soc. 9-28-65
459	Pullman	1914	72	104,300	To Assoc. Metals Sacramento for Scrap 12-6-1960
460	Pullman	1914	72	104,300	To MW 200 9-15-1957
461	Pullman	1914	72	104,300	To SP #1984 7-1-1942; To FdelP 12-21-1951
462	Pullman	1914	72	104,300	To SP #1013 8-30-1935 Leased to Sonora - Baja California Ry. (Mexico) 1-29-1957
463	Pullman	1914	72	104,300	To SP #1985 7-1-1942 Broken Up 11-29-54
464	Pullman	1914	72	104,300	To SP #1986 7-1-1942 To Caboose 997 12-27-52 Sold to Nat. Metals for Scrap 5-31-1957
465	Pullman	1914	72	104,300	To SP #1014 5-25-1935 Sold - Sonora - Baja California Ry. (Mexico)
466	Pullman	1914	72	104,300	To SP #1987 7-1-1942 Leased to W. T. Cox Spray Co. 12-11-50
467	Pullman	1914	72	104,300	To SP #1988 7-1-1942; To FdelP 12-21-1951
468	Pullman	1914	72	104,300	To SP #1015 12-31-1935 Still Active
469	Pullman	1914	72	104,300	To SP #1016 5-25-1935 To Caboose 954 5-20-1954

NOTE: 450-469 were delivered to use Pintsch Gas for lighting. Some were changed to electric lighting before going over to the Southern Pacific. All were changed to electric lighting on the Southern Pacific. No. 453 however, remained Pintsch gas. No. 459 was the only coach to receive the two tone grey on the N.W.P.

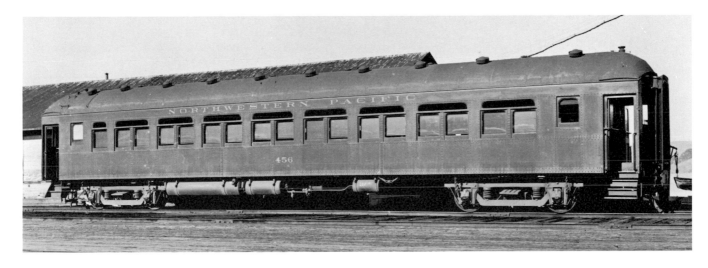

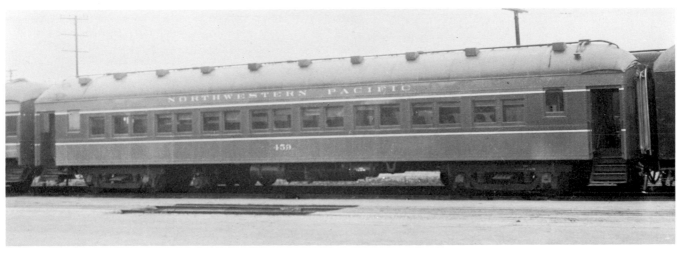

CLOSED VESTIBULE STEEL CHAIR CARS

NO.	BUILDER	DATE	SEATS	WEIGHT	DISPOSITION
550	Pullman	1914	60	105,800	To SP #2688 7-1-1942 To Caboose #955 5-13-1954
551	Pullman	1914	60	105,800	To SP #2689 7-1-1942 To Caboose #999 12-26-1952 Sc. 8-24-1956
552	Pullman	1914	60	105,800	To MW Sold for Scrap 12-6-1960
553	Pullman	1914	60	105,800	To MW Sold for Scrap 12-6-1960

NOTE: 550-553 originally pintsch gas all converted to electric lights. No. 552 only chair car to receive the two tone grey on the N.W.P.

MW — Maintenance of Way.

OBSERVATION CAR — OPEN WOODEN

"MONTESANO" Ex SF&NP Stock Car No. 1228.		36	24,350	From No. 1228, Sept. 1905 To MW 907, Nov. 11, 1908

MAIL, EXPRESS AND BAGGAGE CARS

NO.	FORMER NO.	BUILDER	BUILDER	DATE	WEIGHT	DISPOSITION
600	NWP 1103; SF&NP 10 (Box Car)	OW-Baggage	SF&NP	1887	....	Burned 6-25-1923
601	SF&NP 1	OW-Baggage	Cummings	1869	36,000	Retired 7-7-1923
602	SF&NP 2	OW-Baggage	SF&NP	1884	40,000	Retired 5-31-1932
603	SF&NP 3	OW-Mail & Express	SF&NP	1876	46,000	To MW 238 7-26-1934
604	SF&NP 4	OW-Baggage	SF&NP	1883	42,000	To MW 246 1-24-1936
605	SF&NP 5	OW-Baggage	SF&NP	1892	41,000	Retired 5-31-1932
606	SF&NP 6	OW-Baggage	Pullman	1890	40,000	To MW 251 9-21-1937
607	SF&NP 7	W-Mail & Express	SF&NP	1902	73,500	Retired 5-31-1932
608		W-Baggage	AC&F	1908	79,100	Scrapped 3-17-1941
609		W-Baggage	AC&F	1908	79,100	To MW 252 9-21-1937
610		W-Mail & Express	AC&F	1908	82,300	To MW 247 1-4-1936
611	SF&NW 11	W-Mail & Express	SF&NW	1903	34,700	Retired 5-31-1932 Sold to Sierra Ry. - Movie Use
612	SF&NW 12	W-Mail & Express	SF&NW	1903	37,300	To MW 0208 12-30-1914
613		W-Baggage	AC&F	1911	84,000	Scrapped 1-13-1955
614		W-Baggage	AC&F	1911	84,100	To Nacozari RR 6-14-1954 Scrapped 5-21-1958
615		W-Baggage	AC&F	1911	84,300	To MW 201 2-15-1958
616		W-Baggage & Mail	NWP	1911	87,000	Sold for Scrap 6-10-1941
617		W-Mail & Express	NWP	1911	87,000	To MW 271 10-22-1942
618	No Number issued					
619	NWP 640	S-Baggage	Pullman	1914	99,200	From Mail Car 640 9-11-1950 To MW 202 7-10-1958
620	MW 0253	OW-Baggage	—	1884	26,500	To MW 0115 7-10-1928
625	SP 6259-5291	W-Baggage	S.P.	1901	89,300	From SP 10-23-1931 Returned to S.P. 12-13-1943
626	SP 6260-5301	W-Baggage	S.P.	1901	90,000	From SP 6-9-1931 Returned to S.P. 12-12-1943
627	NS 7; SF&NP Box Car 400	OW-Express	AC&F	1904	34,000	To N.S. 7 7-8-1907 To 627 4-14-1908 Retired 7-31-1914
640		S-Mail & Express	Pullman	1914	99,200	To Baggage 619 9-11-1950
641		S-Mail & Express	Pullman	1914	99,200	To MW 209 6-8-1959
642		S-Mail & Express	Pullman	1914	99,200	To MW 210 6-8-1959
643		S-Mail & Express	Pullman	1914	100,600	To SP 6366 3-22-1943
644		S-Mail & Express	Pullman	1914	100,600	To SP 6367 3-24-1943
645		S-Mail & Express	Pullman	1914	100,600	To SP 6368 3-29-1943
675		S-Baggage	AC&F	1914	93,000	To MW 203 8-12-1957
676		S-Baggage	AC&F	1914	93,000	To MW 206 7-31-1959
677		S-Baggage	AC&F	1914	93,800	To MW 207 11-15-1959
678		S-Baggage	AC&F	1914	93,800	To MW 208 2-6-1960
679		S-Baggage	AC&F	1914	93,800	To MW 204 8-12-1958
680		S-Baggage	AC&F	1914	93,800	To MW 205 12-31-1958

O—Indicates open platform car
W—Indicates Wooden Car
S—Indicates Steel Car

AC&F—American Car and Foundry Co.

Cars built prior to 1908 used oil lamps for lighting - after 1908, pintsch gas.

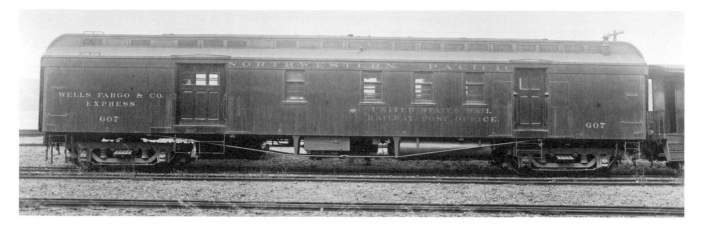

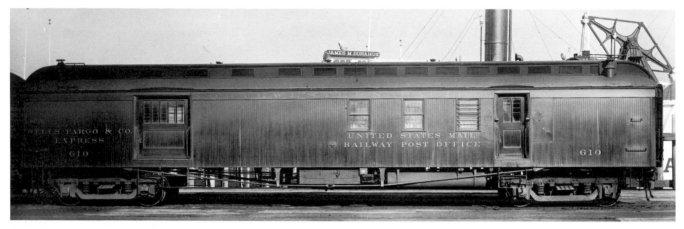

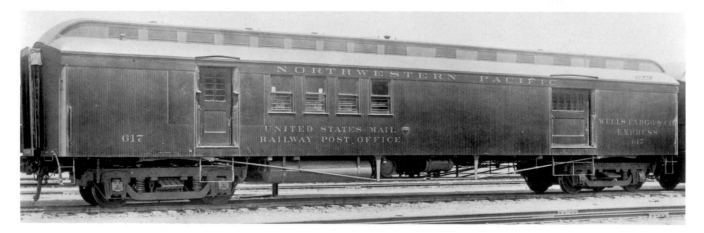

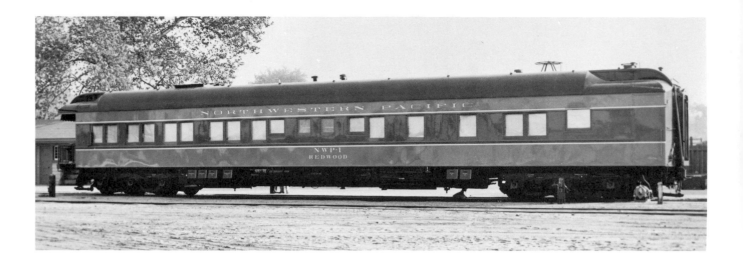

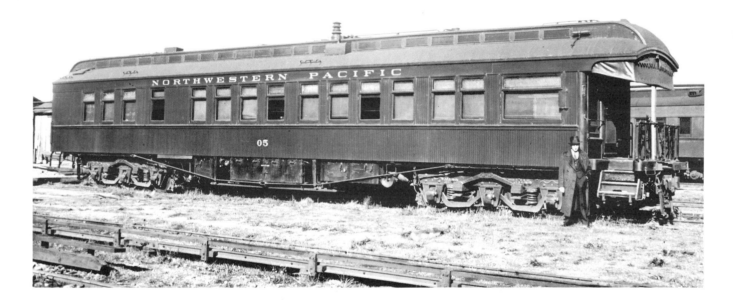

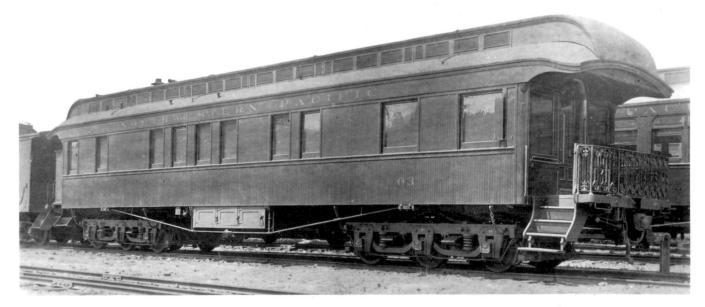

NO.	FORMER NO.	BUILDER	DATE	WEIGHT	DISPOSITION
1	"Redwood" "Balboa"	Pullman	1926	173,760	Purchased by SP 7-12-1954 from Pullman for NWP. Outshopped Sacramento shops 11-4-1954. Returned to S.P.
03	Ex SF&NP "Donahue"	SF&NP	1876	76,900	Retired 1910
04	NWP 69	AC&F	1908	104,000	"Sequoia" to USRA #92 - 1918 & returned. To MW #340 12-26-1946
05	CP 108	Harlan, Hollingsworth	1887	112,900	Sold to SPdeM 9-8-1941
06	T&NO "Victoria" #987-823	Pullman	1916	129,540	To NWP 8-10-1941. Named "Redwood" To MW 211 11-20-1958

NOTE: 03-04-05 were wooden - 1 and 06 steel
SPdeM - Southern Pacific of Mexico
USRA - United States Railroad Administration

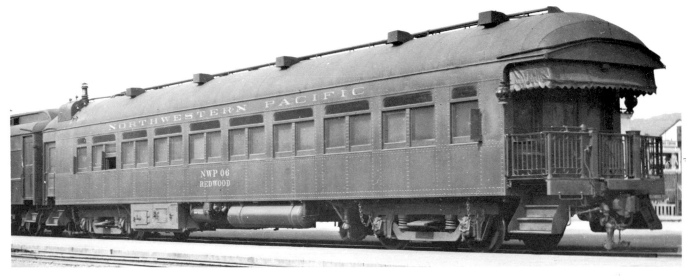

A number of box cars were used in passenger trains on expedited freight service and were distinguished by the "Overnight" paint scheme.

Above, caboose No. 6000 was built by the SF&NP in 1886 as No. 1 and came to the NWP in 1907. No record of disposition.

No. 6007, below, was built in 1905 as logging caboose No. 7. No record of disposition.

OPEN PLATFORM WOODEN TRAILERS

NO.	FORMER NO.	BUILDER	DATE	SEATS	WEIGHT	DISPOSITION
201	NS 101	St. Louis Car Co.	1902	66	46,440	Retired 12-19-1930
202	NS 102	North Shore RR	1902	66	46,440	Retired 12-19-1930
203	NS 103	St. Louis Car Co.	1902	66	46,440	Retired 12-19-1930
204	NS 104	St. Louis Car Co.	1902	66	46,440	To Motor #327 3-20-1915
205	NS 105	St. Louis Car Co.	1902	66	46,440	To Motor #328 3-20-1915
206	NS 106	St. Louis Car Co.	1902	66	46,440	To Motor #321 3-27-1914
207	NS 107	St. Louis Car Co.	1902	66	46,440	To Motor #322 3-24-1914
208	NS 108	St. Louis Car Co.	1902	66	46,440	To Motor #323 2-20-1914
209	NS 109	St. Louis Car Co.	1902	66	46,440	To Motor #324 3-31-1914
210	NS 110	St. Louis Car Co.	1902	66	46,440	To Motor #325 4-14-1914
211	NS 111	St. Louis Car Co.	1902	66	46,440	To Motor #326 3-3-1914
212	NS 112	St. Louis Car Co.	1902	66	46,440	To Motor #320 11-11-1913
213		St. Louis Car Co.	1908	66	56,000	To Motor #319 9-1-1913
214		St. Louis Car Co.	1908	66	56,000	To Motor #317 5-28-1912
215		St. Louis Car Co.	1908	66	56,000	To Motor #318 5-28-1912
216		St. Louis Car Co.	1908	66	56,000	To Motor #316 9-30-1911
217		St. Louis Car Co.	1908	66	56,000	To Motor #314 4-10-1911
218		St. Louis Car Co.	1908	66	56,000	To Motor #315 4-10-1911
219		St. Louis Car Co.	1908	66	56,000	To Motor #312 5-11-1910
220		St. Louis Car Co.	1908	66	56,000	To Motor #313 5-11-1910
221	NS 401-38; NPC 38	Pullman	1897	66	43,600	Retired 10-1-1924
222	NS 402-39; NPC 39	Pullman	1897	66	43,600	Retired 10-21-1924
223	NS 403-40; NPC 40	Pullman	1897	66	43,600	Retired 9-1-1924
224	NS 404-41; NPC 41	Pullman	1897	66	43,600	Retired 9-1-1924
225	NWP 725; NS 35; NPC 35	Pullman	1897	58	43,000	Retired 9-1-1924
226	NWP 726; NS 36; NPC 36	Pullman	1897	58	42,640	Retired 9-1-1924
227	NWP 309; NS 203	Pullman	1897	50	42,600	To Caboose 6202 7-10-1924
228	(No Number issued)					
229	(No Number issued)					
230	NWP 39; SF&NP 44	Carter	1889	62	39,400	Destroyed by fire 12-19-1930
231	NWP 40; SF&NP 46	Carter	1889	62	39,400	Retired 12-31-1930
232	NWP 41; SF&NP 48	Carter	1889	62	39,400	Retired 12-31-1930
233	NWP 42; SF&NP 47	Carter	1889	62	39,400	Retired 12-31-1930
234	NWP 22; SF&NP 22	Wason	1885	62	40,500	Retired 12-31-1930
235	NWP 21; SF&NP 21	Wason	1885	62	40,500	Retired 12-31-1930
236	NWP 19; SF&NP 19	Wason	1885	62	40,500	Retired 12-31-1930
237	NWP 18; SF&NP 18	Wason	1884	62	40,500	Retired 12-31-1930
238	NWP 17; SF&NP 17	Wason	1884	62	40,500	Retired 12-31-1930
239	NWP 20; SF&NP 20	Wason	1885	62	40,500	Burned 2-24-1921
240	NWP 45; CNW 101	Pullman	1902	66	56,500	To Motor 329 5-31-1923
241	NWP 46; CNW 102	Pullman	1902	66	56,500	To Motor #330 7-1-1923
242	NWP 47; CNW 103	Pullman	1902	66	56,500	To Motor #333 11-1-1924
243	NWP 48; CNW 104	Pullman	1902	66	56,500	To Motor #334 11-1-1924
244	NWP 49; CNW 105	Pullman	1902	66	56,500	To Motor #335 11-1-1924

NOTE: Cars 221, 222, 223 and 224 were converted from narrow gauge coaches in 1904; Cars 225 and 226 were converted from narrow gauge coaches in 1910; Car 227 was converted from narrow gauge coach in 1904 to NS Motor 203. Went to NWP 309 in 1908 and to Trailer No. 227 in 1911. Cars 230-239 were converted from steam train coaches to electric in 1911, and 240-244 were converted in 1914.

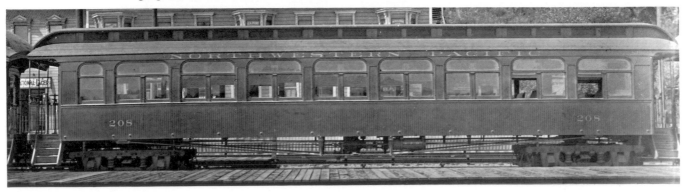

VESTIBULE STEEL TRAILERS

NO.	BUILDER	DATE	SEATS	WEIGHT	DISPOSITION
250	St. Louis Car Co.	1929	103	79,000	To P.E. #4512 4-22-1942
251	St. Louis Car Co.	1929	103	79,000	To P.E. #4513 4-22-1942
252	St. Louis Car Co.	1929	103	79,000	To P.E. #4514 4-22-1942
253	St. Louis Car Co.	1929	103	79,000	To P.E. #4515 4-13-1942
254	St. Louis Car Co.	1929	103	79,000	To P.E. #4516 4-13-1942
255	St. Louis Car Co.	1929	103	79,000	To P.E. #4517 4-13-1942
256	St. Louis Car Co.	1929	103	79,000	To P.E. #4518 4-13-1942

Cars 250-256 were owned by the Southern Pacific. Car 254 became Pacific Electric No. 303, and later Metropolitan Transit 303 and 1502. Operated the last day of rail interurban transportation, Los Angeles—Long Beach Sunday, April 9, 1961.

VESTIBULED STEEL MOTORS

NO.	BUILDER	DATE	SEATS	WEIGHT	DISPOSITION
375	St. Louis Car Co.	1929	98	111,200	To P.E. #4500 4-13-1942
376	St. Louis Car Co.	1929	98	111,200	To P.E. #4501 4-13-1942
377	St. Louis Car Co.	1929	98	111,200	To P.E. #4502 4-13-1942
378	St. Louis Car Co.	1929	98	111,200	To P.E. #4503 4-13-1942
379	St. Louis Car Co.	1929	98	111,200	To P.E. #4504 4-13-1942
380	St. Louis Car Co.	1930	98	111,900	To P.E. #4505 4-13-1942
381	St. Louis Car Co.	1930	98	111,900	To P.E. #4506 4-13-1942
382	St. Louis Car Co.	1930	98	111,900	To P.E. #4507 4-22-1942
383	St. Louis Car Co.	1930	98	111,900	To P.E. #4508 4-22-1942
384	St. Louis Car Co.	1930	98	111,900	To P.E. #4509 4-13-1942
385	St. Louis Car Co.	1930	98	111,900	To P.E. #4510 4-13-1942
386	St. Louis Car Co.	1930	98	111,900	To P.E. #4511 4-22-1942

(375-386 owned by Southern Pacific)

301	NS 301		St. Louis Car Co.	1902	64	65,200	To MW 243 3-16-1936
302	NS 302		St. Louis Car Co.	1902	70	65,200	Retired 3-1-1941
303	NS 303		North Shore RR	1902	70	65,200	To MW 268 1-17-1942
304	NS 304		North Shore RR	1902	70	65,200	Retired 3-1-1941
305	NS 305		North Shore RR	1902	68	65,200	To MW 269 1-17-1942
306	NS 306		North Shore RR	1902	64	65,200	To MW 244 1-11-1936
307	NS 307		North Shore RR	1902	70	65,200	Retired 3-1-1941
308	NS 308		North Shore RR	1902	64	65,200	Burned - Retired 8-6-1913
309	NS 203; NPC Coach		Pullman	1897	50	58,320	To Trailer #227 4-20-1911
310			St. Louis Car Co.	1908	70	70,600	Retired 3-1-1941
311			St. Louis Car Co.	1908	70	70,600	Retired 3-1-1941
312	NWP 219		St. Louis Car Co.	1908	68	75,100	Retired 3-1-1941
313	NWP 220		St. Louis Car Co.	1908	68	75,100	To MW 262 3-28-1941
314	NWP 217		St. Louis Car Co.	1908	68	75,100	Retired 3-1-1941
315	NWP 218		St. Louis Car Co.	1908	68	75,100	Retired 3-1-1941
316	NWP 216		St. Louis Car Co.	1908	68	75,100	Retired 3-1-1941
317	NWP 214		St. Louis Car Co.	1908	68	75,100	Retired 3-1-1941
318	NWP 215		St. Louis Car Co.	1908	68	75,100	Retired 3-1-1941
319	NWP 213		St. Louis Car Co.	1908	68	75,100	Retired 3-1-1941
320	NWP 212; NS 112		St. Louis Car Co.	1902	68	65,500	To MW 245 2-5-1936
321	NWP 206; NS 106		St. Louis Car Co.	1902	68	65,500	Retired 3-1-1941
322	NWP 207; NS 107		St. Louis Car Co.	1902	68	65,500	Retired 3-1-1941
323	NWP 208; NS 108		St. Louis Car Co.	1902	68	65,500	To MW 250 5-14-1937
324	NWP 209; NS 109		St. Louis Car Co.	1902	68	65,500	Retired 3-31-1939
325	NWP 210; NS 110		St. Louis Car Co.	1902	68	65,500	Retired 3-1-1941
326	NWP 211; NS 111		St. Louis Car Co.	1902	68	65,500	Retired 3-1-1941
327	NWP 204; NS 104		St. Louis Car Co.	1902	68	65,500	Retired 3-1-1941
328	NWP 205; NS 105		St. Louis Car Co.	1902	68	65,500	Retired 3-31-1939
329	NWP 240-45; CNW 101		Pullman	1902	67	75,000	To MW 263 9-12-1941
330	NWP 241-46; CNW 102		Pullman	1902	67	75,000	To MW 264 9-24-1941
331	NWP 44; CNW 100		Pullman	1902	70	75,000	Retired 3-1-1941
332	NWP 54; SF&NP 54		Pullman	1902	74	75,000	Retired 3-1-1941
333	NWP 242-47; CNW 103		Pullman	1902	70	75,000	To MW 265 8-23-1941
334	NWP 243-48; CNW 104		Pullman	1902	70	75,000	Retired 3-1-1941
335	NWP 244-49; CNW 105		Pullman	1902	70	75,000	To MW 266 9-22-1941

VESTIBULED WOODEN COMBINATION MAIL, EXPRESS, BAGGAGE & PASSENGER MOTORS

NO.	FORMER NUMBER	BUILDER	DATE	SEATS	WEIGHT	DISPOSITION
350	NWP 501; NS 501	St. Louis Car Co.	1902	36	65,200	From 501 12-16-1913 Retired 5-31-1932
351	NWP 502; NS 502	St. Louis Car Co.	1902	56	65,200	From 502 2-18-1914 Retired 5-31-1932
352	NWP 503; NS 503	St. Louis Car Co.	1902	36	65,200	From 503 1-28-1914 Retired 5-31-1932
353	NWP 504; NS 504	St. Louis Car Co.	1902	56	65,200	From 504 2-10-1914 Retired 5-31-1932
354	NWP 505; NS 505	St. Louis Car Co.	1902	36	65,200	From 505 1-13-1914 To MW 3-28-1941
355	NWP 506; NS 506	St. Louis Car Co.	1902	36	65,200	From 506 1-20-1914 Retired 5-31-1932
356	NWP 507; NS 507	St. Louis Car Co.	1902	36	65,200	From 507 3-9-1914 Retired 3-1-1941
357	NWP 508; NS 508	St. Louis Car Co.	1902	36	65,200	From 508 1-20-1914 Retired 5-31-1932
358	NWP 509; NS 509	St. Louis Car Co.	1902	36	65,200	From 509 4-14-1914 Retired 5-31-1932
....	NWP 510; NS 201	Pullman	1897	32	57,600	Converted from NPC narrow gauge car in 1904. Wrecked & burned-Retired 8-6-1913
359	NWP 511; NS 202	Pullman	1897	32	57,600	Converted from NPC narrow gauge car in 1904. From 511 12-9-1913 To Main line Combo #185 6-11-1920
360	NWP 512	St. Louis Car Co.	1908	36	73,900	From 512 5-2-1914 Retired 5-31-1932
361	NWP 513	St. Louis Car Co.	1908	36	73,900	From 513 3-5-1914 Burned 2-24-1921

WOODEN BAGGAGE AND MAIL MOTOR

NO.	FORMER NUMBER	BUILDER	DATE	SEATS	WEIGHT	DISPOSITION
370	NWP 183; SF&NP 62	Barney & Smith	1903	....	56,300	Retired 3-1-1941

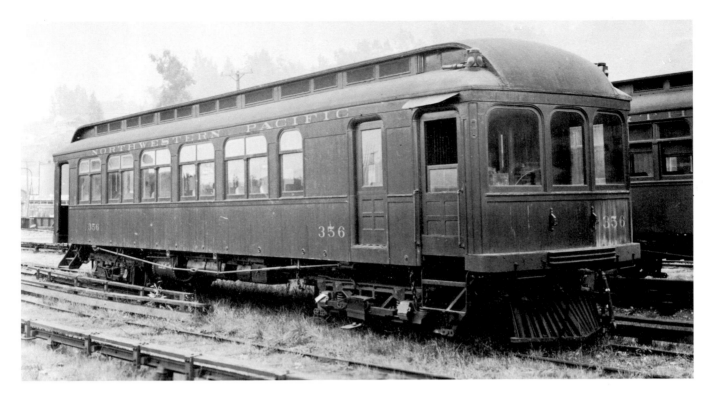

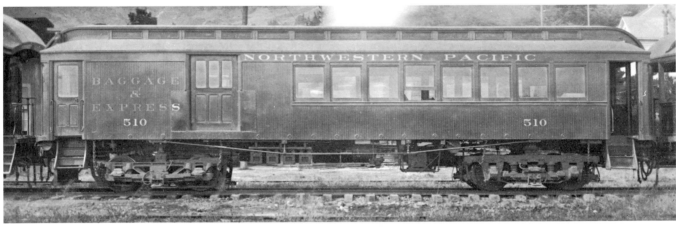

Opening day of broad gauge electric service to Mill Valley, August 20, 1903.

Three-Car train arriving Mill Valley.

Car 370 and three others near Escalle.

Mail for Corte Madera.

Leaving Sausalito, a five car wooden train skirts Richardson's Bay opposite Pine station.

224

A northbound electric train just north of Kentfield. Notice the four rails - narrow and broad gauge, plus forth rail for power.

With "combo" No. 354 in the lead, a three-car train speeds along between Waldo and Manzanita.

Near Escalle.

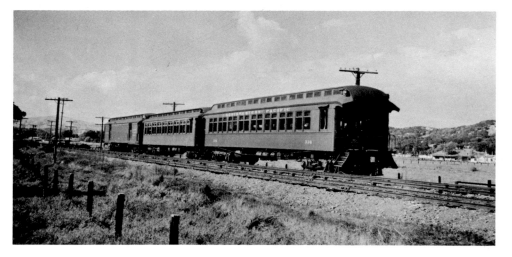

A one-car electric motor takes off from Manor enroute to the Sausalito ferry slip.

Motor No. 318 catches on fire due to a short circuit.

San Anselmo, where trains branched out to Manor and San Rafael.

A five-car special made up of
steel cars speeds along south
of Kentfield. Yes, Marin County
DID have excellent rapid transit at one time.

Mill Valley train stops at
Locust Avenue.

San Rafael-bound from San
Anselmo.

Three car train quietly and fumelessly zips by Pine station.

South Portal of Tunnel No. 1, near Alto. Tunnel was single track, while on either side there were double tracks.

A one-car steel train at the High School station on the Mill Valley line.

228

Wouldn't North Bay commuters welcome this sight again? Fast, comfortable electric cars and pleasant station surroundings. Ross.

Just out of the paint shop at Tiburon. Built to last thirty years or more, these cars were in service on the Northwestern Pacific for only twelve years.

WOODEN COACHES – OPEN PLATFORM

NWP NO.	FORMER NUMBER	BUILDER	DATE	SEATS	WEIGHT	DISPOSITION
701	NWP 6, SPC 5	Carter	1874	46	21,700	Retierd 5-28-1930
702	NWP 7; NS 7; NPC 7	Kimball	1875	33	28,000	Retired 10-5-1923
703	NS 8; NPC 8	Kimball	1875	37	28,000	Sold N-C-O 8-29-1909
704	NWP 10; SPC 8	Carter	1874	46	21,700	Retired 5-28-1930
705	NWP 11; SPC 15	Carter	1874	46	22,500	To MW 027 8-29-1924
706	NWP 12; NS 12; NPC 12	Kimball	1882	31	27,000	To MW 028 8-29-1924
707	NS 13; NPC 13	Carter	1882	48	48,500	Retired 5-28-1930
708	NS 14; NPC 14	Kimball	1882	33	28,000	To MW 029 8-29-1924
709	NS 15; NPC 15	Barney & Smith	1882	39	28,500	To MW 031 8-29-1924
710	NS 17; NPC 17	Barney & Smith	1882	39	28,500	Retired 11-24-1924
711	NS 18; NPC 18	Barney & Smith	1882	44	29,000	Retired 7-5-1923
712	NS 19; NPC 19	Barney & Smith	1882	44	29,000	Retired 7-5-1923
*713	NS 22; NPC 22	Pullman	1893	50	30,500	Sold to White Pass & Yukon 3-29-1930
*714	NS 23; NPC 23	Pullman	1893	50	30,500	Retired 5-28-1930
*715	NWP 24; SPC 29	Carter	1879	40	21,700	To MW 032 8-29-1924
*716	NS 26; NPC 26	Pullman	1893	50	30,500	Sold to White Pass & Yukon 3-29-1930
*717	NS 27; NPC 27	Pullman	1893	50	30,500	Retired 5-28-1930
718	NWP 28; SPC 51	Carter	1883	46	21,700	Retired 5-28-1930
719	NS 29; NPC 29	Kimball	1874	50	29,500	Retired 5-28-1930
720	NS 30; NPC 30	Carter	1893	50	32,500	To #150 Broad Gauge 5-1920
721	NS 31; NPC 31	Carter	1893	50	32,000	To #151 Broad Gauge 9-30-1920
722	NS 32; NPC 32	Carter	1893	50	32,000	To #152 Broad Gauge 5-1920
723	NS 33; NPC 33	Carter	1893	50	32,000	To #153 Broad Gauge 5-1920
724	NS 34; NPC 34	Carter	1893	50	32,000	To #154 Broad Gauge 5-1920
725	NS 35; NPC 35	Pullman	1897	58	33,500	To Electric Trailer #225 6-30-1910
726	NS 36; NPC 36	Pullman	1897	58	35,500	To Electric Trailer #226 6-30-1910
727	NS 37; NPC 37	Pullman	1897	58	35,500	To Broad Gauge #155 5-1920
728	NWP 38; SPC 65	Harlan	1887	50	24,300	Sold to White Pass & Yukon 4-11-1928
729	NWP 39; SPC 74	Carter	1887	46	25,500	Retired 5-28-1930
730	SPC 14	Carter	1878	50	21,700	Retired 5-28-1930
731	SPC 59	Carter	1883	46	25,900	Sold to White Pass & Yukon 2-19-1927
732	SPC 1011	Carter	1884	46	24,900	Sold to White Pass & Yukon 2-19-1927
733	MW 1062; NWP 853; NS 5; NPC 5	Hammond	1888	34	21,700	Retired 6-6-1919 * Indicates Smoker.

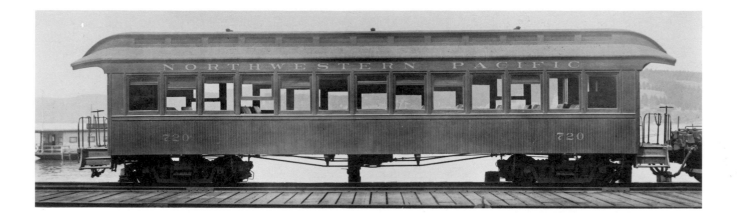

COMBINATION WOODEN OPEN PLATFORM CARS

801	NS 3; NPC 3	Kimball	1872	28	27,000	Retired 7-5-1923
802	NS 20; NPC 20	Carter	1887	22	28,500	To MW 033 8-29-1924
803	NS 21; NPC 21	Kimball	1887	32	29,000	Retired 5-28-1930
804	SPC 62	Carter	1883	28	23,200	Retired 11-15-1926
805	SPC 72	Carter	1887	26	26,700	Sold Northern Redwood Co. 1-27-1928

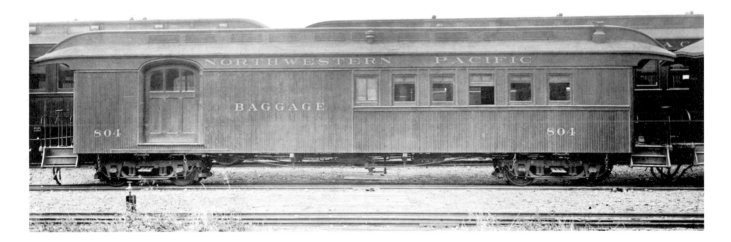

NWP NO.	FORMER NUMBER	BUILDER	DATE	SEATS	WEIGHT	DISPOSITION
825	NS 42; NPC 42	N.P.C.	1895	60	25,000	Retired 5-21-1914
826	NS 43; NPC 43	N.P.C.	1895	60	25,000	To MW 1063 10-15-1908
827	NS 44; NPC 44	N.P.C.	1895	60	25,000	To Lunch Car (MW) 5-2-1914
828	NS 45; NPC 45	N.P.C.	1895	60	25,000	To MW 1064 10-15-1908
839	NS 1247; NS 47; NPC 47	N.P.C.	1895	38	13,000	To Lunch Car (MW) 11-20-1914
840	NS 1249; NS 49; NPC 49	N.P.C.	1895	38	13,000	To Lunch Car (MW) 11-20-1914
841	NS 1251; NS 51; NPC 51	N.P.C.	1895	38	13,000	To MW 1065 10-15-1908
842	NS 1255; NS 55; NPC 55	N.P.C.	1895	38	13,000	Scrapped 10-28-1912
843	NS 1257; NS 57; NPC 57	N.P.C.	1895	38	13,000	Scrapped 10-31-1912
844	NS 1259; NS 59; NPC 59	N.P.C.	1895	38	13,000	Sold for Scrap 3-23-1923
845	NS 1261; NS 61; NPC 61	N.P.C.	1895	38	13,000	Scrapped 10-28-1912
846	NS 1263; NS 63; NPC 63	N.P.C.	1895	38	13,000	Scrapped 3-23-1923
847	NS 1265; NS 65; NPC 65	N.P.C.	1895	38	13,000	Scrapped 10-24-1912
848	NS 1267; NS 67; NPC 67	N.P.C.	1895	38	13,000	To MW 1053 10-15-1908
849	NS 1273; NS 73; NPC 73	N.P.C.	1895	38	13,000	Scrapped 10-28-1912

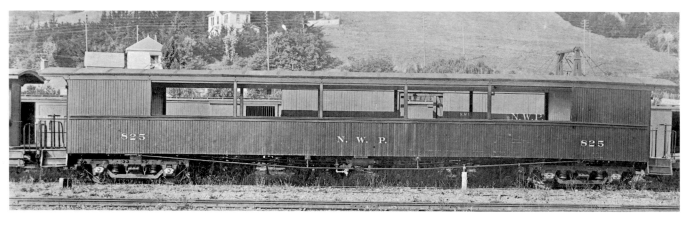

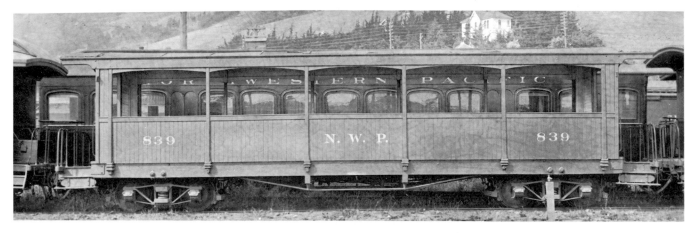

NOTE: North Shore baggage Car No. 8, and former South Pacific Coast coaches 9, 16 and 25, were destroyed by fire at the Sausalito paint shop on September 26, 1907 before being re-stenciled into the N.W.P. numbering system. — Ten cars came from the South Pacific Coast to the North Shore in 1906, but retained their original numbers and lettering until numbered into the N.W.P. roster in 1907.

SECOND CLASS WOODEN COACHES — OPEN PLATFORM

NWP NO.	FORMER NUMBER	BUILDER	DATE	SEATS	WEIGHT	DISPOSITION
851	NS 2; NPC 2	Hammond	1888	42	26,500	To MW 1060 10-15-1908
852	NS 4; NPC 4	Hammond	1888	48	26,500	To MW 1061 10-15-1908
853	NS 5; NPC 5	Hammond	1888	40	26,500	To MW 1062 10-15-1908
						Rebuilt later to Coach 733

| 01 | NS 01; NPC 01 | 1874 | .... | 27,500 | "Club Car" Retired around 1910 |
| 02 | NS 02; NPC 02 | 1892 | .... | 32,000 | "Millwood" Retired in 1923 |

Narrow Gauge Caboose No. 6100 was built in 1877 by the North Pacific Coast Railroad as 2001. Became NWP in 1907 and was renumbered to 5590 around 1915. It remained in existence until the narrow gauge lines were abandoned in 1930.

237

GAS ELECTRICS   (Broad Gauge)

NO.	FORMER NO.	BUILDER	DATE	SEATS	WEIGHT	DISPOSITION
900	Visalia Electric #450	Gen Elect.	1912	73	100,600	In Service NWP 6-14-1921 Sold to S.P. 12-5-1938
901		Pullman	1930	34	158,400	To S.P. #12 6-12-1935
902		Pullman	1930	34	158,400	To S.P. #13 6-9-1935
903		Brill	1930	34	173,820	To S.P. #14 5-6-1941 To P.E. 1648 4-27-1944
904		Brill	1930	34	173,820	To S.P. #15 6-1-1941 To P.E. 1649 4-27-1944
SP 7		Brill	1929	54	166,820	Leased 4-30-1941; Returned 3-13-1942
SP 11		Brill	1930	54	167,500	Leased 4-22-1941; Returned 3-13-1942
SP 10	(Budd Car)	Budd	1954	89	112,660	Rail Diesel Car—RCD Motor Coach Seat Capacity to 68 when Express Compartment added, May, 1959. Leased from S.P. 5-25-1959.

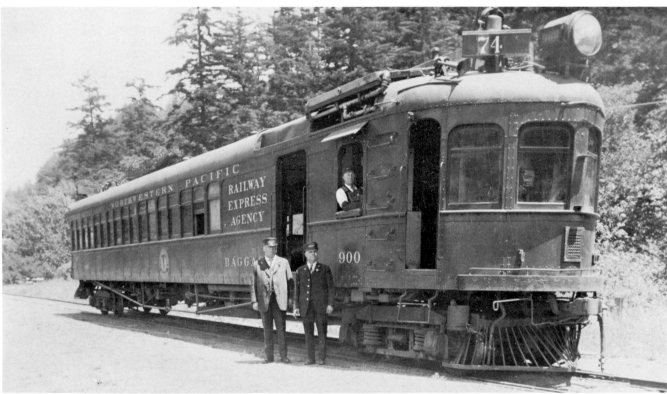

During the last years of operation of the Point Reyes branch, which had been converted from narrow to broad gauge in 1920, some of the passenger assignments were held down by gas electric cars. No. 74 was the daily-except-Sunday run from Manor to Lagunitas.

Gas-electric No. 904 on Train No. 2, the Eureka Passenger, at Willits in 1931. Ahead lies the 145-mile scenic trip along the Eel River to Eureka.

N.W.P. 903

THE J.G. BRILL CO.
ORDER 22789
PHOTO 11974

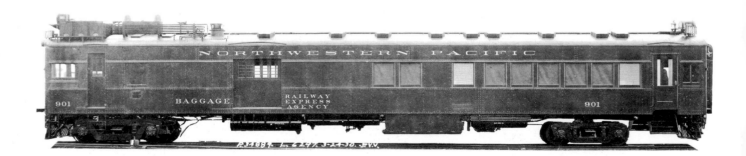

FERRY BOATS

On May 10, 1868, the little single-ended ferry "Princess," under the banner of the Saucelito Land & Ferry Company, backed out of San Francisco's ferry terminal, then located at Meigg's Wharf, and set its bow for Saucelito, thus starting the first regular ferry service to the Redwood Empire. Actually this company was more interested in the real estate it had to sell on the Marin County side of the Golden Gate, and it went into the ferry business only to transport new landowners to and from San Francisco. The company also had an oversized steam launch "Diana," which substituted for the "Princess" whenever the latter was laid up for repairs.

The North Pacific Coast Railroad took over the Land & Ferry Company, but not the boats, when it started service on January 7, 1875. The North Pacific Coast had purchased the "Petaluma" and renamed her the "Petaluma of Saucelito" for its service between Saucelito and San Francisco. This boat was later renamed "Tamalpais" (Number 1). When the North Pacific Coast Railroad acquired the San Rafael & San Quentin Railroad by lease on March 11, 1875, the ferries "Clinton" and "Contra Costa," which earlier had been operating on the ferry route from San Francisco to Haystack Landing for Minturn's Petaluma & Haystack Railroad venture, were also taken into the North Pacific Coast fold.

In 1877, the N.P.C. built the "San Rafael" along with a sister ship, the "Saucelito" (Number 1). Disaster struck the ferry operation with the sinking of the "Clinton" by the "Petaluma of Saucelito" on October 27, 1877, and the burning of the "Saucelito" at San Quentin wharf on February 25, 1884. With the remaining boats the line could not give the service to both Saucelito and San Quentin, so the San Quentin service was discontinued. In 1894, the larger "Sausalito" was built, and in 1901 the larger "Tamalpais" was placed in operation. Before the latter two boats were placed in service, the North Pacific Coast often borrowed the "Bay City" from the South Pacific Coast Railroad on Sundays and holidays to handle the picnic and excursion crowds. Even the old "Amador" of the Southern Pacific was occasionally pressed into service.

With the little single-enders now going out of the picture and more and more commuters living in Marin County, the narrow gauge, under the new name of North Shore, built its last boats: the ferry "Cazadero" in 1903, and the carfloat "Lagunitas," which was a stern-wheeler and handled narrow gauge freight cars. In 1908 she was changed to a broad gauge car float.

The broad gauge operations of the San Francisco & North Pacific Railroad officially started with the secondhand "Antelope" between San Francisco and Donahue Landing on July 9, 1871. In 1875, a larger single-end side-wheeler was built, the "James M. Donahue." In 1884, the larger double-ender "Tiburon" was added, when the terminus of the railroad was moved to Tiburon. This vessel was badly damaged by fire on January 1, 1893, while at the ferry slip in San Francisco. The total cost of rebuilding the steamer was $38,274.73. The huge combination ferry and carfloat "Ukiah" was built in 1890, and began service on January 8, 1891. The steamer was used extensively by the road on Sundays and holidays as a picnic craft. So that the ladies would not trip and fall while boarding the ferry, rope hawsers were laid in the flange grooves of the rails on the lower deck. Because of the heavy service this steamer performed in World War I carrying overloaded freight cars, she became dangerous to operate, so stripped to the hull, this ferry was rebuilt in 1922 and renamed the "Eureka." The new boat was called a "floating palace" and could carry 3,330 passengers. It was the largest ferry ever to operate on San Francisco Bay. When the ferry service to Sausalito ended on Friday, February 28, 1941, it was the "Eureka" that made the last run, leaving the Ferry Building at 11:25 p.m. The next day she made a special trip for some 2,500 invited guests, leaving Sausalito at 12:30 p.m., San Francisco at 1:15 p.m., and taking a tour of the bay. Six veteran ferry skippers took turns operating the boat during the farewell ride. However, it was not the end for the "Eureka." She was transferred to the Southern Pacific, who placed her in operation between San Francisco and Oakland Pier to connect with main line trains. The boat carried on faithfully throughout the years, but on September 30, 1956, the Southern Pacific reduced its passenger service to a one hour and twenty minute headway with the requirement of only one boat - the "Berkeley." The "Eureka" was relegated to standby service. While in substitute service one evening the famous boat broke a crank shaft pin. Repairs were too costly, so the days of the ferries with the "walking beams" were at an end.

When the Northwestern Pacific came into being on January 8, 1907, the following boats were on the marine roster: "James M. Donahue," "Tamalpais," "Sausalito," "Tiburon," "Cazadero" and the carfloats "Ukiah" and "Lagunitas."

In 1909 the Northwestern Pacific added the small "Requa" to the fleet for the Sausalito-Tiburon service, as the "James M. Donahue" was too large for the amount of patronage received. The "Requa" burned to the water line in 1911 and was rebuilt and renamed "Marin."

The early twenties saw the ferries starting to disappear from the scene, and the roster dropped to three boats in the early thirties: the "Eureka," "Tamalpais," and "Cazadero." This was the required number to maintain service, and if one needed repairs a boat was borrowed from the Southern Pacific (in rare instances, the Santa Fe). It was "anything that was available," but usually it was the ex-Western Pacific "Sierra Nevada," known as the fastest boat on the bay. The steamer could clip ten minutes from the standard crossing time of 32 minutes.

It all came to an end on February 28, 1941, when the last segment of electric service to Marin County was abandoned.

Another phase in the life of the Northwestern Pacific ferries was that of the auto boats. With the advent of the auto and the pressure for service, the N.W.P. loaded four autos on the front and six on the after end of each boat. The road was not prone to run additional service, and when the last boat left that was that, leaving many a motorist or horse and buggy waiting at either end until the next morning. After a hard battle, a wide-awake group, known as the Golden Gate Ferry Company, won permission to start service from Sausalito to San Francisco, foot of Hyde Street. From the opening day, May 28, 1922, with the little ferry "Aven J. Hanford" on the initial run, business boomed. The Golden Gate Ferries massed a fleet that gave service "as fast as the boats are loaded" and "all night" if necessary. The N.W.P. management was stunned, and wanting to get into the new lucrative auto trade themselves ordered three large, beautiful boats: "Redwood Empire," "Santa Rosa" and the "Mendocino," which were delivered in 1927. However, the motoring public with long memories, would rather wait in line for the Golden Gate ferries than use the N.W.P. boats. In May, 1929, the Southern Pacific, Northwestern Pacific and the Golden Gate Ferry Company operations were merged to form the largest auto ferry system in the world. But while the ferries were enjoying a tremendous patronage, a shadow of doom was forming just over the hill - the Golden Gate Bridge. When the bridge was opened for traffic May 28, 1937, the auto business diminished almost to nothing. On July 24, 1938, the direct service from Sausalito to Hyde street, San Francisco, was discontinued. The regular boats, though, still hauled autos until the boats' demise on February 28, 1941.

Pulling carts of the San Rafael was the job assigned to a horse named "Dick." The animal was permanently assigned to the vessel, and had a stall on the lower deck.

Left, the EUREKA. Rebuilt from the Ukiah in 1922, the Eureka was the largest ferry to operate on San Francisco Bay. It had a capacity of 3330 passengers and 100 automobiles. It ended the ferry service for the Northwestern Pacific on February 28, 1941, and was donated by the Southern Pacific to the San Francisco Maritime Museum, October 23, 1957. Dedicated by the California Division of Beaches and Parks as part of the San Francisco Maritime Historical Monument, October 2, 1963.

The TAMALPAIS, the second boat of that name, was built in 1901, a product of the San Francisco Union Iron Works. It was the first oil-burning ferry on the Bay, was well liked by passengers, and was in service until N.W.P. ferry operations were abandoned.

Built by John W. Dickie shipyards, Alameda, in 1903, the CAZADERO was named for the northermost point on the narrow gauge line.

The first ferry in service for the North Pacific Coast Railroad between San Francisco and Sausalito was the original TAMALPAIS.

The SAN RAFAEL, with its benches upholstered in deep red velvet, was the word in ferry luxury when this steamer was put into service on August 11, 1877. Twenty-four years later it went to the bottom of the bay after a collision with the Sausalito. The SAUCELITO was a sister ship to the San Rafael. The parts for both were shipped in 239 freight cars from New York and were reassembled in San Francisco. The Saucelito went into service on October 16, 1877. Seven years later it burned to the water's edge at San Quentin.

Located almost eight miles from Petaluma, down Petaluma Creek, was the rail terminal of the San Francisco & North Pacific - Donahue Landing. Here the ferry ANTELOPE in the year 1878 awaits a train load of passengers before departing on the thirty-four mile, two-hour trip to San Francisco.

The North Pacific Coast Railroad had the only "sidewheel" tug on the Bay. Photo shows the tug TIGER and a car float taking cars from Sausalito to San Francisco about the year 1900.

San Francisco & North Pacific ferry JAMES M. DONAHUE at San Francisco slip in 1910.

The three boats pictured on these pages were the last built for the Northwestern Pacific. All were built in 1927 to handle auto traffic across the Golden Gate. Above, the MENDOCINO makes a trial trip before being turned over to the NWP by the builder, Union Iron Works.

Electrically equipped throughout, the SANTA ROSA joined the fleet the latter part of 1927. Twelve years later the bridges had taken their toll and this ferry was sold to the Puget Sound Navigation Company at Seattle and renamed the Enetai.

The REDWOOD EMPIRE was built by Moore Shipyard, Oakland. Sold to the Puget Sound Navigation Company in 1939, becoming the Nisqually.

ROSTER OF FERRY BOATS OF THE NORTHWESTERN PACIFIC
AND ITS PREDECESSOR COMPANIES

STEAMER	BUILT BY	FOR	YEAR	GROSS TONS	LENGTH	HULL	TYPE	PASS. CAP.
CLINTON	D. Marcucci, San Francisco	Charles Minturn	1853	194	128	Wood	SE-SW	......
CONTRA COSTA	John G. North	Charles Minturn	1857	449	158	Wood	SE-SW	......
TAMALPAIS (#1)*	Patrick Tiernan, S. F.	....	1857	365	150	Wood	SE-SW	......
ANTELOPE	(On East Coast)	....	1848	581	202	Wood	SE-SW	......
JAMES M. DONAHUE	E. Collyer	SF&NP	1875	730	228	Wood	SE-SW	870
TIGER (Tug Boat)	San Francisco	....	1875	85	100	Wood	SE-SW	....
SAN RAFAEL	Lawrence & Faulks, N. Y.	NPC	1877	692	220	Wood	SE-SW	950
SAUCELITO	John Engles, Greenpoint, Long Island N.Y.	NPC	1877	692	220	Wood	SE-SW	950
TIBURON	SF&NP	SF&NP	1884	1248	240	Wood	DE-SW	1500
SAUSALITO	John Dickie	NPC	1894	1766	256	Wood	DE-SW	3320
TAMALPAIS (#2)	Union Iron Works San Francisco	NPC	1901	1631	245	Steel	DE-SW	2527
CAZADERO	John Dickie	NS	1903	1682	257	Wood	DE-SW	2000
LAGUNITAS	John Dickie	NS	1903	767	280	Wood	SE-STW	......
MARIN "Requa"	....	NWP	1909	101	97	Wood	SE-PR	220
EUREKA (Ukiah)	S.P. Co.	NWP	1922	2420	300	Wood	DE-SW	3330
MENDOCINO	Union Iron Works, San Francisco	NWP	1927	1025	251	Steel	DE-PR	Auto
REDWOOD EMPIRE	Moore's Shipyard, Oakland	NWP	1927	1025	251	Steel	DE-PR	Auto
SANTA ROSA	General Eng. Alameda	NWP	1927	1025	251	Steel	DE-PR	Auto

*"Petaluma of Saucelito" "Petaluma"

DISPOSITIONS

CLINTON - Leased to San Rafael & San Quentin RR in 1869; to NPC in 1875; in collision with "Petaluma," October 27, 1877, and sunk.

CONTRA COSTA - Leased to SR&SQ 1869. To NPC 1875. Retired 1882.

TAMALPAIS (#1) To SR&SQ 1869. To NPC 1874. Renamed "Tamalpais" 1883. Retired 1895. Scrapped January 30, 1900.

ANTELOPE - Purchased by SF&NP 1871. Retired 1888.

JAMES M. DONAHUE - Retired December 31, 1921.

TIGER - Under NPC and NS ownership for several years hauling car barges between Sausalito and San Francisco. Scrapped in 1917.

SAN RAFAEL - Sunk in collision with "Sausalito" November 30, 1901.

SAUCELITO - Destroyed by fire, San Quentin wharf, February 25, 1884.

TIBURON - Retired September 11, 1925

SAUSALITO - Retired May, 1932

TAMALPAIS (# 2) - Retired March 28, 1941. Sold to U.S. Navy and used as a floating barracks at Mare Island. Scrapped November 28, 1947.

CAZADERO - Retired March 28, 1941. Sold to Western Terminal Co., December 29, 1941 and converted into barge.

LAGUNITAS - Built as narrow gauge car float. Changed to broad gauge 1908. Retired December 31, 1921.

MARIN "Requa" - Built as "Requa". Burned and rebuilt as "Marin" in 1911. Retired October 1, 1934.

EUREKA - Rebuilt March 29, 1922, from "Ukiah" which was built in 1890 as a combination passenger and carfloat ferry by the SF&NP. To Southern Pacific March 2, 1941. Donated to S.F. Maritime Museum October 23, 1957.

MENDOCINO - Sold to Puget Sound Navigation Co., 1939. Renamed "Quinault."

REDWOOD EMPIRE - Sold to Puget Sound Navigation Co., 1939. Renamed "Nisqually."

SANTA ROSA - Sold to Puget Sound Navigation Co., 1939. Renamed "Enetai."

SE	Single Ender	NPC	North Pacific Coast Railroad
DE	Double Ender	NS	North Shore Railroad
SW	Side Wheeler	SPC	South Pacific Coast Railroad
STW	Stern Wheeler	NWP	Northwestern Pacific Railroad
PR	Propeller	SP	Southern Pacific Railroad
SF&NP	San Francisco & North Pacific Railroad	CP	Central Pacific Railroad
SR&SQ	San Rafael & San Quentin Railroad	WP	Western Pacific Railroad

CHARACTERISTICS OF THE THREE FERRY BOATS OF OTHER COMPANIES WHICH SAW THE MOST SERVICE ON THE NORTHWESTERN PACIFIC OR PREDECESSOR COMPANIES

AMADOR	CP	1869	897	199'	Wood	DE-SW	300
SIERRA NEVADA	WP	1913	1578	218'	Steel	DE-PR	1005
BAY CITY	SPC	1878	1283	247'	Wood	DE-SW	1205

AMADOR

Rebuilt from a Sacramento River boat in 1878. Used by North Pacific Coast and North Shore for Sunday excursions. Retired in 1904. During 1915 Panama Pacific Exposition ferry was altered to represent a battleship and was blown up in demonstration.

BAY CITY

Built for the South Pacific Coast Railroad. Used by the North Pacific Coast and North Shore for Sunday and holiday excursions and also as a relief boat. Saw last days of service on the Southern Pacific South Vallejo-Vallejo Junction run. Sold in 1930 and taken near Hunter's Point, San Francisco, where vessel was stripped and finally burned.

SIERRA NEVADA

Built for the Western Pacific. Originally "Edward T. Jeffrey." After First World War renamed "Feather River." When WP trains started operating out of SP Oakland Pier in 1933, ferry was taken over by Southern Pacific and renamed "Sierra Nevada." Was used extensively as a relief boat on the Northwestern Pacific. Leased to Key System in 1939, painted orange, and began service to Treasure Island on February 27. At the conclusion of the Fair in 1940, it went back to Southern Pacific and was used as a relief boat even though painted orange. During World War II taken over by the U.S. Government and sent to Wilmington to operate in shipyard service. Returned to Southern Pacific after the war and then sold to the Richmond-San Rafael Ferry Company, which placed it in auto service on May 30, 1947. Ended service August 31, 1956, when bridge between Richmond and San Rafael replaced ferry service. Sold to Learner Scrap Company on May 6, 1957, and towed to Moore's scrap yard in Alameda. Sold at auction for $19,750 to Ports of Call Village, San Pedro, in October, 1961. Went out of the Golden Gate under tow November 5, 1961, bound for San Pedro where it is now a tourist attraction.

Train time at Monte Rio. In the days of yesteryear the narrow gauge was the popular route to Russian River Points.

Engine #8 was used on all branch lines. This photo taken at Verano station on the Sonoma Valley line in 1909.

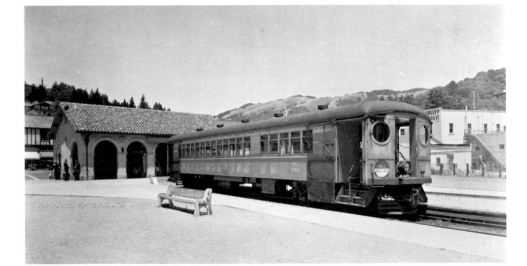

New and modern, a one car electric sits at the Mill Valley station in the year 1931 awaiting its return schedule back to Sausalito for the ferry connection to San Francisco.

The company's paint shops at Tiburon. Open-platform coach gets final trim before going back into service.

Two-car wooden electric train arrives at the old covered San Rafael Union Station in the 'twenties'. View is to the South.

The Point Reyes- Manor local passenger pulls into Lagunitas station. This narrow gauge section was "broad gauged" in April, 1920.

Above, vacationland at Monte Rio, looking west with narrow gauge passenger heading down river to Duncan Mills.

Daily narrow gauge freight from Occidental, with Engine 145 on the point, stops at Fairfax before proceeding to San Anselmo. It returned to Occidental in the afternoon as Train #38.

End of the line. Manor was as far as the electrics went. Photo taken in the 'twenties' of wooden open-platform cars.

Left. End of the Sonoma Valley branch at Glen Ellen - where crew poses for a picture alongside ten-wheeler 101 not long after N.W.P. came into being in 1907.

Right. With the idea of selling view lots, the 1,500 foot Incline Railroad with a 500 foot rise opened operations on August 13, 1913, at Fairfax. It ended in 1929.

Left. Before being sold to the Oahu Railway, Hawaii, in 1890, this engine was Sonoma Valley narrow gauge #3 "General Vallejo." Photo taken at the roundhouse, Honolulu, about 1926.

Right. After steam ended on the N.W.P. some locomotives went over to the S.P. Here N.W.P. #181 is photographed in an unusual duty - on the business end of Train #55, the "San Joaquin Valley Passenger." Tracy, 1954.

Gas Electric #903, a Brill product, has company photo taken at builder's factory before being shipped to the N.W.P.

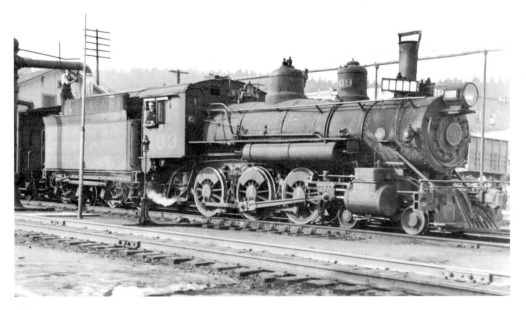

A rare photograph. Engine No. 109 at Truckee, California, December 20, 1944. The locomotive is heading east to Montello, Nevada for stationary boiler service. Note that smoke deflector has been installed because of service in Sierra Nevada snow shed district. Engine returned to N.W.P. April 4, 1945. — Photo by R. B. Trexler, Herb Joiner collection.

Engine 92 takes on passengers for San Francisco at Monte Rio in the year 1908. Monte Rio Hotel is on the left and the order board says "all clear."

Car 7010, top, apparently was for some special service. An old roster lists cars 7000-7008 as water cars.

Narrow gauge stock car No. 4518 was built in 1903 by the North Shore Railroad.

Narrow gauge box car No. 5182 was No. 134 on the North Shore. This was one of the relatively few cars still in existence when the narrow gauge came to an end in 1930.

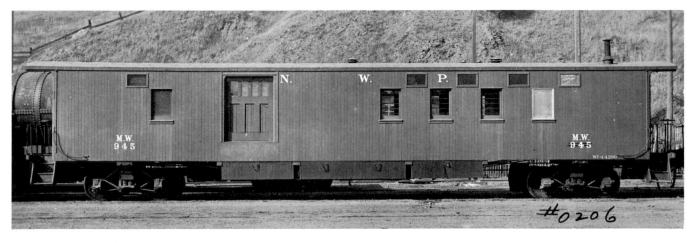

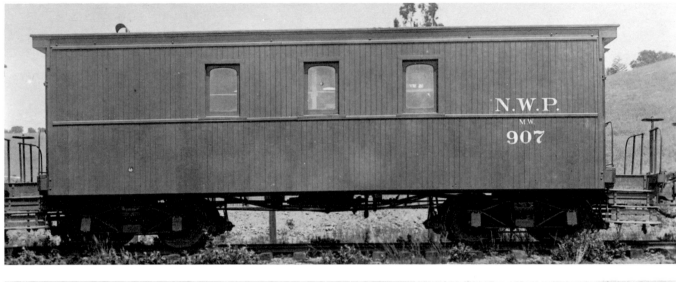

No. 945 was formerly broad gauge passenger car first No. 31, converted to Maintenance of Way service in 1911.

Not much information is available on broad gauge car No. 907. It is unknown whether it was built this way, or converted from a caboose or box car. It was used as sleeping car for section crews.

Caboose No. 6003 was built new by the N.W.P. in 1919 at the Tiburon shops.

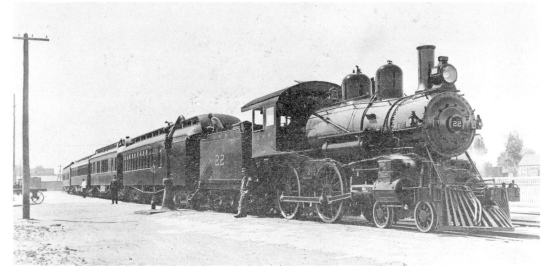

No. 17, a 4-4-0 type passenger engine powers an extra freight in the year 1923. Only known photo showing a smaller N.W.P. passenger engine in freight service. — Bob Parmelee collection.

Four-car Director's Special pauses at Santa Rosa, April 21, 1909, awaiting a southbound meet. Engine No. 22 is brand new, having been delivered less than a year earlier. — D. S. Richter collection.

Train No. 2 made a special stop at Ridge during a snow storm, so the author could capture this March 10, 1942 scene. Two months later the day train to Eureka was discontinued.

Engine crew of 1-223 (first section of Russian River Train.) pause for a photo at Santa Rosa in 1928. Second section was a Boy Scout special. — Bob Parmelee collection.

N.W.P. No. 178 and S.P. No. 2336 pulling a coach, lounge-snack car and Pullman cross Corte Madera Creek in 1949. At San Rafael the Eureka Express will add up to ten head-end cars. Helper No. 178 will assist train over grade north of San Rafael, cut off, and return for freight assignment.

Excursion train on Sonoma Valley branch is powered by venerable No. 112. Photo taken at Schellville, June 9, 1940. — D. S. Richter.

← Arrival at Willits of first through train from San Francisco to Eureka, December 1, 1914. Although the line had been opened October 23, 1914 with the driving of the gold spike at Cain Rock, it was for limited traffic only. Photo courtesy of Tom Williams

Automatic air dump cars are tried out on the N.W.P. during construction of the northern end in 1914.

During construction in 1913 the rugged terrain caused numerous mud and rock slides. Engine No. 103 is partially derailed after hitting a rock at Woodman, thirty-two miles north of Willits.

Engine No. 19 saw service on all N.W.P. branch lines. For a number of years it was used on trains around the Eureka area. Photo taken in 1923 at Willits when locomotive was heading south for transfer to the Southern Division. — Bob Parmelee collection.

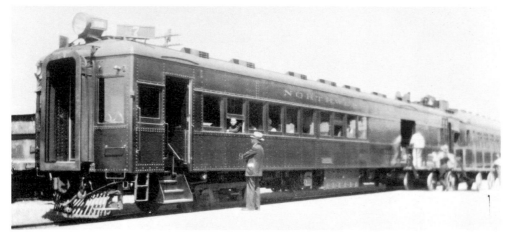

By 1931 the gas electrics started to invade the N.W.P. and took the place of a number of steam-powered passenger trains on the main line, Sausalito to Eureka. Photo shows gas electric No. 901 southbound with the "Healdsburg Passenger" at Santa Rosa.

The place is Monte Rio, the year 1913 and the time is 12:45 PM on a summer day. At the right, broad gauge train No. 222, the Duncan Mills Passenger, behind 4-4-0's No. 20 and 14, a little late on schedule, will shortly depart over the three-rail trackage to Duncan Mills, 3.3 miles to the west, where it will be turned around and become train No. 223 for the return trip to San Francisco via Fulton. To the left, narrow gauge train No. 8, the Cazadero Passenger, also in the tow of a brace of 4-4-0's (Numbers 90 and 85), is just arriving, and will follow No. 222 to Duncan Mills, then strike out north to the narrow gauge end-of-line at Cazadero. A passing thought: Did the unknown photographer who made this picture appreciate what he saw: A scene deep in the redwoods in the leisurely days now so long removed; two wooden-car passenger trains in this remote area at the same time, and four little 4-4-0 type locomotives?

UP DATE TO '82

The end of an era. Over 100 years of passenger service in the Redwood Empire comes to an end. Budd Car No. 10, N.W.P. Train No. 3 southbound on last day of operation, April 30, 1971. Stopping at Fort Seward, Charles Coleman, who had been a conductor on this run for many years, is seen helping a passenger aboard. Note wreath on front door. — Warren Miller photo.

Since the second edition of this book, October, 1966, there have been but a few changes in the physical plant of the Northwestern Pacific Railroad, but of these two have historical significance. On April 30, 1971, the railroad discontinued its tri-weekly passenger service between Eureka and Willits, thus ending a passenger service begun in the Redwood Empire more than 100 years earlier. The service ended due to the passing of the Federal Rail Passenger Service Act and the formation of Railpax (now AMTRAK). Except for certain routes between major cities, AMTRAK eliminated all passenger service by subscribing lines among which were the S.P. and N.W.P. The next historical occasion came a few months later, November 23, 1971, when the last train operation was made between Detour (south of San Rafael) and Sausalito, 7.549 miles, with SP diesel locomotive 2594.

In the 1920s heyday of the Sausalito Terminal there were more than 120 daily train arrivals and departures. On a good Sunday 50,000 persons would crowd ferries and trains as picnickers and vacationers took off for Marin County countryside or Sonoma County resorts. Passenger service to Sausalito had ended November 23, 1941, thirty years before the last train. Other trackage abandonments are shown.

Today the N.W.P. operates no motive power or cars of its own. They are furnished by the parent company, Southern Pacific. Normally assigned to the N.W.P. pool are nine yard or switch engines and forty diesel road engines (SD-9 type-4300 series). In addition many other types find their way to the N.W.P. depending on traffic volume. The road diesels originate either at SP's facility at Roseville or Fresno, California. The S.P. crews change with N.W.P. crews at Schellville, the interchange point. Generally there is one freight a day between Shellville and Eureka and almost every day between Shellville and Willits. There are several local freights and yard assignments on the southern end between San Rafel and Ukiah and the northern end around Eureka.

CONTINUATION OF TRACKAGE ABANDONMENTS FROM PAGES 8 AND 83

SECTION	MILEAGE	DATE
At Santa Rosa (P&SR)	.71	November 15, 1945
Santa Rosa - Leddy (P&SR) (Connection into Santa Rosa made on NWP trackage)	2.68	October 18, 1947
At Park Siding (P&SR) (Connection made with NWP trackage)	.61	June 1, 1969
Ross - Sagu (P&SR) (Sagu signpost established 4.9 miles from Sebastopol)	1.09	June 3, 1969
Tiburon - Meadowsweet (Last freight car barge to Tiburon 9-25-67)	4.9	September 27, 1967
Meadowsweet - Detour	1.3	October 18, 1971
Detour - Sausalito	7.5	November 24, 1971
California Park toward B St. (Old SR&SQ line)	7.8	July 31, 1973
Denman - Turner (P&SR)	7.55	October 31, 1973
Sebastiani - Sonoma	.6	May 7, 1975
Turner - Alten (P&SR)	3.67	February 16, 1978
Alten - Stop 18 (P&SR)	.31	August 8, 1978
Park Siding - Denman (P&SR)	2.38	August 23, 1980
Detour - California Park	1.40	Out of service 8-7-81 (Abandonment pending)

NOTE: After fire destroyed tunnel No. 4 north of San Rafael, July 20, 1961, N.W.P. sought to discontinue line between Hamilton Field and Detour, 9.5 miles. After a four year legal battle waged in federal and state courts and regulatory agencies, the petition for abandonment was denied. The tunnel was rebuilt at the cost of $2.8 million and the section reopened for service September 27, 1967. In 1976 the N.W.P. again filed for discontinuance of this section, but on September 15, 1977 the ICC dismissed the application for procedural reasons. No further application has been made at this time (7-1-82).

We can only thank the unknown photographer for taking these two magnificent views of the Sausalito locomotive and passenger terminal in 1919. Top photo, looking north, shows narrow gauge engine house to left, broad gauge, center, and electric train repair facility to the right. Lower photo, looking south, shows passenger car yard, left, and narrow gauge engine service shed to the right. — D. S. Richter collection.

From an original photograph. The engine was ordered by the North Pacific Coast Railroad in 1875 from William Mason Locomotive Works. The order was subsequently withdrawn and engine resold to the Central Railroad of Minnesota, but not delivered. Altered to broad gauge and sold to Galveston, Harrisburg & San Antonio No. 22 "Dixie Crosby." — Thomas Norrell collection.

North Shore engine No. 13 and five-car passenger train at Cazadero in the year 1903. Note one stall enginehouse in extreme right background. — Roy Graves collection.

On Sundays and holidays in the summertime, two engines were required to handle the large crowd of passengers in the many cars heading for Russian River points. Photo shows narrow gauge engines No. 144 and No. 87 on train No. 8 at Point Reyes Station in the year 1915. — W. A. Silverthorn collection.

Monte Rio was a favorite spot for train crews to pose for pictures. Note oil can on the pilot beam in this 1909 photo. — Roy Graves collection.

Miller's Retreat, a popular summer resort 0.4 mile from end of line at Cazadero. The crew of Train No. 9 with engine No. 92 pose for photograph.

Many model builders and rail buffs have asked about the track arrangement at the Sausalito Terminal. With few cars, this photo gives a good view of the track area and loading platforms.

A slight mishap! A stock car and box car were not properly secured when the ferry boat *Ukiah* backed away from the Tiburon freight car slip with the resulting situation!

When the bridge across the Russian River at Bohemia collapsed, March 19, 1907, a hastily established transfer station was made at a point named River Landing. Photo shows train and steps to the river where boats took passengers to Monte Rio. The facility was in operation for only two years. A new bridge was completed in 1909 and trains then ran through to Monte Rio and Duncan Mills. — Jack Muzio collection.

One of two picnic trains carrying Southern Pacific employees arrives at Guernewood Park for a day's outing at the Russian River resort, September, 1934. — D. S. Richter collection.

Each year the N.W.P. published an attractive Vacation booklet which listed all resorts on the railroad's lines. It gave a concise story of each area, weekly rates and stated whether bus would meet passengers at stations.

Tiburon roundhouse at left with general shops center and right. Year 1922. The shops were destroyed by fire and a new repair facility constructed, as seen in upper photo. — D. S. Richter collection.

An excellent view of Tiburon when railroad activity was at its height in 1924. Photo gives clear sweep from ferry slips to the area where roundhouse and shops are located. Note ferry *San Pablo*, which has been borrowed from the Santa Fe Railroad - a rare occurrence as Santa Fe had only two ferry boats. The ferry without a stack is the *James M. Donahue*, which has been retired. It will become Spencer's Fish Grotto at San Quentin wharf. — D. S. Richter collection.

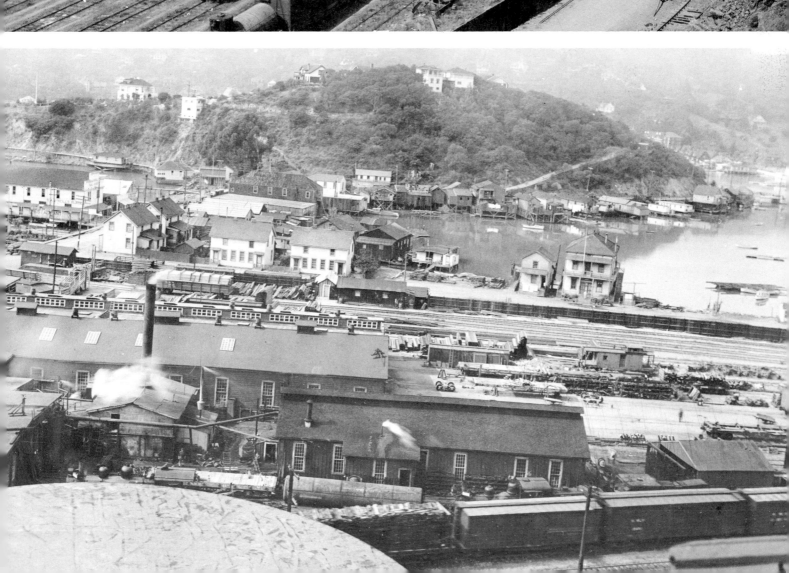

All wooden seven-car consist heads to the Sausalito Terminal during morning commuter hour on N.W.P.'s suburban electric system. At Manzanita in 1939. — W. C. Whittaker photo.

In late afternoon combination car No. 504 and train stops at West End, San Rafael, on its way to Sausalito in 1914. — W. C. Whittaker collection.

Three car wooden train, with baggage-mail motor No. 370 on rear, awaits signal to proceed to Sausalito, 1939. — W. C. Whittaker photo.

San Anselmo was the junction for electric suburban trains. One turned west to proceed to Manor and the other, as this train will do, turned east toward San Rafael. — W. C. Whittaker photo.

FAREWELL CRUISE OF THE S. S. EUREKA

marking the discontinuance of continuous Ferry Service between San Francisco and Marvelous Marin since May 10, 1868.

MARCH 1, 1941

Sponsored by

MARVELOUS MARIN, INC.   OLD TIMERS' COMMITTEE

February 28, 1941, was the last day of electric train service in Marin County, and the last regularly scheduled ferry boat operation between Sausalito and San Francisco. The following day a Farewell Cruise on the ferry boat *Eureka* was sponsored by Marvelous Marin, Inc. and the Old-Timers' Committee.

You are cordially invited on the farewell cruise of the Northwestern Pacific's S. S. Eureka

March 1, 1941

SCHEDULE
Leave Sausalito 12:30 p.m.   Leave San Francisco 1:15 p.m.
Cruise to Tiburon, Belvedere, Golden Gate Bridge
Arrive San Francisco 2:15 p.m.   Arrive Sausalito 3:00 p.m.

This invitation is your ticket

Marvelous Marin, Inc.   Old Timers' Committee

BETWEEN SAN FRANCICO AND EUREKA
(VIA SAUSALITO)

FROM SAN FRANCISCO (READ DOWN) — **TOWARDS SAN FRANCISCO** (READ UP)

12	4	8	6	224	10	222	2	226	220	Miles from S F	STATIONS	Elev.	3	221	7	9	5	223	1	225	11
Sun Only	Daily ★	Daily	Daily	Daily	Daily	Daily	Daily	Daily Ex.Sun	Sun. Only				Daily ★	Daily	Daily	Daily Ex.Sun	Daily	Daily	Daily	Sun. Only	Sun. Only
PM Lv	PM Lv	PM Lv	PM Lv	PM Lv	AM Lv	AM Lv	AM Lv	AM Lv	AM Lv				AM Ar	AM Ar	PM Ar	PM Ar	PM Ar	PM Ar	PM Ar	PM Ar	PM Ar
10 15	8 15	5 15	3 15	1 45	10 45	8 45	7 45	6 45	6 45	0.0	San Francisco	6	9 05	10 35	12 35	3 35	5 05	6 35	7 35	9 05	11 25
10 50	8 55	5 55	3 50	2 20	11 20	9 20	8 25	7 25	7 25	6.5	Sausalito	8	8 30	10 00	12 01	3 09	4 30	6 00	7 00	8 30	10 50
						ff				14.9	Green Brae	29		ff			ff		b		
						ff				15.7	Schuetzen	19									
11 20	9 28	6 26	4 17	2 50	11 47	9 50	8 53	7 54	7 54	17.0	San Rafael	5	7 54	9 25	11 34	2 34	3 56	5 26	6 26	8 00	10 15
						f		f		21.1	Gallinas	12							b		
								f 8 04		21.7	Miller	6					f 3 43		b		
								f		22.0	St. Vincent	8		f					b		
11 37	9 45	6 44	4 37	3 07	12 04	10 07	9 10	8 10	8 10	24.9	Ignacio	17	7 35	9 10	11 18	2 18	3 37	5 08	6 10		9 57
f11 43	f 9 51	6 50	4 44	3 14	12 11	10 14	9 16	8 18	8 18	27.8	Novato	12	7 26	9 01	11 12	2 12	3 30	5 01	b	7 39	9 51
f11 49		f 6 56			f12 17	f10 20		f 8 24	f 8 24	31.3	Burdell	5	f 7 16	f 8 55	f11 06	f 2 06	f 3 23	f 4 52	b		
		f	f		f	f		f		33.1	San Antonio	5	f				f		b		
12 04	10 14	7 13	5 08	3 39	12 34	10 36	9 36	8 41	8 41	38.5	Petaluma	9	7 02	8 41	10 53	1 53	3 09	4 39	5 47	7 20	9 30
										41.0	Crown	30	f						b		
		f 7 21	f 5 16		f12 41					42.0	Ely	39	f 6 49	f 8 31	f10 47	f 1 45	f 2 58		b		
f12 14		7 24	f 5 19	3 49	f12 44	f10 48		8 59	8 52	43.3	Penn Grove	64	f 6 47	8 29	f10 43	f 1 43	2 56	4 24	b		f 9 20
f12 20		f 7 30	f 5 23	3 55	f12 50	f10 54		9 05	8 58	46.1	Cotati	113	f 6 41	8 23	f10 38	f 1 38	2 50	4 18	b		f 9 14
f		f	f		f	f		f		48.7	Wilfred	94	f				f		b		
f12 30		f 7 39	f 5 37	4 15	f 1 00	f11 03		f 9 14	f 9 07	51.3	Bellevue	112	f 6 30	f 8 12	f10 29	f 1 29	f 2 39	f 4 07	b		f 9 04
12 35	10 50	7 48	5 47	4 15	1 05	11 12	10 05	9 35	9 18	53.8	Santa Rosa	150	6 25	8 07	10 25	1 25	2 35	4 02	5 21	6 47	9 00
AM Ar	11 00	7 58	5 57	4 23 PM Ar		11 20	10 15	9 43	9 24	58.5	Fulton	132	6 10	7 55	10 13 PM Lv		2 22	3 50	b	6 32 PM Lv	
	e	f	f		PM Ar	AM Ar		AM Ar	AM Ar	59.8	Mark West	123	f	AM Lv			f	PM Lv	b		
		8 06	6 05				10 22			62.9	Windsor	113	6 00		10 02		2 13		5 04		
	e	f								66.4	Grant	107	f				f		b		
	11 20	8 15	6 16				10 34			68.0	Healdsburg	101	5 50		9 52		2 03		4 54		
	PM Ar									70.2	Chiquita	159	f		AM Lv		f		b		
	e		6 23				10 42			71.9	Lytton	183	f 5 39				1 53		4 44		
		f11 33	6 31				10 50			75.8	Geyserville	203	5 33				1 46		4 37		
	e						f			78.8	Chianti	238	f				f				
		f 6 40					f10 59			81.3	Asti	264	f 5 22				f 1 35		f 4 26		
	11 54	6 50					11 10			85.2	Cloverdale	315	5 15				1 28		4 19		
	e	f					f			86.5	McCray	316	f				f		f		
	e	f 6 55					f11 14			87.1	Preston	329	f 5 08				f 1 21		f 4 13		
	e	f 7 01					f11 21			89.8	Echo	369	f 5 02				f 1 15		f 4 07		
	e						f			91.8	Cummiskey	423	f				f				
	e	f 7 13					f11 34			95.3	Pieta	472	f 4 50				f 1 03		f 3 55		
	e						f			96.8	Fountain	477	f				f				
		f12 30	7 27				11 49			100.1	Hopland	488	4 39				12 52		3 45		
	e		7 36				f11 59			103.9	Largo	522	4 30				f12 43		f 3 36		
	e		7 50				f12 12			109.6	El Roble	562	4 18				f12 31		f 3 24		
	1 05		8 00				12 23			114.0	Ukiah	610	4 10				12 23		3 17		
	e		PM Ar				f12 40			120.1	Calpella	673	f 3 55				PM Lv		f 3 05		
	e						f12 45			122.0	Basil	705	f 3 51						f 3 01		
	e						f12 50			124.0	Laughlin	872	f 3 47						2 57		
	2 00						1 21			131.4	Ridgewood	1913	3 22						2 32		
	2 25						1 45			139.5	Ar‖ Willits..Lv	1365	3 00						2 10		
	2 45						2 05				Lv..Willits..‖ Ar		1 15						1 50		
	2 45						2 05			143.7	Outlet	1339	f 1 05						1 40		
	f 2 54						f 2 14			148.7	Arnold	1232	f12 55						f 1 30		
	f 3 04						f 2 24			152.5	Longvale	1164	12 45						1 20		
	3 14						2 34			158.2	Farley	1071	f12 34						f 1 10		
	f 3 24						f 2 44			161.8	Tatu	1014	f12 24						f 1 01		
	f 3 33						f 2 53			166.5	Dos Rios	924	12 12						12 49		
	3 45						3 05			175.5	Nash	811	f11 51						f12 29		
	f 4 05						f 3 25			180.0	Spyrock	769	11 41						12 19		
	4 15						3 35			184.3	Bell Springs	704	f11 31						f12 10		
	f 4 25						f 3 45			189.3	Ramsey	620	f11 18						f11 58		
	f 4 36						f 3 56			194.5	Island Mtn.	550	11 03						11 44		
	4 49						4 09			200.3	Kekawaka	431	f10 44						f11 26		
	f 5 05						4 25			209.1	Alderpoint	341	10 21						11 05		
	5 25						4 45			216.6	Fort Seward	322	10 01	155					10 45		
	5 45					156	5 05			228.3	Tanoak										
	f 6 15					Daily	f 5 35			230.1	Sequoia	196	f 9 27	Daily					f10 12		
	f 6 20					PM Lv	f 5 40			232.2	McCann	185	f 9 21 PM Ar						f10 06		
	6 30					1 35	5 50			237.3	South Fork	169	9 11	1 05					9 56		
	f					f				242.3	P. L. Spur	151	f	f							
	6 50					1 55	6 10			245.6	Shively	149	8 50	12 42					9 35		
	f 7 00					f 2 05	f 6 19			250.0	Elinor	125	f 8 39	f12 31					f 9 24		
	7 12					2 20	6 30			255.6	Scotia	101	8 28	12 20					9 13		
	f					f 2 35 f k..				260.2	Metropolitan	84	f 8 11	f12 02							
	7 33					2 41	6 50			262.7	Alton	65	8 06	11 57					8 51		
	f 7 37					f 2 45	f 6 54			264.5	Rohnerville	48	f 8 01	f11 52					f 8 46		
	7 42					2 50	6 59			266.1	Fortuna	53	7 57	11 48					8 42		
	7 48					2 57	7 05			268.7	Fernbridge	35	7 51	11 42					8 36		
						f 2 58				269.5	Singley	31		f11 39							
	7 56					3 05	7 13			271.0	Loleta	56	7 44	11 35					8 29		
	f 8 04					3 13	f 7 21			273.9	Beatrice	17	f 7 36	11 27					f 8 21		
	8 15					3 21	7 30			277.8	South Bay	9	7 30	11 20					8 15		
	8 30					3 35	7 45			284.1	Eureka	9	7 15	11 05					8 00		
	AM Ar					PM Ar PM Ar							PM Lv AM Lv							AM Lv	

‖Lunch Counter. fTrains stop only on signal or to discharge passengers.
e Stops only to discharge passengers boarding train at Santa Rosa and south
‡Will not stop on Saturdays or Sundays.

b Stops only to discharge passengers boarding train beyond Healdsburg. †Daily Except Sunday.
★No. 3 and 4 carry sleeping cars and coaches between Sausalito and Eureka and Fort Bragg.

Shown on these two pages are N.W.P. main line and branch line schedules for the summer of 1923, the year when N.W.P. scheduled the most passenger trains. The Camp Meeker, Monte Rio and Cazadero schedule in lower left, opposite page, is operated by narrow gauge trains between Point Reyes and Cazadero. Note schedule to Mt. Tamalpais and Muir Woods via Mt. Tamalpais & Muir Woods Railway, shown on opposite page.

SAN FRANCISCO, WOODACRE, LAGUNITAS, SAN GERONIMO AND POINT REYES

FROM SAN FRANCISCO (READ DOWN)														TOWARD SAN FRANCISCO (READ UP)									
84-86	82	62-80	78	76	74	70-72	68	60	66	64	Miles from S. F.	STATIONS	Elev.	63	65-69	67	71	73-75	77-79	81-83	85	61	87-89
Daily a	Daily Ex. Sun.	Daily Ex. Sun.	Daily Ex. Sat & Sun.	Sun. Only g	Sat. Only g	Daily o	Sun. Only	Daily	Sun. Only	Daily Ex. Sun.				Daily Ex. Sun.	Daily Ex. Sun.	Sun. Only	Sun. Only	Daily	Daily Ex. Sun.	Daily Ex. Sun.	Sun. Only	Daily	Daily
PM Lv	PM Lv	PM Lv	PM Lv	PM Lv	PM Lv	AM Lv	AM Lv	AM Lv	AM Lv	AM Lv				AM Ar	AM Ar	AM Ar	PM Ar	PM Ar	PM Ar	PM Ar	PM Ar	PM Ar	PM Ar
5 45	4 45	2 45	1 45	12 45	12 45	10 45	9 15	8 15	7 15	......	0.0	....San Francisco....	6	7 35	8 35	8 35	12 35	1 35	3 35	5 05	5 35	7 35	8 05
6 18	5 21	3 18	2 18	1 18	1 18	11 18	9 50	8 55	7 51	......	6.5	......Sausalito......	8	7 00	8 00	8 00	12 01	1 00	3 00	4 30	5 00	7 00	7 30
6 39	5 48	3 46	2 46	1 39	1 39	11 39	10 18	9 18	8 18	......	16.5	....San Anselmo....	47	6 32	7 28	7 28	11 32	12 28	2 28	3 58	4 28	6 28	6 58
6 56	5 56	3 56	2 56	1 56	1 56	11 56	10 26	9 26	8 26	6 28	18.8	.......Manor.......	147	6 23	7 21	7 21	11 23	12 21	2 21	3 51	4 21	6 21	6 51
f 7 07	f 6 12	f 4 07	f 3 06	f 2 07	f 2 10	f12 10	f10 37	f 9 37	f 8 37	f 6 38	21.5	...Woodacre Lodge...	402	f 6 10	f 7 08	f 7 10	f11 08	f12 10	f 2 10	f 3 40	f 4 10	f 6 12	f 6 40
f.....	f.....	f.....	f.....	f.....	f.....	f.....	f.....	f.....	f.....	f.....	22.0	......Woodacre......	368	f.....	f.....	f.....	f.....	f.....	f.....	f.....	f.....	f.....	f.....
7 13	f.....	4 13	f.....	f 2 13	f....	12 16	10 43	9 43	8 43	f.....	23.1	....San Geronimo....	306	6 05	7 03	7 05	11 03	12 05	2 05	3 35	4 05	6 06	6 35
f.....	f.....	f.....	f.....	f.....	f.....	f.....	f.....	f.....	f.....	f.....	24.5	....Forest Knolls....	240	f.....	f.....	f.....	f.....	f.....	f.....	f.....	f.....	f.....	f.....
7 20	6 21	4 20	3 16	2 20	2 20	12 23	10 50	9 50	8 50	6 48	25.2	......Lagunitas......	219	5 58	6 56	6 58	10 56	11 58	1 58	3 28	3 58	5 57	6 28
f.....	PM Ar	f.....	PM Ar	f.....	PM Ar	f.....	AM Ar	f.....	f.....	AM Ar	27.9	....Camp Taylor....	138	f.....	AM Lv	f.....	AM Lv	f.....	f.....	PM Lv	f.....	f.....	f d...
f.....	......	f.....	......	f.....	......	f.....	......	f.....	f.....	......	31.2	......Tocaloma......	87	f.....	......	f.....	......	f.....	f.....	......	f.....	f.....	f d...
..7 57	......	4 57	......	2 57	......	1 00	......	10 43	9 27	......	36.4	....Point Reyes....	31	5 20	......	6 20	......	11 20	1 20	......	3 20	5 19	d 5 50
PM Ar	......	PM Ar	......	PM Ar	......	PM Ar	......	AM Ar	AM Ar	......				AM Lv	......	AM Lv	......	AM Lv	PM Lv	......	PM Lv	PM Lv	PM Lv

f Trains stop only on signal or to discharge passengers.
a On week days use electric train to Manor and transfer to steam train.
g Use electric train to Manor and transfer to steam train.
o On Sundays use eiectric train to Manor and transfer to steam train.
d Runs beyond Lagunitas on Sunday only.

GUERNEVILLE BRANCH

FROM SAN FRANCISCO (READ DOWN)							TOWARDS SAN FRANCISCO (READ UP)			
224	222	226	220	Miles from S. F.	STATIONS	Elev.	221	227	223	225
Daily	Daily	Daily Ex. Sun.	Sun. Only				Daily	Daily Ex. Sun.	Daily	Sun. Only
PM Lv	AM Lv	AM Lv	AM Lv				AM Ar	PM Ar	PM Ar	PM Ar
1 45	8 45	6 45	6 45	00.0	..San Francisco..	6	10 35	5 05	6 35	9 05
4 15	11 12	9 35	9 18	53.8	...Santa Rosa...	150	8 07	2 20	4 02	6 47
4 25	11 22	9 45	9 26	58.5	.....Fulton.....	132	7 55	2 12	3 50	6 32
f 4 29	f11 26	f 9 49	f 9 31	60.6	....Meacham....	87	f 7 48	f 2 05	f 3 43	f 6 25
f 4 31	f11 28	f 9 51	f 9 33	61.4	....Woolsey....	81	f 7 45	f 2 02	f 3 40	f 6 22
f 4 37	f11 34	f 9 57	f 9 39	63.9	....Trenton....	63	f 7 38	f 1 55	f 3 32	f 6 14
f 4 42	f11 39	f10 02	f 9 44	65.8	...Forestville...	62	f 7 33	f 1 50	f 3 26	f 6 08
f.....	f.....	f.....	f.....	66.4	.....Mirabel.....		f.....	f.....	f.....	f.....
f 4 47	f11 44	f10 08	f 9 49	67.5	..Green Valley..	64	f 7 28	f 1 45	f 3 21	f 6 03
f.....	f.....	f.....	f.....	68.7	.....Cosmo.....		f.....	f.....	f.....	f.....
f 4 52	f11 49	f10 16	f 9 54	69.4	.....Hilton.....	69	f 7 23	f 1 40	f 3 15	f 5 57
f.....	f.....	f.....	f.....	70.9	.....Korbel.....	67	f.....	f.....	f.....	f.....
4 59	11 56	10 27	10 01	72.2	.....Rionido.....	57	7 15	1 32	3 05	5 47
5 05	12 04	10 38	10 09	73.9	...Guerneville...	52	7 10	1 27	3 00	5 38
f.....	f.....	f.....	f.....	74.7	.Guernew'd P'k.	48	f.....	f.....	f.....	f.....
f.....	f.....	f.....	f.....	75.2	....Graystone....	52	f.....	f.....	f.....	f.....
f.....	f.....	f.....	f.....	75.6	...Montesano...	52	f.....	f.....	f.....	f.....
f.....	f.....	f.....	f.....	75.9	.Russian R. Hts..	52	f.....	f.....	f.....	f.....
f 5 20	f12 22	f10 57	f10 27	76.9	...Rio Campo...	48	f 6 56	f 1 13	f 2 42	f 5 20
5 25	12 29	11 05	10 34	78.1	...Monte Rio...	41	6 53	1 10	2 38	5 16
f.....	f.....	f.....	f.....	79.0	..Villa Grande..	40	f.....	f.....	f.....	f.....
5 35	12 39	11 17	10 46	81.5	Ar Duncan Mills Lv	26	6 43	1 00	2 24	5 02
......	12 55	......	......	81.5	Lv Duncan Mills Ar	26	......	......	2 19	......
......	1 22	......	......	88.7	....Cazadero....	106	......	......	1 53	......
PM Ar	PM Ar	AM Ar	AM Ar				AM Lv	PM Lv	PM Lv	PM Lv

f Trains stop only on signal or to discharge passengers.

SONOMA VALLEY BRANCH

FROM SAN FRANCISCO (READ DOWN)								TOWARD SAN FRANCISCO (READ UP)			
148	146	144	142	140	Miles from S. F.	STATIONS	Elev.	141	143	145	147
Daily	Sat. Only	Daily	Daily	Sun. Only				Daily	Daily	Daily	Sat. and Sun.
PM Lv	PM Lv	AM Lv	AM Lv	AM Lv				AM Ar	PM Ar	PM Ar	PM Ar
4 45	1 15	10 45	8 15	7 15	00.0	..San Francisco..	6	9 35	1 35	6 05	8 35
5 20	1 50	11 21	8 50	7 50	6.5	....Sausalito....	8	9 00	1 00	5 30	8 00
......	......	f†			14.9	...Green Brae...	29	......	......	......	......
......	......	f†....	......	......	15.7	....Schuetzen....	19	......	......	......	......
5 50	2 20	11 52	9 25	8 26	17.0	...San Rafael...	5	8 26	12 32	4 57	7 26
f....	......	f.....	......	f.....	21.1	....Gillinas....	12	f....	f.....	f....	......
f6 01	......	......	......	f 8 37	21.7	.....Miller.....	6	f....	f12 21	f4 44	......
f....	......	f.....	......	f.....	22.0	...St Vincent...	8	f....	f.....	f....	......
6 10	2 44	12 14	9 43	8 45	24.9	.....Ignacio.....	17	8 10	12 16	4 37	7 10
f6 17	f2 51	f12 21	f 9 50	f 8 52	28.5	...Black Point...	8	f8 01	f12 07	f4 26	f7 01
f6 23	f2 57	f12 27	f 9 56	f 8 58	30.8	...Reclamation...	1	f7 55	f12 01	f4 20	f6 55
f6 29	f3 03	f12 33	f10 02	f 9 04	33.4	...Sears Point...	8	f7 49	f11 56	f4 14	f6 49
f....	f....	f.....	f.....	f.....	35.2	....Fairville....	4	f....	f.....	f....	f....
f....	f....	f.....	f.....	f.....	36.0	....Quarries....	2	f....	f.....	f....	f....
f....	f....	f.....	f.....	f.....	36.7	.....McGill.....	1	f....	f.....	f....	f....
f6 39	f3 13	f12 43	f10 12	f 9 14	37.8	.....Wingo.....	6	f7 39	f11 46	f4 04	f6 39
6 46	3 19	12 50	10 19	9 21	40.4	....Shellville....	10	7 32	11 39	3 57	6 32
6 51	3 24	12 55	10 24	9 26	42.2	....Vineburg....	49	7 27	11 34	3 52	6 27
f....	f....	f.....	f.....	f.....	43.5	...Buena Vista...	106	f....	f.....	f....	f....
6 58	3 30	1 02	10 31	9 33	44.8	.....Sonoma.....	97	7 20	11 27	3 43	6 20
f7 03	f3 36	f 1 07	f10 36	f 9 38	46.1	......Verano.....	116	f7 14	f11 22	f3 36	f6 14
7 04	3 38	1 08	10 37	9 39	46.4	..Coney Island..	.....	7 13	11 21	3 35	6 13
7 06	3 40	1 10	10 39	9 41	46.8	..Boyes Springs..	129	7 12	11 20	3 34	6 12
7 08	3 42	1 12	10 41	9 43	47.4	.Fetters Springs.	126	7 10	11 18	3 32	6 10
f7 10	f3 44	f 1 14	f10 43	f 9 45	47.7	..Agua Caliente..	131	f7 08	f11 16	f3 30	f6 08
f....	f....	f.....	f.....	f.....	48.5	.....Watriss.....	149	f....	f.....	f....	f....
f7 15	f3 49	f 1 19	f10 48	f 9 50	49.1	....Madrone....	169	f7 03	f11 12	f3 25	f6 03
f....	f....	f.....	f.....	f.....	49.8	....Eldridge....	191	f....	f.....	f....	f....
7 20	3 54	1 24	10 53	9 55	51.2	...Glen Ellen...	228	6 58	11 08	3 20	5 58
PM Ar	PM Ar	PM Ar	AM Ar	AM Ar				AM Lv	AM Lv	PM Lv	PM Lv

f Train stops only on signal or to discharge passengers.
† Daily except Sunday.

CAMP MEEKER, MONTE RIO AND CAZADERO

FROM SAN FRANCISCO (READ DOWN)						TOWARD SAN FRANCISCO (READ UP)			
	62	60	Miles from S. F.	STATIONS	Elev.	61	37		
	Sat. Only	Daily				Daily	Daily Ex. Sun		
	PM Lv	AM Lv				PM Ar	AM Ar		
......	2 45	8 15	0.0	......San Francisco......	6	7 35	......	......	......
......	3 20	8 55	6.5	........Sausalito........	8	7 00	......	......	......
......	5 19	10 43	36.4	......Point Reyes......	31	5 19	10 00	......	......
......	f 5 29	f10 53	40.5	........Millerton........	17	f 4 52	9 43	......	......
......	5 42	11 06	45.4	........Marshall........	7	4 36	9 25	......	......
......	f 5 53	f11 17	49.4	.........Hamlet.........	7	f 4 21	9 10	......	......
......	f.....	f.....	51.2	......Camp Pistolesi......	9	f.....	9 01	......	......
......	6 05	11 29	53.1	........Tomales........	115	4 09	8 58	......	......
......	6 10	11 34	55.2	.........Fallon.........	67	3 59	8 45	......	......
......	6 22	11 46	59.5	......Valley Ford......	45	3 45	8 30	......	......
......	6 29	11 53	62.2	.......Bodega Road.......	176	3 34	8 15	......	......
......	6 35	11 59	63.7	........Freestone........	222	3 29	8 06	......	......
......	6 50	12 14	67.6	........Occidental........	570	3 14	7 50	......	......
......	6 55	12 19	69.0	......Camp Meeker......	402	3 07	AM Lv	......	......
......	fh....	f.....	72.4	.........Tyrone.........	62	f.....	......	......	......
......	h7 15	12 39	73.8	........Monte Rio........	41	2 46	......	......	......
......	fh....	f.....	74.3	........Fern Cove........	41	f.....	......	......	......
......	fh....	f.....	74.6	.......Villa Grande.......	40	f.....	......	......	......
......	fh....	f.....	75.5	........Sheridan........	35	f.....	......	......	......
......	h7 27	12 55	77.1	......Duncan Mills......	26	2 34	......	......	......
......	fh....	f.....	81.6	.........Watsons.........	61	f.....	......	......	......
......	fh....	f.....	83.5	...Cazadero Redwoods...	90	f.....	......	......	......
......	fh....	f.....	83.9	.....Miller's Retreat.....	101	f.....	......	......	......
......	h7 55	1 22	84.3	........Cazadero........	106	1 53	......	......	......
......	PM Ar	PM Ar				PM Lv			

h Will run beyond Camp Meeker only until September 8, Incl.
f Train stop only on signal or to discharge passengers.

To Mt. Tamalpais and Muir Woods

Daily

Leave San Francisco	Arrive Mill Valley	Arrive Summit	Arrive Muir Woods
8 45	9 35	10 40	10 26
9 45	10 35	11 40	11 23
10 45	11 35	12 40	12 26
11 45	12 35	1 40	1 30
1 45	2 35	3 40	3 26
2 45	3 35	4 40	4 30
4 45	5 35	6 40	

Leave Summit	Leave Muir Woods	Leave Mill Valley	Arrive San Francisco
10 43	....	11 43	12 35
11 43	....	12 43	1 35
1 43	1 40	2 43	3 35
2 43	....	3 43	4 35
4 43	4 40	5 43	6 35
5 43	5 40	6 43	7 35
6 43	....	7 43	8 35

Leave Summit	Arrive Muir Woods
10 43	11 26
11 43	12 26
12 43	1 30
*1 40	*2 21
1 43	2 26
2 43	3 26
3 43	4 30
4 43	5 30

*Sunday only.

1929 ROUND TRIP FARES

FROM SAN FRANCISCO to and return	16-Day Exc.	3-Mo. Exc.
Agua Caliente⑦	†1.95	2.35
Albion①③	11.00	12.15
Alderpoint	11.40	13.70
Alton	14.90	17.85
Arcata	16.40	19.70
Arnold	6.30	7.55
Asti	†3.30	3.95
Austin Creek	†3.20	3.85
BartlettSprings②	14.10	14.90
Basil	4.95	5.95
Beatrice	15.50	18.60
Bellevue	†2.10	2.50
Bell Springs	9.10	10.90
Black Point	†1.20	1.45
Boonville①	8.00	8.70
Bothin	† .80	.85
Bottini	†1.05	1.25
Boyes Springs⑦	†1.95	2.35
Bridgeport③	14.90	16.05
Buena Vista⑦	†1.80	2.20
Burdell	†1.30	1.55
Byron	13.75	16.50
Calpella	4.90	5.85
Camp Rest	7.90	9.45
Camp Taylor	†1.15	1.40
Casper①③	11.00	12.15
Cazadero	†3.40	4.10
Cazadero Redwoods	†3.40	4.10
Chianti	†3.20	3.85
Chiquita	†2.90	3.45
Cloverdale	†3.50	4.20
Cotati	†1.90	2.25
Covelo	10.90	12.40
Crown	†1.70	2.00
Cummiskey	†3.75	4.50
Deer Lodge	7.90	9.45
Dos Rios	7.40	8.90
Duncan Mills	†3.15	3.80
Echo	†3.60	4.35
Eel Rock	12.50	15.00
Eldridge⑦	†2.00	2.40
Elinor	14.15	17.00
Elk①	11.00	11.70
El Roble	†4.40	5.30
Ely	†1.75	2.10
Essex	16.70	20.00
Eureka	16.00	19.20
Fairville	†1.50	1.80
Farley	6.90	8.25
Fernbridge	15.15	18.20
Fern Cove	†3.00	3.60
Fetters' Springs⑦	†1.95	2.35
Forest Knolls	†1.00	1.20
Forestville	†2.70	3.20
Ft. Bragg	11.00	12.15
Fort Ross④	6.15	6.80
Fort Seward	11.95	14.35
Fortuna	15.00	18.00
Fountain	†3.95	4.75
Fulton	†2.40	2.90
Gallinas	† .90	1.05
Garcia	†1.35	1.60
Geyserville	†3.10	3.70
Glen Ellen⑦	†2.10	2.50
Grant	†2.70	3.20
Graystone	†3.00	3.60
Green Valley	†2.75	3.30
Gualala④	10.85	11.50
Guerneville	†3.00	3.60
Guernewood Pk	†3.00	3.60
Hacienda	†2.80	3.40
Healdsburg	†2.75	3.30
Highland Spgs②	10.10	10.90
Hilton	†2.80	3.40
Hopland	†4.10	4.90
Ignacio	†1.00	1.20
Indian Springs	7.90	9.45
Island Mountain	10.10	12.10
Jenner④	4.15	4.80
Jewell	†1.20	1.45
Kekawaka	10.60	12.75
Kelseyville②	8.10	8.90
Kidd Creek	†3.30	3.95
Korbel	†2.85	3.45
Lagunitas	†1.00	1.20
Lakeport②	8.10	8.90
Larabee	13.60	16.35
Largo	†4.20	5.05
Laughlin	5.00	6.00
Little River①③	11.00	12.15
Loleta	15.30	18.35
Longvale	6.50	7.80
Lytton	†2.95	3.55
Madrone⑦	†2.00	2.40
Mark West	†2.40	2.90
McCann	13.00	15.60
McCray	†3.50	4.20
McGill⑦	†1.55	1.85
Meacham	†2.50	3.00
Mendocino①③	11.00	12.15
Miller	† .95	1.15
Miller Retreat	†3.40	4.10
Mirabel	†2.70	3.20
Monte Rio	†3.00	3.60
Montesano	†3.00	3.60
Moscow	†3.10	3.70
Muir Woods	.....	2.48
Mt. Tamalpais	.....	2.48
Nashmead	8.30	9.95
Navarro①	10.00	10.70
NavarroRiver①	11.00	12.15
Northspur	8.85	10.00
Novato	†1.15	1.40
Olde Camp 7	9.05	10.20
Ornbaun Road①	6.75	7.45
Outlet	5.95	7.15
Penngrove	†1.75	2.10
Petaluma	†1.60	1.95
Pieta	†3.90	4.65
Philo①	8.50	9.20
Plantation	7.80	8.50
Point Arena④	14.05	14.70
Point Reyes	†1.50	1.80
Preston	†3.55	4.25
Quarries	†1.50	1.80
Ramsey	9.55	11.45
Reclamation	†1.30	1.55
Ridge	5.30	6.35
Rio Campo	†3.00	3.60
Rionido	†2.95	3.55
River Rest①	9.50	10.20
Rohnerville	14.95	17.95
Roys	† .80	.85
Russian R. Hts	†3.00	3.60
San Antonio	†1.35	1.60
San Geronimo	† .95	1.10
Santa Rosa	†2.20	2.65
Scotia	14.50	17.40
Sears Point	†1.40	1.70
Sea View	5.80	6.50
Sebastopol⑤	†2.50	3.00
Sebastopol⑥	†2.50	2.91
Shellville⑦	†1.70	2.00
Sheridan	†3.10	3.70
Shively	13.90	16.65
Skaggs Springs	5.60	6.20
Sonoma⑦	†1.80	2.20
South Bay	15.70	18.80
South Fork	13.35	16.00
Spyrock	8.70	10.40
St. Vincent	† .95	1.15
Stewart's Point④	8.85	9.50
Tatu	7.15	8.60
Taylorville	†1.20	1.45
The Geysers①	7.00	7.70
Tocaloma	†1.30	1.55
Trenton	†2.60	3.15
Trinidad	17.50	21.00
25 Junction	17.40	20.90
Ukiah	†4.60	5.55
Upper Lake②	9.60	10.40
Van Zandt①	8.50	9.20
Verano⑦	†1.90	2.25
Villa Grande	†3.00	3.60
Vineburg⑦	†1.75	2.10
Watriss⑦	†2.00	2.40
Watson	†3.30	3.95
Wilfred	†2.00	2.40
Willits	5.60	6.75
Windsor	†2.55	3.05
Wingo⑦	†1.55	1.85
Woodacre	† .90	1.00
Woodacre Lodge	† .90	1.00
Woodman	7.90	9.45
Woolsey	†2.50	3.00
Yorkville①	6.50	7.20

†Tickets will also be sold at this fare on Monday, Tuesday, Wednesday and Thursday, good to return within 4 days, including day of sale.
① Via Cloverdale and stage. ② Via Hopland and stage.
③ Via Ft. Bragg and stage. ④ Via Duncan Mills and stage.
⑤ Via Santa Rosa. ⑥ Via Petaluma and P. & S. R. R. R.
⑦ Tickets also sold to go and return on Sunday of sale, $1.50.

Sale dates—May 1 to September 30, 1929 inclusive.

Sixteen-day Excursion Tickets will be sold for use leaving selling station on Friday, Saturday or Sunday. Return limit 16 days.

Three-months Excursion Tickets will be sold daily. The going and return trips must be completed within 3 months. Stopovers allowed within limit, except at interurban stations.

The limit of short limit tickets will be extended on payment of difference between the fare paid and 3-months' fare between the same stations. Consult our agents.

Tickets to Guerneville, Rio Campo and intermediates will be honored without additional charge returning from Monte Rio. **Tickets to other stations** will be honored returning from Monte Rio at small additional cost. Consult our agents.

The N.W.P. had aready planned the demise of the narrow gauge between Point Reyes and Camp Meeker in 1929, so no fares to narrow gauge points were shown in the "Round Trip Fares" listing. However, the narrow gauge did operate in 1929 and roundtrip fares to various stations from San Francisco were as follows: Millerton $1.70; Marshall $1.90; Hamlet $2.00; Tomales $2.15; Fallon $2.30; Valley Ford $2.40; Freestone $2.60; Occidental $2.75 and Camp Meeker $2.80. All fares on 16-day excursion basis.

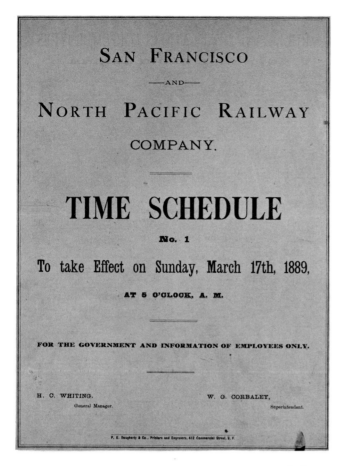

SAN FRANCISCO

—AND—

NORTH PACIFIC RAILWAY

COMPANY.

TIME SCHEDULE

No. 1

To take Effect on Sunday, March 17th, 1889,

AT 5 O'CLOCK, A. M.

FOR THE GOVERNMENT AND INFORMATION OF EMPLOYEES ONLY.

H. C. WHITING,
General Manager.

W. G. CORBALEY,
Superintendent.

P. E. Dougherty & Co., Printers and Engravers, 412 Commercial Street, S. F.

California Northwestern Railway Co.

LESSEE OF

San Francisco and North Pacific Railway Co.

TIME TABLE

No. 1,

To take effect on Sunday, October 16, 1898,

AT 5 O'CLOCK, A. M.

For the government and information of employees only, and not intended for the use of the public. The company reserves the right to vary from this schedule as circumstances may require.

H. C. WHITING,
General Manager.

F. K. ZOOK,
Superintendent.

H. S. Crocker Company Print, 215, 217 and 219 Bush St., S. F.

The San Francisco & North Pacific Railway was incorporated December 19, 1888, as a consolidation of 15 southern area roads, and its first operating timetable became effective March 17, 1889. It was an 8-page affair, size 10 x 14 inches. Three pages were devoted to rules and regulations; one page published the schedules of the Sonoma Valley, Guerneville and Donahue branches; and two pages listed the 28 main line trains (including trains both from and toward San Francisco), of which 24 were passenger, 2 were freight and 2 were mixed. At the time this schedule became effective, trains operated only as far as Cloverdale, 84 miles from San Francisco, but stations and mileages were shown all the way to Ukiah, 113 miles.

The California Northwestern Railway was incorporated March 17, 1898, and on September 30, 1898, took over, by lease, the operation of the San Francisco & North Pacific Railway. The first operating timetable was published effective October 16, 1898, and included not only the Sonoma Valley, Guerneville and Donahue branches, but the Sebastopol branch as well. By now forty trains were listed on the main line, including one passenger and one freight all the way to Ukiah. All trains, however, were not daily, and some operated only as far as San Rafael, and two others only as far as Cloverdale. The total of forty includes trains in both directions.

Another of the several timetables No. 1 became effective June 16, 1928 when the Northern and Southern Divisions were abolished and all Northwestern Pacific trains, other than suburban, were operated under one timetable. There were several timetables numbered 1, the original Southern Division, original Western Division and original Northern Division. Also a No. 1 was issued on May 31, 1970 when P&SR trackage was included with the N.W.P. The inter-urban lines had their own timetable. In addition, there was a No. 1 timetable for the Northern and Southern Divisions and the inter-urban lines under the United States Railroad Administration, effective 1918.

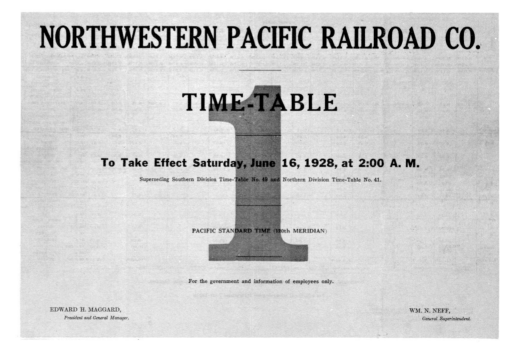

NORTHWESTERN PACIFIC RAILROAD CO.

TIME-TABLE

To Take Effect Saturday, June 16, 1928, at 2:00 A. M.

Superseding Southern Division Time-Table No. 49 and Northern Division Time-Table No. 41.

PACIFIC STANDARD TIME (120th MERIDIAN)

For the government and information of employees only.

EDWARD H. MAGGARD,
President and General Manager.

WM. N. NEFF,
General Superintendent.

Car No. 458 was donated in September, 1965, by the Southern Pacific Company to the Pacific Coast Chapter, Railway & Locomotive Historical Society. It was built by Pullman in 1914 as N.W.P. No. 458, was renumbered to SP 1012 on August 30, 1935, serving in commute work for thirty years. It was restored to its original number and appearance by Bethlehem Shipyard.

Caboose No. 5591, shown here beautifully restored by the Railway & Locomotive Historical Society. It was one to two caboose units on the narrow gauge. This caboose will be on display at the California State Railroad Museum at Sacramento.

Engine No. 112, the only N.W.P. locomotive in existence. Donated by the railroad to the Pacific Coast Chapter, Railway & Locomotive Historical Society, June 18, 1953. Photo taken on May 18, 1965, the day restoration was completed. Engine is now on display at the California State Railroad Museum, Sacramento.

The Floods

At the little isolated station of South Fork, forty-seven miles south of Eureka, Manuel Rubira, retired water service mechanic of the Northwestern Pacific, took a concerned look at the Eel River on the afternoon of Monday, December 21, 1964. Manuel, who had worked for the NWP for nearly thirty-four years, had established a modest home at South Fork, just below the station, and had been through many winters with the rising waters of the Eel. There had been floods before, but now there was an ominous feeling of impending disaster. Rain had pelted the area for the past three days, and on this afternoon it was reaching cloudburst proportions. (Between December 17, 1964 and January 8, 1965, the recorded rainfall for the area was thirty-one inches - over 400% of normal.) At 5 PM the Eel started to rise at a rate of two feet an hour. At 10 PM, with water lapping at his front door, Manuel knew it was time to gather his family and flee to higher ground. At 2 AM December 22, the waters broke over the level of the track at the station; at 7 AM there was twenty-one-and-a-half feet over the track! The entire hundred miles of the track from just south of Dos Rios to north of Scotia were at the mercy of the rampaging torrent. The muddy waters ripped out track, bridges, communication lines, stations, living quarters and maintenance buildings. At Island Mountain Bridge, rails that normally stand eighty-four feet above the surface of the river were torn out and the entire 620-foot structure was knocked off its foundations and thrown into the river. One tunnel had water in it nearly twenty feet deep. Virtually none of the track escaped damage as heavy mud slides, triggered by incessant rains, boomed down canyon slopes to erase long stretches of road-bed and riprap retaining walls were cut away by the swirling river. At Scotia, Agent Stuart Pritchett reported that the waters went ten and a half feet over the track at that point, washing the historic station across the tracks and breaking it up beyond repair. At this point also - across the river, a huge section of mountain slid into the Eel River, forcing water to roar down the NWP tracks and adjacent street, lifting three homes from their foundations and crushing them like match sticks, and destroying remaining homes in the block-long area. The town of Pepperwood was completely wiped out and much damage was done to the nearby communities of Weott and Rio Dell.

When the flood waters subsided, the tough little NWP was in shambles. Three major bridges - Island Mountain, Cain Rock and South Fork - had been virtually wiped out and nearly one hundred miles of

track needed rebuilding. The river had erased some thirty miles of roadbed so completely that in places only the canyon walls were left. In a few days, Charles Neal, Vice President and General Manager of the road, made a preliminary survey by helicopter to assess the damage. The photographs in this special added section of this book, show part of the story of destruction. Most of the stations and waiting sheds were gone - Alderpoint, McCann, South Fork and Scotia to name a few. But by a quirk, the station at Fort Seward remained unharmed. Approximately five hundred culverts were either destroyed or left in need of repair. Fortunately no train crews had been caught in the canyon. There had been some wash-outs before the tremendous surge of the Eel, so trains had been annulled with the exception of one stranded at Bell Springs, and the engine managed to get to safety before the flood waters struck. The Budd Car passenger train made its last trip on Sunday, December 20, from Eureka to Willits, the return trip to Eureka the next day being annulled. (In June, 1965, the NWP, through the Southern Pacific, applied to discontinue this sole remaining passenger service altogether; however, after extensive hearings the State Public Utilities Commission said "no" to the SP, and service was resumed April 22, 1966.)

After estimating what had to be done to get the railroad back in operation, calls went out for the necessary men and materials. Responding to the emergency, NWP employees from every craft volunteered to do anything necessary. Trainmen, enginemen, machinists, electricians, clerks, telegraphers and others served as track foremen, equipment operators, timekeepers, carpenters, laborers and truck drivers. Called in to provide extra help were such experienced contractors as Morrison-Knudsen, American Bridge Company, International Engineering and Tudor Engineering. Headquarters were set up in the Willits station.

As the river went back to its more normal meandering, but with rains still falling, repair work moved forward both at Dos Rios and Scotia, on the extreme ends of the damaged line. Fighting mud and rain, railroaders and construction men converted some thirty-five miles of trails through the rugged mountain terrain into emergency roads so that heavy equipment could be trucked to the isolated line. At the same time, tons of bridge and track material were barged to Eureka for the restoration project.

As repair work swung into full stride, 850 men - nearly half of them railroaders - began attacking the damage at twenty-two points along the canyon route. Over 500 pieces of work equipment were pressed into service. Much of this, including three twenty-five-ton locomotives and twenty-five rail cars of various types, had to be trucked in over the tough access roads on lowboy rigs.

To house and feed the workers, temporary "towns" were built at Spy Rock, Island Mountain and Kekawaka. Smaller camps were set up at twelve other locations.

Rebuilding of the line required, for example, the installation of: Sixty miles of bank protection in the canyon, totaling millions of cubic yards of rock; 40,000 railroad ties; almost 25,000 linear feet of culvert pipe; nearly 6,000 cubic yards of concrete (in bridge piers). Most of this material had to be trucked in.

A survey of railroad equipment that was caught in the canyon showed that thirty-five cars were lost and 250 others damaged. Stranded on the Eureka end of the line were twelve locomotives and 903 freight cars.

About a hundred miles of pole line communications system were replaced by new microwave and VHF radio network between Willits and Eureka. The three wrecked bridges required months of work. At Island Mountain, two hundred foot trusses from the 620-foot bridge were swept from their piers; two girder spans totaling 160 feet were lost, and a concrete pier was torn from its base. At Cain Rock, three girders at one end and two at the other end of the 1100-foot bridge were toppled from their piers. At South Fork, two two-hundred foot spans and one ninety-foot-high pier were ripped out of the 780-foot bridge. What track remained in the hundred-mile stretch was filled with debris or stacks of logs. In fact, the track area between McCann and South Fork became a "sea" of logs when the waters receded, and all had to be bulldozed out of the way. Repair materials, particularly in the early stages of reconstruction, had to be transported part way by rail and part by truck, with the Pacific Motor Trucking Company,

a subsidiary of the Southern Pacific, hauling about six hundred loads over the access roads, including girders up to sixty feet long.

In only 177 days - December 21, 1964 to June 16, 1965 - the reconstruction forces in spite of adverse weather and the rampaging river, and continuing problems of remoteness, inaccessibility and rugged terrain, completed one of the most monumental repair jobs in railroad history. A newspaper editorial exclaimed in part: "—the men had matched the mountains." And the cost: nearly twelve million dollars.

On October 23, 1914 there had been a "Gold Spike" ceremony at Cain Rock heralding completion of the Redwood Empire Route. With the finishing of the rebuilding of the line destroyed in the Christmas flood of 1964, it was proclaimed that another "gold spike" ceremony be in order. The original spike used in 1914, for years reposing in a safe at Southern Pacific headquarters in San Francisco, was once again used, the festivities taking place at South Fork Wednesday, June 16, 1965. The program got under way at 11:30 AM with speeches by prominent civic and rail officials, with about three thousand persons in attendance. Promptly at 12:30 PM Southern Pacific President B. F. Biaggini and United States Congressman Don H. Clausen - with alternate blows of the spike mauls - drove the historic spike into a tie of polished redwood. (The spike was later presented to the Humboldt County Board of Supervisors, which accepted it on behalf of the people of the area, and placed it on display at the Clark Memorial Museum in Eureka.) The "first" train was then signaled by Mr. Neal to come forward for proper christening. Lead Diesel, No. 5287, draped with bunting and a big "177" on its pilot, signifying the number of days it took to reopen the road, had a bottle of California champagne smashed on its nose by Miss Pamela Schmidt, "Miss Humboldt Chamber of Commerce" - and the train with its seventy-six cars, called the "North Coast Lumber Special" was on its way, while the Pacific Lumber Company's Scotia band played the familiar tune I've Been Working on the Railroad.

The crowd then headed for the adjacent picnic area for a barbecue provided by the NWP and SP. Consumed at the picnic tables were some 3,000 chickens, 600 pounds of ham, 600 pounds of baked beans, almost a ton of macaroni salad, and 6,000 cans of beer and soft drinks. And in the distance the blast from the air horn of Diesel 5287 (helped by units 5290 and 5332) signaled that the Northwestern Pacific, which moves eighty-percent of the Redwood Empire's forest products, was again open for through traffic.

The Scotia station rests in shambles "the morning after," having been battered by logs and flood waters 180 feet from its foundation to the center of the roadway. Agent Stuart Pritchett in foreground.

At McCann Mile Post 232.2, a large portion of the mountainside was washed down over the N.W.P. tracks.

A sea of logs, mud and debris covers the right of way at Camp Grant, Mile Post 233.4.

A complete section destroyed at the Jerry Pagh ranch between Farley and Dos Rios, Mile Post 162.8.

Ballast gone, the rails and ties were left hanging on a washed out section between Farley and Dos Rios, Mile Post 162.9.

A heavy rush of water from this normally placid little creek erased a whole section of roadbed. Mile Post 183.25, between Spyrock and Bell Springs.

A freight train caught in a slide at Bell Springs station, Mile Post 184.3. Altogether 903 freight cars were stranded between Dos Rios and Eureka for six months until the line could be reopened.

Hundreds of feet of right-of-way were destroyed in the section between Bell Springs and Ramsey.

Toppled span of the Island Mountain bridge.

One of the first passenger trains through Island Mountain tunnel shortly after the road was opened in 1914. Photo courtesy Tom Williams

Two piers remain of the Island Mountain Bridge. You can see right through the tunnel, 4313 feet. At this point the railroad went over the longest bridge into the longest tunnel on the system.

At Island Mountain, Mile Post 194.5, the high bridge has been washed away and is lying in the river over a hundred feet downstream. Section hands who had scampered from their Maintenance of Way quarters to higher ground said the backup of logs and debris pushing against the spans caused them to fall.

At Alderpoint the station was completely wiped out, and approximately one mile north the railroad was practically obliterated, as indicated in above picture.

Scene showing havoc at Denmark Sink, Mile Post 222.1, between Fort Seward and Eel Rock.

At South Fork, the raging Eel rose 21 feet above the tops of the rails, washing away a gasoline storage and distribution plant and tearing away two big truss spans from the long bridge that crossed the main Eel River at its confluence with the south fork. A 200-foot and a 180-foot span, including the center pier, were carried away when water rose into the spans and caused tremendous jams of logs and debris. Note the debris and logs jammed into the remaining spans and onto the right-of-way beyond the bridge.

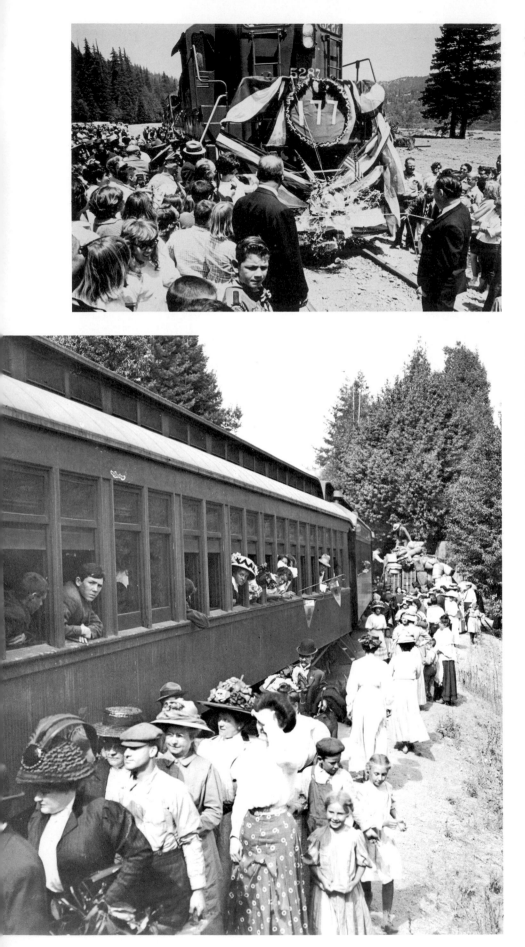

SP Diesel No. 5287 heads a 76-car freight train ready to start service again after 177 days of reconstruction of the line. It is being christened with the traditional bottle of champagne during the finale of railroad ceremonies at South Fork, June 16, 1965. Performing the honors before a crowd of some three thousand was Miss Pamela Schmidt, 19, a representative of the Humboldt Chamber of Commerce. Photo courtesy of Eureka Newspapers, Inc.

Vacationers boarding train at Guernewood Park on their way back to the city. The scene was repeated many times at other Russian River station stops and northern California resort areas. But, like the stage coach that preceeded it, the roar of the "iron horse" and the railroad passenger car in the Redwood Empire are but memories.

INDEX

303